SATANISM
AND WITCHCRAFT

SATANISM
AND WITCHCRAFT

A Study in Medieval Superstition

by

JULES MICHELET

TRANSLATED BY A. R. ALLINSON

THE CITADEL PRESS · New York

A 48-8022

CONTENTS

Contents

INTRODUCTION

Sᴘʀᴇɴɢᴇʀ said, before 1500: "We should speak of the *Heresy of the Sorceresses,* not of the Sorcerers; the latter are of small account." So another writer under Louis XIII.: "For one Sorcerer, ten thousand Sorceresses."

"Nature makes them Sorceresses,"—the genius peculiar to woman and her temperament. She is born a creature of Enchantment. In virtue of regularly recurring periods of exaltation, she is a Sibyl; in virtue of love, a Magician. By the fineness of her intuitions, the cunning of her wiles—often fantastic, often beneficent—she is a Witch, and casts spells, at least and lowest lulls pain to sleep and softens the blow of calamity.

All primitive peoples start alike; this we see again and again in the accounts given by travellers. Man hunts and fights. Woman contrives and dreams; she is the mother of fancy, of the gods. She possesses glimpses of the *second sight,* and has wings to soar into the infinitude of longing and imagination. The better to count the seasons, she scans the sky. But earth has her heart as well. Her eyes stoop to the amorous flowers; a flower herself in her young beauty, she learns to know them as playfellows and intimates. A woman, she asks them to heal the men she loves.

Pathetic in their simplicity these first beginnings of Religion and Science! Later on, each province will be separated, we shall see mankind specialise—as medicine-man, astrologer or prophet, necromancer, priest, physician. But in these earliest days woman is all in all, and plays every part.

A strong and bright and vigorous religion, such as was Greek Paganism, begins with the Sibyl, to end with the Sorceress. The first, a virgin fair and beautiful, brilliant in the full blaze of dawn, cradled it, gave it its charm and glamour. In later days, when sick and fallen, in the gloom of the Dark Ages, on heaths and in forests, it was concealed and protected by the Sorceress; her dauntless pity fed its needs and kept it still alive. Thus for religions it is woman is mother, tender protectress and faithful nurse. Gods are like men; they are born and they die on a woman's breast.

But what a price she paid for her fidelity! . . . Magian queens of Persia, enchanting Circé, sublime Sibyl, alas! how are you fallen, how barbarous the transformation you have suffered! . . . She who, from the throne of the Orient, taught mankind the virtues of plants and the motions of the stars, she who, seated on the Delphic tripod and, illumined by the very god of light, gave oracles to a kneeling world,—is the same that, a thousand years later, is hunted like a wild beast, chased from street to street, reviled, buffeted, stoned, scorched with red-hot embers! . . .

The clergy has not stakes enough, the people insults, the child stones, for the unhappy being. The poet, no less a child, throws yet another stone at her, a crueller one still for a woman. Gratuitously insulting, he makes her out always old and ugly. The very word Sorceress or *Witch* calls up the image of the Weird Sisters of *Macbeth*. Yet the cruel witch trials prove exactly the opposite; many perished just because they were young and pretty.

The Sibyl foretold the future; but the Sorceress makes it. Here is the great, the vital distinction. She evokes, conjures, guides Destiny. She is not like Cassandra of old, who foresaw the coming doom so clearly, and deplored it and awaited its approach; she creates the future. Greater than Circé, greater than Medea, she holds in her hand the magic wand of natural miracle, she has Nature to aid and abet her like a sister. Foreshadowings of the modern Prometheus are to be seen in her,—a beginning of industry, above all of the sovereign industry that heals and revivifies men. Unlike the Sibyl, who seemed ever gazing towards the dayspring, she fixes her eyes on the setting sun; but it is just this sombre orb of the declining luminary that shows long before the dawn (like the glow on the peaks of the High Alps) a dawn anticipatory of the true day.

The Priest realises clearly where the danger lies, that an enemy, a menacing rival, is to be feared in this High-priestess of Nature he pretends to despise. Of the old gods she has invented new ones. Beside the old Satan of the past, a new Satan is seen burgeoning in her, a Satan of the future.

For a thousand years the people had one healer and one only, —the Sorceress. Emperors and kings and popes, and the richest barons, had sundry Doctors of Salerno, or Moorish and Jewish physicians; but the main body of every State, the whole world we may say, consulted no one but the *Saga*, the *Wise Woman*. If her cure failed, they abused her and called her a Witch. But more generally, through a combination of respect and terror, she was spoken of as the *Good Lady*, or *Beautiful Lady* (Bella Donna), the same name as that given to fairies.

Her fate resembled that which still often befalls her favourite herb, the belladonna, and other beneficent poisons she made use of, and which were antidotes of the great scourges of the Middle Ages. Children and ignorant passers-by cursed these sombre flowers, without understanding their virtues, scared by their suspicious colour. They shudder and fly the spot; yet these are the Comforting plants (*Solanaceæ*), which, wisely administered, have worked so many cures and soothed so much human agony.

They are found growing in the most sinister localities, in lonely, ill-reputed spots, amid ruins and rubbish heaps,—yet another resemblance with the Sorceress who utilises them. Where, indeed, could she have taken up her habitation, except on savage heaths, this child of calamity, so fiercely persecuted,

so bitterly cursed and proscribed? She gathered poisons to heal
and save; she was the Devil's bride, the mistress of the Incarnate Evil One, yet how much good she effected, if we are to
credit the great physician of the Renaissance! Paracelsus, when
in 1527, at Bâle, he burned the whole pharmacopœia of his day,
declared he had learned from the Sorceresses all he knew.

Had they not earned some reward? Yes! and reward they had.
Their recompense was torture and the stake. New punishments
were devised for their especial benefit, new torments invented.
They were brought to trial *en masse,* condemned on the slightest pretext. Never was such lavish waste of human life. To say
nothing of Spain, the classic land of the *auto-da-fé,* where Moor
and Jew are always associated with Witches, seven thousand
were burned at Trèves, and I know not how many at Toulouse;
at Geneva five hundred in three months (1513); eight hundred
at Wurzburg, in one batch almost, and fifteen hundred at Bamberg,—both of these quite small bishoprics! Ferdinand II. himself, the bigot, the cruel Emperor of the Thirty Years' War, was
forced to restrain these worthy bishops, else they would have
burned all their subjects. I find, in the Wurzburg list, a wizard of
eleven, a schoolboy, and a witch of fifteen, at Bayonne, two
sorceresses of seventeen, damnably pretty.

Mark this, at certain epochs the mere word of *Sorceress* or
Witch is an arm wherewith Hate can kill at discretion. Female
jealousy, masculine avarice, are only too ready to grasp so convenient a weapon. Such and such a neighbour is rich? . . .
Witch! witch! Such and such is pretty? . . . *Ah! witch!* We
shall see Murgin, a little beggar-girl, casting this terrible stone
at a great lady, whose only crime was being too beautiful, the
Châtelaine de Lancinena, and marking her white forehead with
the death sign.

Accused of sorcery, women anticipate, if they can, the torture that is inevitable by killing themselves. Remy, that worthy
judge of Lorraine who burned eight hundred of them, boasts of
this Reign of Terror: "So sure is my justice," he declared, "that

sixteen witches arrested the other day, never hesitated, but strangled themselves incontinently."

In the long course of study for my history during the thirty years I have devoted to it, this horrible literature of Sorcery, or Witchcraft, has passed through my hands again and again. First I exhausted the Manuals of the Inquisition, the asinine collections of the Dominicans—the *Whips, Hammers, Ant-Swarms, Fustigations, Lanterns,* etc., to give some of the absurd titles these books bear. Next I read the men of the Law, the lay judges who take the place of these monks, and who despise them without being much less idiotic themselves. I say a word or two of these elsewhere; for the present I have only one observation to make, viz. that from 1300 down to 1600, and even later, the administration of justice is identically the same. With the exception of one small interlude in the *Parlement* of Paris, we find always and everywhere the same ferocity of folly. Ability and talent make no difference. The wise and witty De Lancre, a magistrate of Bordeaux under Henri IV., a man of enlightened ideas in politics, directly he has to deal with witchcraft, falls back to the level of a Nider or a Sprenger, two imbecile monks of the fifteenth century.

One is filled with amazement to see all these widely different epochs, all these men of varying cultivation, unable to make one step in advance. But the explanation is simple; they were one and all arrested, let us rather say, blinded, hopelessly intoxicated and made cruel savages of, by the poison of their first principle, the doctrine of Original Sin. This is the fundamental dogma of universal injustice: "All lost for one alone, not only punished but deserving punishment, undone even before they were born and desperately wicked, dead to God from the beginning. The babe at its mother's breast is a damned soul already."

Who says so? All do, even Bossuet. A Roman theologian of weight, Spina, Master of the Sacred Palace, formulates the doctrine in precise words: "Why does God permit the death of the innocent? He does so justly. For if they do not die by reason of the sins they have committed, yet they are guilty of death by reason of original sin" [1]

From this monstrous theory two consequences follow, in justice and in logic. The judge is always sure of doing justice; anyone brought before him is inevitably guilty, and if he defends himself, doubly guilty. No call for Justice to sweat, and rack its brains in order to distinguish true and false; in every case the decision is a foregone conclusion. The logician likewise and the schoolman may spare themselves the trouble of analysing the soul of man, of examining the phases through which it passes, of considering its complexity, its internal disparities and self-contradictions. No need, as *we* feel ourselves bound to do, to explain how, by slow and subtle degrees, the soul may grow vicious instead of virtuous. These refinements, these doubts and difficulties and scruples, if they understood them at all, how they would laugh at them, and shake their heads in scorn, and how gracefully would the fine long ears that ornament their empty pates waggle to and fro!

Particularly when the *Compact with the Devil* comes into question, that ghastly covenant where, for some small ephemeral gain, the soul sells itself into everlasting torment, we philosophers should endeavour to trace out the accursed path, the appalling ladder of calamities and crimes, capable of having brought it so low. But our theologian can ignore all such considerations! For him Soul and Devil were created for each other; so that at the first temptation, for a caprice, a sudden longing, a passing fancy, the soul flies headlong to this dreadful extremity.

Nor can I see any traces of modern writers having made much inquiry into the moral chronology of Sorcery. They confine themselves far too much to the connections between the Middle

---

[1] *De Strigibus,* ch. 9.

Ages and Classical Antiquity. The connection is real enough, but slight and of quite minor importance. Neither the ancient Enchantress, nor yet the Celtic and Germanic Seeress, are yet the true Sorceress. The harmless *Sabasia* (festivals of Bacchus Sabasius), a miniature rustic "Sabbath" which survived down to Mediæval times, are far from identical with the *Black Mass* of the fourteenth century, that deliberate and deadly defiance of Jesus. These gloomy conceptions were not passed on down the long thread of tradition; they sprang ready made from the horrors of the time.

From when does the Sorceress date? I answer unhesitatingly, "From the ages of despair."

From the profound despair the World owed to the Church. I say again unhesitatingly, "The Sorceress is the Church's crime."

I pass over the string of plausible explanations by which the priests attempt to mitigate her guilt: "Weak and frivolous by nature, open to every temptation, women were led astray by concupiscence." Alas! in the wretchedness and famine of those dreadful times, this was no force sufficient to rouse to demoniac frenzy. Loving women, jealous and forsaken, children driven out of doors by a cruel stepmother, mothers beaten by their sons (all hackneyed subjects of legendary tales), may indeed have been tempted to invoke the Evil Spirit; but all this does not constitute the Sorceress, the Witch. Because the unhappy creatures call upon Satan, it does not follow that he accepts their service. They are still far, very far, from being ripe for him. They have yet to learn *to hate God.*

To understand this better, read the accursed Registers still extant of the Inquisition, not in the extracts compiled by Llorente, Lamotte-Langon, etc., but in what is extant of the original Registers of Toulouse. Read them in their vapid sameness, their dismal aridity, their shocking unconscious savagery. A few pages, and you are cold at heart, a cruel chill strikes home to the vitals. Death, death, always death, you feel it in every page. You are already in the tomb, or immured in a little chamber of stone with damp-stained walls. The happiest gate is death. The dreadful thing is the *in pace*. One word recurs continually, like a bell of horror tolled, and tolled again, to drive the dead in life into despair,—always the same word, *Immured*.

Dread apparatus for crushing and annihilating souls, cruel press for breaking hearts. The screw turns, and turns, till breath fails and the very bones crack, and she springs from the horrid engine a mystery in an unknown world!

The Sorceress has neither father nor mother, neither son, nor mate, nor kindred. She appears none knows from whence, a monster, an aërolite from the skies. Who so bold, great God! as to come nigh her?

Where is her lurking-place? In untracked wilds, in impenetrable forests of bramble, on blasted heaths, where entangled thistles suffer no foot to pass. She must be sought by night, cowering beneath some old-world dolmen. If you find her, she is isolated still by the common horror of the countryside; she has, as it were, a ring of fire round her haunts.

'Tis hard to credit it, but she is a woman still. Even this fearful life has its spring of womanhood, its feminine electricity, in virtue of which she is dowered with two gifts—

The salf-sane, half-insane madness, illuminism, of the seer, which according to its degree is poetry, second sight, preternatural vision, a faculty of speech at once simple and astute, above all else the power of believing in her own falsehoods. This gift is unknown to the male Sorcerer; the Wizard fails to comprehend its very elements.

From it flows a second, the sublime faculty of *solitary conception*, that parthenogenesis our physiologists of to-day recognise as existing among the females of numerous species. The same fecundity of body is no less procreative where conceptions of the spirit are involved.

All alone, she conceived and brought forth. Whom or what? Another of her own kind, so like the original as to cheat the eyes.

Child of hate, conceived of love; for without love nothing can be created. The Sorceress, terror-struck as she is at her strange offspring, yet sees herself so faithfully reproduced, finds such content in contemplating this new idol, that instantly she sets it on the altar, worships it, immolates herself to it, giving her own body as victim and living sacrifice.

We shall often and often find her telling the judge: "There is only one thing I am afraid of,—not to suffer enough for him." [2]

Do you know how the newborn infant salutes the new world he enters? With a horrid scream of laughter. And has he not good cause to be glad, there on the free and open plains, far from the dungeons of Spain, and the *immured* victims of Toulouse? His *in pace* is wide as the world itself. He comes and goes, roaming where he will. His the boundless forest! his the vast heath that stretches away to the farthest horizon! his the round world and the riches thereof! The Sorceress calls him tenderly, *"Robin,* Robin mine!"—from the name of that gallant outlaw, the gay Robin Hood, that lived under the greenwood tree. Another pet name she loves to give him is *Verdelet, Joli-Bois, Vert-Bois.* The green woods, indeed, are the frolicsome scamp's favourite haunts; one glimpse of bush and briar, and he is off, a wild truant of Nature.

The astounding thing is that at the first essay the Sorceress really and truly made a living being. He has every mark of actuality. He has been seen and heard, and everybody can describe him.

The saints, those children of affection, the sons of the house, pay little heed, only watch and dream; they *wait in patient waiting,* confident of getting their share of the Elect in God's

---

[2] Lancre.

good time. The small degree of activity they possess is concentrated within the narrow circle of *Imitation*—the word sums up the Middle Ages. But for him, the bastard all curse, whose share is only the lash, he has no thought of waiting. He is for ever prying and searching, never an instant still, trying all things in heaven and earth. He is to the last degree curious and inquisitive, scrutinising, rummaging, sounding, poking his nose everywhere. At the solemn *Consummatum est* he grins, and makes a derisive mow. His word is always "Not yet!" and "Forward still!"

All the same, he is not hard to please. Nothing rebuffs him; what Heaven throws in his way, he picks up with alacrity. For instance the Church has rejected Nature as something impure and suspect. Satan seizes on it, and makes it his pride and ornament. Better still, he utilises it, turns it to profit, originates the arts from it, accepting gladly the great name they would fain cast at him as a stigma and a disgrace, that of *Prince of this World.*

"Alas for them that laugh!"—they had declared with startling unwisdom; for what was this but giving Satan a fine initial advantage to start with, the monopoly of laughter, and proclaiming him *amusing?* Let us say *necessary* at once; for laughter is an essential function of human nature. How support life at all, if we cannot laugh,—at any rate when we are in sorrow?

The Church, which sees in our life below only a test and trial for one to come, takes care not to prolong it needlessly. Her medicine is resignation, a waiting and a hoping for death. Here is a great field opened to Satan; he becomes physician, healer of living men. Nay more! consoler as well; he has the compassion to show us our dead, to evoke the shades of the dear ones we have loved and lost.

Another trifle the Church has cast away and condemned—Logic, the free exercise of Reason. Here again is an appetising dainty *the Enemy* snaps up greedily.

The Church had built of solid stone and tempered mortar a

narrow *in pace,* vaulted, low-browed and confined, lighted by the merest glimmer of day through a tiny slit. This they called the *schools.* A few shavelings were let loose in it, and told "to be free"; they one and all grew halting cripples. Three hundred, four hundred years, only made them more helplessly paralysed. Between Abelard and Occam the progress made is—nil!

A pretty tale, to say we must look there for the origin of the Renaissance! The Renaissance came about, no doubt of that; but how? by the satanic effort of men who broke through the vault, the struggles of condemned criminals who *would* see the light of heaven. It came about in the main far away from schools and scholastics, in that school of wild nature where Satan lectured a truant band of Sorceresses and shepherd lads.

A dangerous curriculum, if ever there was one! But its very risks stimulated the love of knowledge, the frantic longing to see and know. It was there began the black sciences, the forbidden Chemistry of poisons, and the accursed thing, Anatomy. The shepherd, first to scan the stars, along with his discoveries in Astronomy, brought to the common stock his sinister recipes and his experiments on animals. Then the Sorceress would contribute a corpse filched from the nearest graveyard; and for the first time—at the risk of the stake—men could contemplate that miracle of God's handicraft "which" (as M. Serres so well said) "we hide in silly prudishness instead of trying to understand."

The only Doctor admitted to these classes, Paracelsus, noted a third as well, who now and again would glide in to join the sinister conclave, bringing Surgery with him as his contribution. This was the surgeon of those gentle times,—the Public Executioner, the man of unflinching hand, whose plaything was the branding-iron, who broke men's bones and could set them again, who could slay and make alive, and hang a felon up to a certain point and no further.

This criminal University of the Sorceress, the Shepherd, and the Hangman, by means of its experiments—a sacrilege every one—emboldened the other and rival seat of learning and forced its scholars to study. For each was fain to live; and otherwise the Witch would have monopolised all, and the Schoolmen turned their backs for good and all on Medicine. The Church *had* to submit, and wink at these crimes. She allowed there were *good poisons* (Grillandus); she permitted dissection in public, though reluctantly and under dire constraint. In 1306 the Italian Mondino opened and dissected a woman, and another in 1315. It was a solemn and beneficent revelation, the veritable discovery of a new world,—far more so than Christopher Columbus's. Fools shuddered, and howled in protest; wise men dropped on their knees.

With victories like these to his credit, Satan could not but live. Alone the Church would never have had strength to crush him. Fire and stake were of no avail, but a certain line of policy was more successful.

With no little astuteness the kingdom of Satan was divided against itself. In opposition to his daughter and bride, the Sorceress, was set her son, the Healer.

The Church, deeply and from the bottom of her heart as she hated the latter, none the less established his monopoly, to secure the Sorceress's ruin. She declares, in the fourteenth century, that if a woman dare to cure *without having studied,* she is a Witch and must die.

But how should she study publicly? Imagine the scene, at once ludicrous and terrible, that would have occurred if the poor savage creature had ventured to enter the schools! What merriment and wild gaiety! In the bale-fires of St. John's day, cats chained together were burned to death. But think of the Sorceress bound to this caterwauling rout of hell, the Witch screaming and roasting in the flames, what a treat for the gentle band of young shavelings and sucking pedants!

We shall see Satan's decadence all in good time,—a sorry tale. We shall see him pacified, grown a *good old sort.* He is robbed and pillaged, till at last, of the two masks he wore at the Witches' Sabbath, the foulest is adopted by Tartuffe.

His spirit is everywhere. But for himself, for his own personality, in losing the Witch, he lost all. The Wizards were bores, and nothing more.

Now that his fall has been so far consummated, do his foes quite realise what they have done? Was he not a necessary actor, an indispensable factor in the great engine of religious faith,—something out of gear nowadays? Every organism that works well is double, has two sides; life is hardly possible otherwise. A certain balance between two forces is necessary, forces mutually opposed and symmetrical, but unequal. The inferior acts as counterpoise, corresponding to the other. The superior grows impatient at the check, and is for abolishing it altogether. But the wish is a mistaken one.

When Colbert, in 1672, shelved Satan with so little ceremony, forbidding the Judges of the Realm to hear cases of Witchcraft, the Norman *Parlement,* in its obstinate conservatism, its sound Norman logicality, demonstrated the dangers attending such a decision. The Devil is nothing less than a dogma closely bound up with all the rest. Touch the vanquished of the ages—are you not touching the victor too? Doubt the acts of the one—is not this paving the way to doubt those of the other, those very miracles he did to fight the Devil? The pillars of heaven are based in the abyss. The rash man who shakes this infernal foundation may well crack the walls of paradise.

Colbert paid no heed; he had so many other things to do. But it may be the Devil heard. And his wounded spirit is greatly consoled. In the petty trades where he now gains his living—Spiritualism, Table-turning, and the like—he resigns himself to insignificance, and thinks, at any rate, he is not the only time-hallowed institution that is a-dying.

SATANISM
AND WITCHCRAFT

PART ONE

DEATH of the GODS

THERE are authors who assure us that a little while before the final victory of Christianity a mysterious voice was heard along the shores of the Ægean Sea, proclaiming: "Great Pan is dead!"

The old universal god of Nature is no more. Great the jubilation; it was fancied that, Nature being defunct, Temptation was dead too. Storm-tossed for so many years, the human soul was to enjoy peace at last.

Was it simply a question of the termination of the ancient worship, the defeat of the old faith, the eclipse of time-honoured religious forms? No! it was more than this. Consulting the earliest Christian monuments, we find in every line the hope expressed, that Nature is to disappear and life die out—in a word, that the end of the world is at hand.

The game is up for the gods of life, who have so long kept up a vain simulacrum of vitality. Their world is falling round them in crumbling ruin. All is swallowed up in nothingness: "Great Pan is dead!"

It was no new evangel that the gods must die. More than one ancient cult is based on this very notion of the death of the gods. Osiris dies, Adonis dies—it is true, in this case, to rise again. Æschylus, on the stage itself, in those dramas that were played only on the feast-days of the gods, expressly warns them, by the voice of Prometheus, that one day they must die. Die! but how?—vanquished, subjugated to the Titans, the antique powers of Nature.

Here it is an entirely different matter. The early Christians,

3

as a whole and individually, in the past and in the future, hold Nature herself accursed. They condemn her as a whole and in every part, going so far as to see Evil incarnate, the Demon himself, in a flower.[1] So, welcome—and the sooner the better—the angel-hosts that of old destroyed the Cities of the Plain. Let them destroy, fold away like a veil, the empty image of the world, and at length deliver the saints from the long-drawn ordeal of temptation.

The Gospel says: "The day is at hand." The Fathers say: "Soon, very soon." The disintegration of the Roman Empire and the inroads of the barbarian invaders raise hopes in St. Augustine's breast, that soon there will be no city left but the City of God.

Yet how long a-dying the world is, how obstinately determined to live on! Like Hezekiah, it craves a respite, a going backward of the dial. So be it then, till the year One Thousand,—but not a day longer.

Is it so certain, as we have been told over and over again, that the old gods were exhausted, sick of themselves and weary of existence? that out of sheer discouragement they as good as gave in their own abdication? that Christianity was able with a breath to blow away these empty phantoms?

They point to the gods at Rome, the gods of the Capitol, where they were only admitted in virtue of an anticipatory death, I mean on condition of resigning all they had of local sap, of renouncing their home and country, of ceasing to be deities representative of such and such a nation. Indeed, in order to receive them, Rome had had to submit them to a cruel operation, that left them poor, enervated, bloodless creatures. These great centralised Divinities had become, in their official life, mere dismal functionaries of the Roman Empire. But, though fallen from its high estate, this Aristocracy of Olympus had in nowise involved in its own decay the host of indigenous gods, the crowd

---

[1] Compare Muratori, *Script. It.*, i. 293, 545, on St. Cyprian; A. Maury, *Magie*, 435.

of deities still holding possession of the boundless plains, of woods and hills and springs, inextricably blended with the life of the countryside. These divinities, enshrined in the heart of oaks, lurking in rushing streams and deep pools, could not be driven out.

Who says so? The Church herself, contradicting herself flatly. She first proclaims them dead, then waxes indignant because they are still alive. From century to century, by the threatening voice of her Councils,[2] she orders them to die. . . . And lo! they are as much alive as ever!

"They are demons . . ."—and therefore alive. Unable to kill them, the Church suffers the innocent-hearted countryfolk to dress them up and disguise their true nature. Legends grow round them, they are baptised, actually admitted into the Christian hierarchy. But *are* they converted? Not yet by any means. We catch them still on the sly continuing their old heathen ways and Pagan nature.

Where are they to be found? In the desert, on lonely heaths, in wild forests? Certainly, but above all in the house. They cling to the most domestic of domestic habits; women guard and hide them at board and even bed. They still possess the best stronghold in the world—better than the temple, to wit the hearth.

History knows of no other revolution so violent and unsparing as that of Theodosius. There is no trace elsewhere in antiquity of so wholesale a proscription of a religion. The Persian fireworship, in its high-wrought purity, might outrage the visible gods of other creeds; but at any rate it suffered them to remain. Under it the Jews were treated with great clemency, and were protected and employed. Greece, daughter of the light, made merry over the gods of darkness, the grotesque pot-bellied Cabiri; but still she tolerated them, and even adopted them as working gnomes, making her own Vulcan in their likeness. Rome,

---

[2] See Mansi, Baluze; Council of Arles, 442; Tours, 567; Leptines, 743; the *Capitularies*, etc. Gerson even, towards 1400.

in the pride of her might, welcomed not only Etruria, but the rustic gods as well of the old Italian husbandman. The Druids she persecuted only as embodying a national resistance dangerous to her dominion.

Victorious Christianity, on the contrary, was fain to slaughter the enemy outright, and thought to do so. She abolished the Schools of Philosophy by her proscription of Logic and the physical extermination of the philosophers, who were massacred under the Emperor Valens. She destroyed or stripped the temples, and broke up the sacred images. Quite conceivably the new legend might have proved favourable to family life, if only the father had not been humiliated and annulled in St. Joseph, if the mother had been given prominence as the trainer, the moral parent of the child Jesus. But this path, so full of rich promise, was from the first abandoned for the barren ambition of a high, immaculate purity.

Thus Christianity deliberately entered on the lonely road of celibacy, one the then world was making for of its own impulse— a tendency the imperial rescripts fought against in vain. And Monasticism helped it on the downward slope.

Men fled to the desert; but they were not alone. The Devil went with them, ready with every form of temptation. They must needs revolutionise society, found cities of solitaries,—it was of no avail. Everyone has heard of the gloomy cities of anchorites that grew up in the Thebaïd, of the turbulent, savage spirit that animated them, and of their murderous descents upon Alexandria. They declared they were possessed of the Devil, impelled by demons,—and they told only the truth.

There was an enormous void arisen in Nature's plan. Who or what should fill it? The Christian Church is ready with an answer: The Demon, everywhere the Demon—*Ubique Dæmon.*[3]

Greece no doubt, like all other countries, had had its *energu-*

---

[3] See the *Lives of the Fathers of the Desert,* and the authors quoted by A. Maury, *Magie,* 317. In the fourth century the Messalians, believing themselves to be full of demons, were constantly blowing their noses, and spitting unceasingly, in their incredible efforts to expectorate these.

mens, men tormented, possessed by spirits. But the similarity is purely external and accidental, the resemblance more apparent than real. In the Thebaïd it is no case of spirits either good or bad, but of the gloomy children of the pit, wilfully perverse and malignant. Everywhere, for years to come, these unhappy hypochondriacs are to be seen roaming the desert, full of self-loathing and self-horror. Try to realise, indeed, what it means,—to be conscious of a double personality, to really believe in this second self, this cruel indweller that comes and goes and expiates within you, and drives you to wander forth in desert places and over precipices. Thinner and weaker grows the sufferer; and the feebler his wretched body, the more fiercely the demon harries it. Women in particular are filled, distended, inflated by these tyrants, who impregnate them with the infernal *aura*, stir up internal storm and tempest, make them the sport and plaything of their every caprice, force them into sin and despair.

Nor is it human beings only that are demoniac. Alas! all Nature is tainted with the horror. If the devil is in a flower, how much more in the gloomy forest! The light that seemed so clear and pure is full of the creatures of night. The Heavens full of Hell,—what blasphemy! The divine morning star, that has shed its sparkling beam on Socrates, Archimedes, Plato, and once and again inspired them to sublimer effort, what is it now?—a devil, the great devil *Lucifer*. At eve, it is the devil *Venus*, whose soft and gentle light leads mortals into temptation.

I am not surprised at such a society turning mad and savage. Furious to feel itself so weak against the demons, it pursues them everywhere, in the temples and altars of the old faith to begin with, later in the heathen martyrs. Festivals are abolished; for may they not be assemblages for idolatrous worship? Even the family is suspect; for might not the force of habit draw the household together round the old classic Lares? And why a family at all? The empire is an empire of monks.

Yet the individual man, isolated and struck silent as he is, still gazes at the skies, and in the heavenly host finds once more the old gods of his adoration. "This is what causes the famines," the Emperor Theodosius declares, "and all the other scourges of the Empire,"—a terrible dictum that lets loose the blind rage of the fanatic populace on the heads of their inoffensive Pagan fellow-citizens. The Law blindly unchains all the savagery of mob-law.

Old gods of Heathendom, the grave gapes for you! Gods of Love, of Life, of Light, darkness waits to engulf you! The cowl is the only wear. Maidens must turn nuns; wives leave their husbands, or if they still keep the domestic hearth, be cold and continent as sisters.

But is all this possible? Who shall be strong enough with one breath to blow out the glowing lamp of God? So reckless an enterprise of impious piety may well bring about strange, monstrous, and astounding results. . . . Let the guilty tremble!

Repeatedly in the Middle Ages shall we find the gloomy story recurring of the Bride of Corinth. First told in quite early days by Phlegon, the Emperor Hadrian's freedman, it reappears in the twelfth century, and again in the sixteenth,—the deep reproach, as it were, the irrepressible protest of outraged Nature.

"A young Athenian goes to Corinth, to the house of the man who promises him his daughter in marriage. He is still a Pagan, and is not aware that the family he hopes to become a member of has just turned Christian. He arrives late at night. All are in bed, except the mother, who serves the meal hospitality demands, and then leaves him to slumber, half dead with fatigue. But hardly is he asleep, when a figure enters the room,—a maiden, clad in white, wearing a white veil and on her brow a fillet of black and gold. Seeing him, she raises her white hand in surprise: 'Am I then already so much a stranger in the house? . . . Alas! poor recluse. . . . But I am filled with shame, I must begone.' 'Nay! stay, fair maiden; here are Ceres and Bacchus, and with *you*, love! Fear not, and never look so pale!' 'Back, back, I say! I have no right to happiness any more. By a vow my sick mother made, youth and life are for ever fettered. The gods are no more, and the only sacrifices now are human souls.' 'What! can this be you? You, my promised bride I love so well, promised me from a child? Our fathers' oath bound us indissolubly together under Heaven's blessing. Maiden! be mine!' 'No! dear heart, I cannot. You shall have my young sister. If I groan in my chill prison-house, you in her arms must think of me, me who waste away in thoughts of you, and who will soon be beneath the sod.' 'No! no! I call to witness yonder flame; it is the torch of Hymen. You shall come with me to my father's house. Stay with me, my best beloved!' For wedding gift he offers her a golden cup. She gives him her neck-chain; but chooses rather than the cup a curl of his hair.

" 'Tis the home of spirits; she drinks with death-pale lips the dark, blood-red wine. He drinks eagerly after her, invoking the God of Love. Her poor heart is breaking, but still she resists. At last in despair he falls weeping on the bed. Then throwing herself down beside him: 'Ah! how your grief hurts me! Yet the horror of it, if you so much as touched me! White as snow, and cold as ice, such alas! and alas! is your promised bride.' 'Come to me! I will warm you, though you should be leaving the very tomb itself. . . .' Sighs, kisses pass between the pair. 'Cannot you feel how I burn?' Love unites them, binds them in one close embrace, while tears of mingled pain and pleasure flow. Thirstily she drinks the fire of his burning mouth; her chilled blood is fired with amorous ardours, but the heart stands still within her bosom.

"But the mother was there, though they knew it not, listening to their tender protestations, their cries of sorrow and delight. 'Hark! the cock-crow! Farewell till to-morrow, to-morrow night!' A lingering farewell, and kisses upon kisses!

"The mother enters furious,—to find her daughter! Her lover strives to enfold her, to hide her, from the other's view; but she struggles free, and towering aloft from the couch to the vaulted roof: 'Oh! mother, mother! so you begrudge me my night of joy, you hunt me from this warm nest. Was it not enough to have wrapped me in the cold shroud, and borne me so untimely to the tomb? But a power beyond you has lifted the stone. In vain your priests droned their prayers over the grave; of what avail the holy water and the salt, where youth burns hot in the heart? Cold earth cannot freeze true Love! . . . You promised; I am returned to claim my promised happiness. . . .

"'Alack! dear heart, you must die. You would languish here and pine away. I have your hair; 'twill be white to-morrow.[4] . . . Mother, one last prayer! Open my dark dungeon, raise a funeral pyre, and let my loving heart win the repose the flames alone can give. Let the sparks fly upward and the embers glow! We will back to our old gods again.' "

---

[4] At this point of the story I suppress an expression that may well shock us. Goethe, so noble in the form of his writings, is not equally so in the spirit. He quite mars the wonderful tale, fouling the Greek with a gruesome Slavonic notion. At the instant when the lovers are dissolved in tears, he makes the girl into a vampire. She curses because she is athirst for blood, to suck his heart's blood. The poet makes her say coldly and calmly this impious and abominable speech: "When he is done, *I will go on to others;* the new generation shall succumb to my fury."

The Middle Ages dress up this tradition in grotesque garb to terrify us with the devil *Venus.* Her statue receives from a young man a ring, which he imprudently places on her finger. Her hand closes on it, she keeps it as a sign of betrothal; then at night, comes into his bed to claim the rights it confers. To rid him of his hellish bride, an exorcism is required (S. Hibb., part iii. chap. iii. 174). The same story occurs in the *Fabliaux,* but absurdly enough applied to the Virgin. Luther repeats the classical story, if my memory serves me, in his *Table-talk,* but with great coarseness, letting us smell the foulness of the grave. The Spaniard Del Rio transfers the scene from Greece to Brabant. The affianced bride dies shortly before the wedding-day. The passing-bell is tolled; the grief-stricken bridegroom roams the fields in despair. He hears a wail; it is the loved one wandering over the heath. . . . "See you not," she cries, "who my guide is?" "No!" he replies, and seizing her, bears her away to his home. Once there, the account was very near growing over tender and touching. The grim inquisitor, Del Rio, cuts short the thread with the words, "Lifting the veil, they found a stake with a dead woman's skin drawn over it." The Judge Le Loyes, though not much given to sensibility, nevertheless reproduces for us the primitive form of the legend. After him, there is an end of these gloomy story-tellers, whose trade is done. Modern days begin, and the Bride has won the day. Buried Nature comes back from the tomb, no longer a stealthy visitant, but mistress of the house and home.

2

WHAT DROVE the MIDDLE AGES to DESPAIR

"BE YE like unto new-born babes" (*quasi modo geniti infantes*); be little children for innocence of heart, and peacefulness and forgetfulness of all causes of offence, calm and serene, under the hand of Jesus.

Such is the sweet counsel the Church gives this stormy world on the morrow of the great catastrophe. In other words: "Volcanoes, scoriæ, ashes, lava, grow green and lush with grass. Fields burned up with fire, come, carpet yourselves with flowers."

One circumstance, it is true, then was promised the peace that revivifies,—all the schools were ended, the path of logic abandoned and deserted. A method of infinite simplicity rendered all discussion futile, and set before the feet of all the easy downward road they must needs follow henceforth. If the *Credo* was of doubtful interpretation, still life was all traced out plainly enough in the track of legend. The first word, and the last, was the same,—*Imitation*.

"*Imitate*, and all will be well; only repeat and copy." Yes! but is this really and truly the way of genuine *infancy*, the infancy that vivifies the heart of man, makes him find new sources of refreshment and fertility? To begin with, I can see in this world that moulds childhood and infancy only attributes of senility, over-refinement, servility, impotence. What is this literature compared with the sublime monuments of Greeks and Jews? even compared with the Roman genius? We find precisely the same literary decline that befell in India, from Brahminism to Buddhism; a garrulous verbiage succeeding to lofty inspiration. One book plagiarises another, till presently they cannot even copy correctly. They rob one from the other, and the marbles of Ravenna are torn down to adorn Aix-la-Chapelle. The whole fabric of society is of a piece; the bishop who is lord of a city, the barbarian prince of a half-savage tribe, model themselves on the Roman magistrature. Our monks we think so original, are only repeating in their monastery the *villa* of an earlier day, as Chateaubriand well observes. They have no notion of fashioning a new society, any more than of refertilising the old. Mere imitators of the Eastern monks, they would fain have had their dependants poor monkish taskmen, a sterile population of celibate lay brothers. It was in their despite family life renewed itself, and so renewed the world.

When we observe how quickly these old monks are ageing, how in a single century the level drops from the wise monk St. Benedict to the pedant Benedict of Ariane, we clearly realise that these gentry were purely and entirely innocent of the grand popular creation that grew up about the ruins; I refer to the Lives of the Saints. The monks wrote them, but it was the people made them. This young vegetation may throw its luxuriance of leaf and blossom over the crumbling walls of the old Roman building converted into a monastery, but it does not grow out of it, we may be very sure. It has roots deep in the soil; the people sowed it there, the family worked the ground, all took a hand in its production—men, women, and children. The precarious, restless life of those times of violence made these poor countryfolk imaginative, ready to put faith in their own dreams that consoled them in their misery,—wild dreams, teeming with wonders and full of absurdities, equally ludicrous and delightful.

These families, living isolated in the woods or on the mountains (as men live still in the Tyrol and the High Alps), coming down to the plains but one day in the week, were filled with the hallucinations their loneliness encouraged. A child had seen this, a woman had dreamed that. A brand-new Saint arose in the district; his story ran through the countryside, like a ballad, in rough-and-ready rhyme. It was sung and danced at evening under the oak by the fountain. The priest who came on Sunday to say Mass in the forest chapel found the legendary song in every mouth already. Then he said to himself: "Well! after all, the tale is a beautiful one and an edifying; . . . it does honour to the Church. *Vox populi, vox Dei!* . . . But however did they come across it?" Then would they show him authentic witnesses, of unimpeachable veracity,—the tree, the rock, that saw the apparition, the miracle. What more could be said after that?

Reported at the Abbey, the legend will soon find a monk, *good for nothing better,* whose only craft is the pen, both curious and credulous, ready to believe anything and everything miraculous. He writes it all out, embroiders the simple tale with his vapid rhetoric, spoils it somewhat. But at any rate here it is duly recorded and recognised, read in refectory, and before long in church. Recopied, loaded, overloaded with embellishments, often grotesque embellishments, it will descend from age to age, till at last it takes honourable rank and place in the *Golden Legend.*

Even to-day, when we read these beautiful tales, when we listen to the simple, artless, solemn melodies into which these rustic populations put all their young enthusiasm, we cannot but recognise a very real inspiration, and bewail the irony of fate when we think what was to be their eventual lot.

These people had taken literally the Church's touching appeal: "Be ye as little children." But they applied it to the very thing least dreamed in the original conception. The more Christianity had feared and abhorred Nature, the more these folk loved her and held her good and harmless,—even sanctified her, giving her a part to play in the legend.

The animals which the Bible so harshly calls *hairy beasts,* and which the monk mistrusts, fearing to find demons incarnated in them, come into these charming tales in the most touching way, as, for instance, the hind that warms and comforts Geneviève de Brabant.

Even apart from the life of legends, in everyday existence,
these humble fireside friends, these gallant helpers in the day's
work, gain a higher place in men's esteem. They have their proper rights,[1] and their proper estate. If in God's infinite goodness
there is room for the lowliest, if He ever seems to have a preference for such out of pity, why should not my ass be allowed in
church? He has his defects, no doubt,—which makes him only
the more like me. He is a sturdy fellow to work, but thick-
skulled; he is intractable and obstinate, in one word, he is my
very counterpart.

Hence those grand festivals, the most beautiful of the Middle
Ages, of the *Innocents,* of *Fools,* of the *Ass.* It is the very people
of that day which in the ass presents its own likeness in person
before the altar, ugly, ludicrous, and down-trodden! Truly a
touching sight! Led by Balaam, he enters solemnly between the
Sibyl and Virgil,[2] enters to bear witness. If of old he kicked
against Balaam, this was because he saw flashing before him the
sword of the old Law. But here the Law is abrogated and done
with, and the world of Grace seems to open wide its doors to receive the lowliest, the simple ones of the earth. The people
believes it all in the innocency of its heart. Hence the sublime
canticle, in which it addressed the ass, as it might have addressed
itself:—

> A genoux, et dis *Amen!*
> Assez mangé d'herbe et de foin!
> Laisse les vieilles choses, et va! [3]

---

[1] See J. Grimm, *Rechts Alterthümer,* and Michelet, *Origines du Droit.*

[2] From the ritual of Rouen. See Ducange, under *Festum;* Carpentier, under
Kalendæ, and Martène, iii. 110. The Sibyl was crowned, followed by Jews and
Gentiles, by Moses and the Prophets, Nebuchadnezzar, etc. From the earliest
times, and from century to century, the seventh to the sixteenth, the Church
endeavours vainly to proscribe the great popular festivals of the Ass, of the
Innocents, of Children, and of Fools. She meets with no success, previously to
the rise of the modern spirit.

[3] "Down on your knees, and *Amen* say!
Enough you've eat of grass and hay!
Leave go old things, and up, away!

> Le neuf emporte le vieux!
> La vérité fait fuir l'ombre!
> La lumière chasse la nuit![3]

What insolence and wrong-headedness! Is *this* what they required of you, disobedient, unruly children, when they told you to be as little children? They offered you milk; you drink strong wine instead. They would lead you gently, bridle in hand, by the narrow way. Gentle, timid creatures, you seemed afraid to put one foot before another. Then behold! of a sudden the bridle is broken . . . one leap, and you swap over the course.

Ah! how unwise it was to let you invent your saints, and raise your altar, then bedeck and load and bury it in flowers, till its original form is all but indistinguishable. What *can* be discerned is the old heresy, long ago condemned by the Church, the *innocence of Nature*. An old heresy do I say? Nay! rather a new heresy that will live many a long day yet,—the *emancipation of mankind*.

Now listen and obey:

It is expressly forbidden to invent, to create. No more originality; no more legends; no more new saints. There are enough already. Forbidden to innovate in the forms of worship with new melodies; inspiration is prohibited. Any martyrs that should come to light are to keep quiet in their graves, and wait with becoming humility till the Church recognises them. Forbidden for clergy or monks to confer on peasants the tonsure that enfranchises them. Such the narrow, timid spirit of the Carlovingian Church,[4] which deliberately contradicts herself, gives herself the lie, now says to little children, "Be ye old men!"

---

[3] The new world puts the old to flight!
  Truth turns the gloomy dusk to light!
  Dawn's brightness drives away the night!"
     Vetustatem novitas,
     Umbram fugat claritas,
     Noctem lux eliminat.
          (Rouen Ritual.)

[4] See the *Capitularies* passim.

What a change is here! But can it be meant seriously? Did they not tell us to be young? Nay! the priest is no longer indentical with the people. A mighty divorce is beginning, an infinite gulf of separation. Henceforth the priest, a great lord now or a prince, will sing the Office in a golden cope, using the sovereign tongue of the great empire that is no more. We, poor cattle of the field, having lost the language of mankind, the only one God will deign to hear, what can we do now but low and bleat, in company with the innocent companion that never scorns us, that in wintertime warms us in the stall and covers us with his fleece? We will live with the dumb beasts, and be dumb ourselves.

In very truth, we have then the less need to go to Church. But she will not let us off; she orders us back, to listen to words we cannot understand.

From that day forth a monstrous fog, a heavy, grey, leaden fog, enwraps the world. Say, for how long? for a thousand long, dreary, terrible years! For ten whole centuries, a languor no previous age has known oppressed the Middle Ages, even to some extent later times, in a condition midway between sleep and waking, under the empire of a dismal, an intolerable phenomenon,— that convulsion of supreme boredom we call a yawn.

The indefatigable church bell rings out the accustomed hours, —and folks yawn; a nasal chant drones on in antiquated Latin, —and folks yawn. Everything is foreseen; no room is left for hope in all the world. Day after day events will recur in indentically the same way. The inevitable oppression of to-morrow makes men yawn before to-day is done, and the never-ending perspective of days, and years, of weary sameness still to come, weighs on the spirits beforehand and sickens of life. From brain to stomach, from stomach to mouth, the automatic, the fatally irresistible, convulsion travels, distending the jaws in an endless and cureless gape. A veritable disease, which pious Bretons openly avow, imputing it, it is true, to the Devil's machinations. He lies crouching in the woods, say the Breton peasants; to the herdsman as he passes with his beasts, he sings Vespers and all the other Offices, and sets him yawning, yawning till he is like to die.[5]

To be old is to be feeble. When the Saracens, when the Northmen, threaten us, what will be our fate, if the people is still old and decrepit? Charlemagne weeps unavailing tears, and the Church with him, confessing that the holy relics, against these barbarian demons, can no longer protect the altars.[6] Were it not well to appeal to the arm of the intractable child they were going to bind, the arm of the young giant they were fain to paralyse? A self-contradictory movement marks the ninth century throughout,—at one time the people is held back, at another pushed forward, at one time feared, at another appealed to for help. With the people's aid, by the people's hands, barriers are thrown up, shelters contrived, to stop the barbarian invaders, to protect the priests, and the saints, escaped from their churches.

Despite the Bald Emperor's prohibition, a castle-keep rises on the mountain height. There the fugitive arrives, "Take me in, in God's name,—at any rate my wife and children. I will camp with my bestial in your outer bailey." The castle restores his courage and he feels himself a man at last. It shelters him; he defends it, and so protects his protector.

In earlier days the poor, under stress of famine, surrendered themselves to the rich and powerful as serfs. Now it is very different; he gives himself as *vassal,* that is to say, brave and valiant champion.[7]

He gives himself, yet remains his own man, keeping the right to renounce his allegiance. "I am for higher things; the world is

---

[5] A very famous Breton (Renan), last man of the Middle Ages, but who was nevertheless a friend of my own, on the occasion of the quite ineffectual journey he made for the conversion of Rome, received brilliant offers when in the Eternal City. "What would you have?" the Pope asked him. "One thing and one thing only: a dispensation from the Breviary . . . I am sick to death of it."

[6] Such was Hincmar's well-known admission.

[7] A distinction too little appreciated, too little noticed, by writers who have enlarged upon *personal surrender, "recommendation" to a superior,* etc.

wide. I too, as well as another, may raise my castle on the steep.
. . . I have defended the outside; I shall know how to guard my
head in the inside."

Here we have the grand, noble origin of the Feudal world. The
man of the keep received his vassals, but said to them, "You
shall leave me when you will, and I will even help you to do it, if
needful; so far, indeed, that if you are mired, I will get down off
my horse myself to succour you." This is the ancient formula
word for word.[8]

But one morning what is this I see? Do my eyes deceive me?
The Lord of the Valley sallies forth to raid the lands round about,
sets up landmarks none may overpass, and even invisible lines of
demarcation. "What is it? What does it mean?" . . . It means
that the Lordship is enclosed: "The Feudal Lord, under lock and
key, holds all immured, between sky and earth."

Alas! alas! By virtue of what right is the *vassus* (the valiant
man, that is) henceforth to be a prisoner? Nay! *vassus,* they will
maintain, may equally be equivalent to *slave.*

In the same way *servus,* meaning *servant* (often a high-born
servant, a Count or Prince of the Empire), will signify for the
weak and lowly, a *serf,* a villein whose life is valued at a denier.

This is the hateful net they are taken in. But yonder on his
plot of ground is one who maintains his land is free, an *allod*
(*allodium, aleu*), a "fief of the sun." He sits on his boundary-
stone, crushes his hat down firm on his head, and watches the
Feudal Lord, the Emperor himself, pass by.[9]

"Go your ways, ride on, Emperor, you sit tight in your saddle,
and I on my boundary-stone yet tighter. You pass, but I remain.
. . . For I am Freedom."

But . . . I have not the heart to tell the man's eventual fate.
The air thickens round him, and his breath fails more and more.
He seems *bewitched.* He cannot move, he is as if paralysed. His

---

[8] Grimm, *Rechts Alterthümer;* Michelet, *Origines du Droit.*

[9] Grimm, on the word *aleu* (*allodium*).

beasts too grow thinner and thinner, as though a spell were on them. His servants die of hunger. His land is fallen barren. He is hag-ridden o' nights.

Still he holds on; he says, "A poor man's house is his castle."

But they will not leave him alone. He is cited, and must answer, to the Imperial Court. He repairs thither, a survival from a vanished world, a spectre of the past, a thing unrecognisable. "What is it?" the younger men ask each other. "He is neither Seigneur nor serf! Why, then, what is he? He is nothing."

" 'Who am I?' ask you? I am he who built the first castle-keep, and defended it in your behoof; he who, leaving its walls, strode bravely to the bridge to meet the heathen Northmen. . . . More than that, I dammed the river, I reclaimed the alluvial waste, I created the very soil, like God who made 'the dry land appear.' . . . This soil, who shall drive me off it?"

"Nay, my friend," answered his neighbour, "you shall not be driven off it. You shall cultivate it still, this soil . . . only on other conditions from what you think. . . . Remember, good friend, how in the heedlessness of youth (it is fifty years agone now) you wedded Jacqueline, a little maid of my father's serfs. . . . Remember the maxim: 'Who treads my hen, is my cock.' You belong to my hen-roost. Come, off belt and away sword! . . . Henceforth you are my serf."

There is no invention here; it is all bare truth. The atrocious story recurs over and over again in the Middle Ages. And what a bitter weapon of tyranny it was! I have abridged and omitted much, for every time one returns to these incidents, the same sharp point of pity and indignation pierces the heart.

One there was who, under so dire an outrage, fell into such a passion of fury he could find never a word to say. 'Twas like Roland betrayed at Roncesvaux. All the blood of his body rose to his throat and choked him. . . . His eyes flashed fire, his poor dumb mouth, dumb but so fiercely eloquent, turned all the assemblage pale. . . . They shrank back in terror. . . . He was dead. His veins had burst. . . . His arteries shot the red blood into the very faces of his murderers.[10]

This instability of condition and tenure, this horrid, shelving declivity, down which a man slips from free man to *vassal*,—from vassal to *servant*,—from servant to *serf*, is the great terror of the Middle Ages, the basis of its despair. There is no way of escape; one step, and the man is lost. He is an *alien*, a *waif and stray*, a head of *wild game;* serfdom or death, these are the only alternatives. The heavy soil clogs the feet, and entangles and engulfs the passer-by in its miry depths. The poisoned air kills him, lays its *dead hand* on him, turns him into a dead man, a non-entity, a brute beast, a life priced at ten farthings,—a life anyone may take and expiate the murder for ten farthings down. Such were the two main, external features of Mediæval wretchedness, the two great hardships that drove men to give themselves to Satan. Now to look at the internal aspect, to examine the foundations of life and character, and sound the depths of human existence, at the same unhappy period.

[10] This is what happened to the Comte d'Avesnes, when his free land was declared a mere fief, and himself a mere vassal, the *man* of the Comte de Hainault. Read also the terrible history of the Grand Chancellor of Flanders, the First Magistrate of Bruges, who for all this was nevertheless claimed, and successfully claimed, as a serf (Gualterius, *Scriptores Rerum Francicarum*, xiii. 334).

3

The LITTLE DEMON
of the HEARTH and HOME

THE early centuries of the Middle Ages, when the legends were in making, give all the impression of a dream. Among rustic populations, deeply submissive to the Church and of a gentle spirit (the legends themselves attest this), we would gladly assume a high degree of innocence. Surely it must have been God's own time, this. Nevertheless, in the *Penitentiaries,* where the most ordinary sins are noted down, strange and dishonouring forms of depravity are mentioned too, of rare occurrence under the reign of Satan.

This is due to two causes—utter ignorance, and the habit of living in common, which brought near relatives into the closest contiguity. They seem to have had scarce an inkling of our morality. Their own, in spite of ecclesiastical prohibitions, appears to have been that of the Patriarchs, of the remotest antiquity, which looks upon marriage with strange women as wicked, and only allows the kinswoman to be a lawful bride. Allied families formed only a single household. Not daring as yet to disperse their dwellings over the wastes that surrounded them, tilling merely the outlying demesne of a Merovingian palace or of a monastery, they retired every night together with their beasts under the roof of a vast *villa.* Hence inconveniences similar to those of the *ergastulum* of classical antiquity, in which slaves were herded promiscuously. More than one of these communities still existed in the Middle Ages, and even later. The Lord of the Soil recked little of what resulted from the arrangement. He regarded as forming a single family this tribe, this mass of human beings "getting up and going to bed together,"—"eating bread off one platter and meat out of one pot."

In this indiscriminate way of living, woman met with very little care or protection; the place she occupied was an extremely humble one. True, the virgin, the ideal woman, rose higher from century to century, but the woman of real life counted for mighty little in these rustic communities, these massed aggregates of men and cattle. Such was the unhappy but inevitable outcome of a state of things which could only change for the better when the common habitation was subdivided, when at length men plucked up courage to live apart, in separate hamlets, or to settle as isolated cultivators of fertile lands at a distance, and build huts in clearings of the forest. The separate hearth created true family life; the nest made the bird. Henceforth they have ceased to be chattels—they are living souls. . . . The wife and mother has come into existence.

A touching moment. At length she has a *home;* she can therefore be pure and holy at last, poor creature. She can brood quietly over a thought, and undisturbed, as she sits spinning, dream dreams while he is abroad in the forest. The hut is wretched enough, damp and ill-built, and the winter wind whistles through it; but to make up for all defects it is silent. There are dim corners in it where her dreams can find a lodgement.

She is an owner now, possesses something of her very own. *Distaff, bed, chest* is all the household has, as the old song says.[1] But soon a table will be added, a bench, or a couple of stools. . . . A poorly appointed house! but its furniture includes a living soul. The firelight heartens it; the consecrated bush of box guards the bed, to which is often added a pretty bunch of ver-

---

[1] Trois pas du côté du banc,   "Three steps towards the bench,
   Et trois pas du côté du lit,   Three steps towards the bed,
   Trois pas du côté du coffre   Three steps towards the chest,
   Et trois pas, revenez ici.   And three steps back again."
                                  (Old French song of *The Dancing-Master.*)

vain. The lady of this palace sits spinning at her door, watching a few sheep the while. They are not rich enough yet to keep a cow; but this will come in time, if God blesses the house. The forest, a bit of pasture land, a hive of bees that feed on the heath are their livelihood. They do not grow much wheat yet, having no certainty of reaping a crop so long in growing. This life, poverty-stricken as it is, is yet less hard upon the wife. She is not broken with fatigue, made old and ugly before her time, as she will be when the time of farming on a large scale has arrived. And she has more leisure too. Beware of judging her in any way by the coarse literature of the *Noëls* and *fabliaux,* the silly laughter and licence of the broad tales composed at a later date. She is alone, without neighbours. The evil, unhealthy life of dark little shut-in towns, the prying into each other's affairs, the pitiful, perilous scandal-mongering,—none of this is begun yet! There is no old harridan yet, coming creeping at dusk down the narrow, gloomy street to tempt the young wife and tell her *someone* is a-dying of love for her. The serf's wife we are describing now has no friend but her dreams, no one to gossip with but her beasts or the forest trees.

They talk to her,—we know not what about. They awake in her things her mother told her, her grandmother—old, old things that for century after century have been handed on from woman to woman. Harmless memories come back of the ancient spirits of the country, a gentle, genial family religion, which in the common life just quitted and its noisy promiscuity, had doubtless lost most of its force, but which now returns like a ghost and haunts the lonely cabin.

A strange, dainty world of fairies and elves, made to appeal to a woman's soul. Directly the great stream of invention that produced the saintly legends runs dry and stops, these other legends, older and equally poetical, but in a totally different way, come to share their vogue with them, and reign softly and secretly in gentle hearts. They are the woman's especial treasure, which she fondles and caresses. A fairy is a woman too, a fantastic mirror in which she sees her own self, only fairer and daintier than the reality.

What were the Fairies? What we are told is that in old days, queens of the Gauls, proud and fantastic princesses, at the coming of Christ and His apostles, were wickedly impertinent and turned their backs. In Brittany they were dancing at the time, and never stopped. Hence their cruel sentence; they are doomed to live on till the Day of Judgment.[2] Many of them are reduced to the tiny dimensions of a rabbit or a mouse; for instance, the kowrig-gwans (fairy dwarfs), who at night-time, at the foot of old Druidical stones, ring you round with their elvish dances; or to take another example, the lovely Queen Mab, who makes her royal coach out of a walnut-shell. They are a trifle capricious, and sometimes mischievously disposed,—and what wonder, considering their unhappy destiny? Whimsical and tiny as they are, they possess a heart, and crave to be loved. Sometimes kindly, sometimes the reverse, they are full of fancies. At the birth of a child they come down the chimney, endow the babe with gifts good or bad, and fix its fate. They love good spinsters, and spin divinely themselves. *To spin like a fairy,* the goodwives say.

In the *Fairy Tales,* disencumbered of the absurd ornaments the latest editors have dressed them out in, is found the people's very inmost heart. They mark a poetical period between the coarse promiscuity of the primitive *villa* and the licence of the days when a rising *bourgeoisie* produced the cynical *fabliaux.*

These Tales *have* a historical side, recalling the great famines, —in the ogres and so on. But as a rule they float in a higher ether than common history, soaring on the wings of Fantasy through the realms of eternal Poesy, expressing the desires of men's hearts, which are ever the same and have an unchanging history of their own.

---

[2] The authorities of all dates have been brought together in M. Alfred Maury's two learned books, *Les Fées,* 1843, and *La Magie,* 1860. Consult also, for the North, Grimm's *Mythologie.*

The longing of the poor serf to get breathing time, to find rest, to discover a treasure that shall end his wretchedness, recurs again and again in them. More often still, by a nobler aspiration, this treasure trove is a soul to boot, a treasure of sleeping love that must be awaked,—as in "The Sleeping Beauty"; though often the charming heroine is found hidden under a mask by reason of a fatal spell. Whence that touching Trilogy, that admirable *crescendo,—Riquet of the Tuft, Ass's Skin, Sleeping Beauty*. Love will take no denial; under all these hideous disguises, it pursues, and wins, the hidden fair one. The last of these three tales reaches the true sublime, and I suppose no one has ever been able to read it without tears.

A very real and very genuine passion underlies it, that of unhappy, quite hopeless love, one that cruel Nature often sows between pure souls of too widely separated ranks, the poignant regret of the peasant woman that she cannot make herself fair and desirable, to be loved of the knight; the stifled sighs of the serf, as looking down his furrow, he sees riding by on a white horse a too, too charming vision, the beautiful, the adored, mistress of the castle and the lands he tills. It is like the Eastern fable, the melancholy idyll of the impossible loves of the Rose and the Nightingale. But there is one great difference; the bird and the flower are both beautiful, equal even in beauty. But here the inferior being, so low placed in the scale of rank, confesses humbly, "I am plain and homely, a monster of ugliness!" The pity of it! . . . But all the same, with a persistency and a heroic power of will unknown to the East, and by the very ardour of his longing, he breaks through the silly obstacles in his way. He loves so truly he is loved in turn, this monster; and Love makes him beautiful.

There is an infinite tenderness in it all. This soul of enchantment turns her thoughts to others besides herself; and is eager to save all nature and all society as well. All the victims of those rough days are her especial favourites,—the child beaten by a cruel stepmother, the youngest sister scorned and ill-treated by the others. She extends her pity even to the lady of the castle herself, compassionating her for being in the hands of the ferocious baron, Blue Beard. She commiserates the brutes, and comforts them for the misery of still wearing the shapes of animals. They must be patient, a brighter time is coming; one day their captive souls will take wings and be free, lovable and beloved. This is the other side of *Ass's Skin* and other similar stories. Here at any rate is evidence of a woman's tender-heartedness. The rude field labourer is brutal enough with his beasts; but woman is different, she sees something else than beasts in them. She judges them as a child does, observes the human and spiritual elements in them, ennobles the whole animal world with her sympathy. Oh! happy spell! Lowly as she is, and convinced of her own plainness, yet she has invested all Nature with her beauty, and the charm of her personality.

But *is* she so plain, this little peasant wife, whose dreaming imagination feeds on all these fancies? I have described her life, how she keeps house, how she spins as she watches her sheep, how she trips to the forest and gathers her little bundle of firewood. No very hard work is hers as yet; she is not the repulsive-looking countrywoman of a later time, disfigured by unremitting labour in the wheat fields. Neither is she the heavy citizen's dame, fat and indolent, of the towns, who formed the subject of so many appetising stories amongst our forefathers. Our heroine is timid, and has no sense of security; soft and gentle, she is conscious of being in God's hand. On the mountain crag she sees the black and lowering castle, whence a thousand dangers may at any moment descend. She fears and honours her husband; a serf elsewhere, by her side he is a king. For him she keeps the best, living on almost nothing herself. She is slim and small, like the pictured saints in church windows. The meagre fare of those days is bound to make fine-strung creatures, but having only a frail vitality. Witness the enormous infant mortality. These pale-faced blossoms are nothing but nerves. At a later date this will break out in the epileptic dances of the fourteenth century. At present in the twelfth and thereabouts, two weaknesses are connected with this condition of semi-starvation: at night, somnambulism, and by day, hallucination, dreamy reverie, and the gift of tears.

All innocence as the woman is, still she has a secret—we have said so before—a secret she never, never confesses at church. She carries shut within her breast a fond remembrance of the poor ancient gods,[3] now fallen to the estate of spirits, and a feeling of compassion for them. For do not for an instant suppose, because they are gods, they are exempt from pain and suffering. Lodged in rocks, in the trunks of oaks, they are very unhappy in winter. They greatly love heat, and prowl round the houses; they have been surprised in stables, warming themselves beside the cattle. Having no more incense, no more victims, poor things, they sometimes take some of the housewife's milk. She, good managing soul, does not stint her husband, but diminishes her own portion, and when evening comes, leaves a little cream behind in the bowl.

These spirits, which no longer appear except by night, sadly regret their exile from the day, and are eager for lights. At nightfall the goodwife hardens her heart and sallies out fearfully, bearing a humble taper to the great oak where they dwell, or the mysterious pool whose surface will double the flame in its dark mirror to cheer the unhappy outlaws.

---

[3] Nothing can be more touching than this fidelity to the old faith. In spite of persecution, in the fifth century, the peasants used still to carry in procession, under the form of poor little dolls of linen and flour, the deities of the great old religions—Jupiter, Minerva, Venus. Diana was indestructible, even in the remotest corner of Germany (see Grimm). In the eighth century some pagan processions are still performed. In some humble cabins, sacrifices are still made and auguries taken, etc. (*Indiculus paganiarum,* Council of Leptines in Hainault). The *Capitularies* threaten death in vain. In the twelfth century Burchard of Worms mentions the various prohibitions and declares they were all unavailing. In 1389 the Sorbonne once more condemns the remaining traces of Paganism, and about 1400 Gerson (*Contra Astrol.*) mentions Astrology as an actual superstition still obstinately surviving.

Great heavens! if she were discovered! Her husband is a prudent man, and has a holy terror of the Church's anger; he would
most certainly beat her, if he knew. The priest makes fierce war
on the poor spirits, and hunts them out of every corner. Yet
surely they might be let live in peace in the old oaks. What harm
do they do in the forest? But no! Council after Council launches
its anathemas against them. On certain days the priest even goes
to the oak, and mumbles prayers and sprinkles holy water to
drive away the evil spirits.

What would become of them if there were no kind soul to pity
them? But *she* is their protection; good Christian as she is, she
yet has a warm corner in her heart for them. None other is to be
trusted with sundry little intimate secrets of her woman's nature,
innocent enough secrets for a chaste wife like her, but which the
Church would be sorely scandalised if it heard. They are her
confessors, to whom she does not fear to make these touching
feminine confidences. She thinks of them as she lays the Yule log
on the fire. It is Christmas, but it is the old Feast of the Spirits of
the North as well, the *Feast of the Longest Night*. The same of
the *Vigil of May Night,* the *pervigilium* of Maïa, when the mystic tree is planted. The same again, the fires of St. John's Eve, the
true festival of life and flowers and new-born love. Above all,
the childless wife makes it a duty to love these feasts, and observe
them piously. A vow to the Virgin might not perhaps be successful; she is hardly in full sympathy with such a case. Whispering
low, the anxious wife prefers to address her prayer to some old-
world deity, adored as a rustic god of yore, and whom such-and-
such a church has been good-natured enough to make into a
saint.[4] Thus bed and cradle, the tenderest mysteries a chaste and
fond soul broods over, all this is still the province of the gods of
ancient days.

Nor are the spirits ungrateful. One day she wakes, and lo!
without her putting a hand to anything, the household tasks are

[4] A. Maury, *Magie,* 159.

done. She is struck dumb, crosses herself, and says nothing. When her man is gone to work she asks herself what it means, but can find no answer. It must be a spirit. "What is he? what is he like? . . . Oh! how I should love to see him! . . . But I am afraid. . . . They say folks die who see a spirit." Meantime the cradle moves, rocks all by itself. . . . She is lost in wonder, and presently hears a tiny, soft, soft voice, so low she might almost think it spoke within her own breast. It says, "Dear, dearest mistress, if I love to rock your child, 'tis because I am a little child myself." Her heart beats wildly, but soon she gathers better courage. The harmless innocence of the act makes the spirit seem harmless too; he must be good and gentle, one God must surely tolerate at least.

Henceforth she is no longer alone. She plainly feels his presence, and he is never far from her. He rubs against her skirt, she can hear the rustle he makes. He is for ever on the move about her, and evidently cannot quit her side. If she goes to the stable, there he is again. And she is almost sure, the other day, he was in the butter-firkin.[5]

What a pity she cannot catch him and have a good look at him! Once, all of a sudden, when she stirred the live embers, she thought she saw him dancing an elfin dance among the sparks. Another time she all but captured him in a rose. Small as he is, he works away, sweeping and tidying and sparing her a world of trouble. All the same he has his faults. He is volatile and over-bold, and if he *were* caught he would most likely escape. Also he sees and hears too much. Sometimes he repeats in the morning some little word she has said quite low, low down, at bedtime, after the light was out. She knows for certain he is very indis-

---

[5] This is one of the little glutton's favourite hiding-places. The Swiss, who know his likings, to this day make him presents of milk. Their name for him is *troll;* among the Germans he is called *kobold, nix;* among the French, *follet, goblin, lutin;* among the English, *Puck, Robin Goodfellow.* Shakespeare makes him oblige sleepy maidservants by pinching them black and blue to wake them in the mornings.

creet, and most inquisitive. It troubles her to feel herself followed about everywhere; she complains how annoying it is, and likes it all the while. Sometimes she will threaten him and send him about his business. At last she is really alone, and quite reassured at the thought. But next moment she feels on her cheek a light caressing breath, a touch like a bird's wing. He was under a leaf, the rogue. . . . He laughs, and his sweet voice—no mockery in it now—tells her his delight in having stolen a march on his modest, modest mistress. Now she is really angry; but the rascal only trills, "No! no! little mistress, darling little mistress, you are not angry,—not at a thing like that!"

She is ashamed and dares say no more. But she has her suspicions he loves her over-well. Her scruples are awaked,—and she loves him all the more. At night she thought she felt him in bed, that he had slipped in between the sheets. She was afraid, offered a prayer to God, and pressed close to her goodman's side. What is she to do? She has not the heart or the courage to tell the priest. So she tells her husband, who laughs at first in sheer incredulity. Then she confesses a little more,—that Robin Goodfellow is a sly fellow, sometimes too bold by half. . . . "What matter? he is so wee!" Thus her husband himself reassures her.

Are we also to be reassured, we who can see more plainly? Yes! she is still perfectly good and innocent. She would shudder to imitate the great lady up yonder in the castle, who under her very husband's eyes, has her court of lovers and her page. Still we must allow the elfin lover has made good progress already. Impossible to have a less compromising page than one who can lie hid in a rose. And there is much that is love-like about him too. Few can be more encroaching; so tiny he is, he can slip in anywhere.

He slips even into the husband's heart, pays court to him, wins his good graces. He looks after his tools, works in his garden, and of evenings for his reward, behind the child and the cat, crouches in the chimney corner. His little voice makes itself heard, for all the world like a cricket's, but he is seldom seen, except when a struggling beam of light falls upon a particular crack where he loves to lie. Then they catch a glimpse, or think they do, of a sharp, whimsical little face; and cry, "Ah, ha! little one, we saw you."

All very well to tell them at church they must beware of evil spirits, that one they think quite harmless, one that slips into the house like a puff of wind, may really and truly be a demon. They take good care not to believe a word of it. Why! his littleness is proof enough of innocence; and certainly they have prospered more since he came. The husband is as sure of it as the wife, perhaps surer. He is firmly convinced the dear, frolicsome little Brownie makes the happiness of their home.

4

TEMPTATIONS

I HAVE omitted from the above picture the deep shadows of that cruel period, as these would have darkened it unduly. I refer especially to the uncertainty in which the rustic household habitually lived as to its lot, the suspense, the chronic terror of the savage violence that might burst at any moment on their unoffending heads from the castle above.

The feudal régime involved precisely the two things of all others that go farthest to make a hell on earth; on the one hand, the *extreme of immobility,*—the man was nailed to the soil, and emigration utterly impossible; on the other, a high degree of *uncertainty* as to the continuance of existing conditions.

Optimistic historians who talk so glibly of fixed quit-rents, and charters, and purchases of emancipation, forget the paucity of guarantees forthcoming for it all. So much is bound to be paid to the Feudal Lord,—but he can take all the rest too, if he likes. This is called in so many words *the right of prehension.* Work away, goodman! And while you are abroad in the fields, the dreaded troop from the heights may swoop down on your house and carry off what it pleases "for the service of the Seigneur."

No wonder, if you look at him the fellow is gloomy over his furrow, and hangs his head! . . . Yes! and he is always like that, with anxious brow and heavy heart, like a man constantly expecting bad news.

Is he pondering revenge? Not he; but two thoughts fill his mind, two anxieties trouble him alternately. The first, "In what condition will you find your house when you go back to-night?" The other, "Ah! if only the clod I turn would let me see a treasure underneath! if the kind Devil would give me wherewith to buy our freedom!"

It is said that at this appeal (like the Etruscan "genius" that emerged one day from under the ploughshare in the shape of a child) a dwarf, a gnome, would often lift its tiny figure from the soil and standing up in the furrow ask him, "What will you of me then?" But the poor man would be dumbfoundered, and wanted nothing now. He turned pale and crossed himself, and then the whole vision was gone.

Was he sorry afterwards? Did he never say to himself, "Fool, fool, do you mean then to be for ever unhappy?" I can well believe it, but I am no less convinced an unsurmountable barrier of terror prevented him from going further. I do not think for an instant, as the monks would have us believe, who have given accounts of Sorcery and Witchcraft, that the pact with Satan was a mere caprice, a sudden impulse of a lover or a miser. We need only consult common sense and human nature to be certain of the contrary, that people never resorted to such extremes except as a last resource, in utter despair, under the awful pressure of unending wrong and wretchedness.

"But," they tell us, "these excessive miseries must have been largely diminished as we near the days of St. Louis, who forbade private wars between great lords." My own opinion is exactly the opposite. During the eighty or a hundred years which intervened between this prohibition and the English Wars (1240–1340), the seigneurs, no longer having their customary amusement of burning and pillaging the lands of the neighbouring lord, were ferocious in the treatment of their vassals. St. Louis's peace was their war.

The ecclesiastical seigneurs, the monkish seigneurs, and the like, make the reader of the *Journal d'Études Rigault* (published recently) fairly shudder. The book gives a revolting picture of wild, barbarian licence. The monkish seigneurs showed especial violence towards the nunneries. The austere Rigault, Confessor of the sainted King and Archbishop of Rouen, makes a personal investigation into the condition of Normandy. Every night he rides up to the door of a fresh monastery. Everywhere he finds the monks leading the bold, bad life of feudal nobles, going armed, drinking, duelling, hunting recklessly over waste and cornland alike, the nuns living with them in indiscriminate concubinage, and everlastingly with child by them.

Such was the Church! What must the lay nobles have been? What was the inside like of those gloomy towers that, viewed from the plain below, inspired mere panic terror? Two tales, true history doubtless both of them, *Blue Beard* and *Griselda*, tell us something. What was he for his vassals, his serfs, this torturer, who treated his own family with such refinement of cruelty? We can judge from the only one of them brought to trial, and that not till the fifteenth century, Gilles de Ritz, the kidnapper of children. Sir Walter Scott's *Front de Bœuf*, the barons of melodrama and romance, are poor creatures compared to these terrible realities. The Templar in *Ivanhoe* is an equally feeble and an entirely artificial portrait. The author has not dared to face the foul actualities of celibacy among the Knights of the Temple, and of life inside the fortified castle, where very few women were allowed, as being mere useless mouths. The Romances of Chivalry give exactly the opposite of the truth. Indeed, it has often been observed how literature in many cases expresses the entire contrary of contemporary life and character; as, for instance, the insipid pastoral plays of the Florian type that held the stage during *the Terror* of the Revolutionary Period.

The domestic arrangements of these mediæval castles, where they can still be traced, tell us more than all the books put together. Men-at-arms, pages, serving-men, packed together at night under low-browed vaults, by day stationed on the battlements, on narrow terraces, suffering the most atrocious boredom, found breath and life only in their sallies on to the plain below— no longer now warlike expeditions against neighbouring lands, but hunting parties, *man*-hunting parties, exactions, outrages, without number on the households of the surrounding serfs. The Lord knew perfectly well himself that a mass of men like this without women could only be kept in hand on condition of occasional licence.

The appalling notion of a hell where God uses the wickedest souls, the most sinful of all there, to torture the less sinful, delivered up to them as playthings, this noble dogma of the Middle Ages was literally realised. Men felt instinctively God was far from them. Each razzia was another proof of the domination of Satan, a convincing proof it was to him they must henceforth address their prayers.

To add insult to injury, there was much coarse laughter and ribald wit indulged in. "But surely the serf women were too unattractive," it may be objected. The answer is, it was no question of beauty; the pleasure consisted in outraging, beating, and making women cry. As late as the seventeenth century, the great Court ladies would almost die of laughing to hear the Duke of Lorraine describe how his fellows raided peaceable villages, killing and torturing every woman, old women included.

Outrage was especially rife, as may be supposed, among the well-to-do households, of a relatively superior rank, which were to be found among the serfs, families of serfs supplying mayors to the community from generation to generation, such as are found as far back as the twelfth century taking the first place in the villages. The nobility hated, mocked, and would fain have ruined these. Their new sense of moral dignity was an unpardonable offence; it was unforgivable that their wives and daughters should be chaste and virtuous women. What right had they to be respectable? Their honour was not theirs to keep. *Serfs of the body,* that was the cruel phrase everlastingly thrown in their teeth.

It will be hard to believe in days to come that, among Christian people, the Law did a worse thing than any it did to the slaves of Antiquity,—that it expressly sanctioned as a right the most deadly outrage that can wring a human being's heart.

The ecclesiastic seigneur, no less than the lay, possesses this foul prerogative. In a parish in the neighbourhood of Bourges, the curé, being a seigneur, laid express claim to the *firstfruits* of every bride, though in practice he was quite willing to sell his wife's virginity to the husband for money down.[1]

The theory has been too readily accepted that this outrage was only formal, never actually done. But the price named in certain countries for release from it was far beyond the means of almost any peasant. In Scotland, for instance, the Feudal Superior claimed "several cows,"—an enormous, an impossible price. Thus the poor young peasant's wife was at her Lord's discretion. Moreover, the *Fors du Béarn* state in so many words that the right was literally exacted. "The peasant's eldest son is always reckoned the Seigneur's child, for he may be of his engendering."[2]

All feudal customs, even where this is not mentioned, invariably impose an obligation on the newly made bride to go up to the castle to present the *marriage meat-offering*. An odious practice to force the poor trembling creature thus to run the gauntlet of anything it might enter the heads of the wild pack of insolent, wifeless retainers that harboured there to do to her.

One can still see the shameful scene,—the young husband bringing his bride to the castle. One can imagine the guffaws of the knights and squires, the ribald tricks of the pages, that welcomed the unhappy pair. "At any rate the presence of the Lady of the Castle will keep them in check," you say. Not a bit of it. The fair châtelaine the romances would have us think so delicate,[3] but who was quite capable of taking command of the garri-

---

[1] Laurière, ii. 100, under word *Marquette;* Michelet, *Origines du Droit,* 264.

[2] This work was not published till (1842) subsequently to the *Origines* (1837).

[3] This delicacy and refinement is well instanced in the treatment the ladies of the Court were for inflicting with their own hands on Jean de Menny, their poet, the author of the *Roman de la Rose* (about 1500). They would certainly

son in her Lord's absence; who was used to judging, punishing, ordering torture or death; who had a hold over the Baron himself by means of the fiefs she brought him—she was no tender-hearted protectress, least of all for a serf, who perhaps was a pretty woman too. Flaunting publicly, as was the habit of the time, her favoured knight and her page, she was not sorry to justify the liberties she allowed herself by similar misdemeanours on her husband's part.

She will be no obstacle to the game in hand, the amusement they are getting out of the poor trembling fellow eager to redeem his wife. They begin by bargaining with him, laughing at the agonies of the "hard-fisted peasant," and end by sucking his very marrow and blood. Why this dead set at the pair? Because he is fittingly dressed, an honest man of respectable position, a notable person in his village. Because she is pious, chaste, and modest, because she loves him, because she is afraid and in tears. Her pretty eyes ask for pity,—in vain.

The unfortunate man offers all he possesses, even the dowry itself. . . . No use! it is not enough. Angered at the injustice of such harsh treatment, he urges, "But my neighbour, he paid nothing." . . . Ho! ho! argufying now, the insolent scoundrel! Then the whole pack crowds round him, shouting; sticks and brooms belabour him with a hail of blows. Finally he is hustled and kicked out of doors, and they scream after him: "Jealous brute, with your ugly, lenten looks, who's stealing your wife? You shall have her back to-night, and to cap the favour, with child! . . . Say thank you; why! you're nobles now. Your firstborn will be a Baron!" All crowd to the windows to see this ludicrous figure, death in his heart, wedding-clothes on his back. . . . Peals of laughter pursue him, and the roystering mob, down to the meanest scullion, gives chase to the "poor cuckold!" [4]

have carried out their intention, had it not been for the witty poet's clever subterfuge.

[4] Nothing can be merrier than the old French *Contes;* but they have a certain monotony. The jokes are limited to three: the injured husband's

The man would have died on the spot of rage and chagrin, but for one hope,—of the Devil's help. He goes home alone, and finds his house, how empty, how deserted! No! not empty; there is someone there. Satan sits at the hearth-side.

Presently she returns too, pale, disordered, in pitiful estate! . . . She throws herself on her knees, and craves his pardon. At this the man's heart is like to burst. . . . He puts his two arms round her neck, and weeps and sobs and cries aloud till the very walls tremble. . . .

Still her coming brings God back to the house. Whatever she may have endured, she is pure, innocent, and holy yet. Satan will get nothing to-day. The *Pact* is not ripe for signing yet.

Our silly national *Fabliaux* and ridiculous *Contes* without exception assume that under this mutual injury and all subsequent ones she will have to affront, the wife is on the side of her outragers and against her husband; they would have us believe that the poor girl, bullied and shamefully used, made a mother in spite of herself, is delighted and overjoyed at it all. Can anything be more improbable? No doubt rank, politeness, elegance were likely enough to seduce her; but no one took the trouble to use these means. They would have much fine fun indeed of anyone who for a serf's wife should have played the high-bred lover. All the rout, chaplain, cellarer, down to the very serving-men, thought they were honouring her by outrage. The humblest page fancied himself a great Lord, if only he seasoned his love-making with insults and blows.

One day, when the poor woman had been maltreated in her husband's absence, she was heard to exclaim, as she recoiled her

---

despair, the squalls of the victim of the lash, the grimaces of the fellow on the gallows. The first is funny; the second sets you laughing till you cry; but there! the third caps all, and you hold your sides in inextinguishable merriment! Mark now, the three are only one after all. It is always the man who is down, the weakling that can be outraged without risk of retaliation, the person who is incapable of self-defence.

long hair, "Oh, miserable Saints of wood, of what avail to make vows to them? Are they deaf? or are they grown old? . . . Why have I not a Spirit to protect me, strong and powerful,—if an evil Spirit, I cannot help it? I see them many a one carved in stone at the church door. What are they doing there? Why do they not fly to their proper home, the castle yonder, to carry off these miscreants and roast them in hell? . . . Oh for strength and power! Who can give me these? I would gladly give my whole self in exchange. . . . Alas! what could I give? What have I to give? I have nothing left. Woe on me, body and soul,—on my soul that is but ashes! Why—why cannot I have, instead of my elfin friend, who is good for nothing, a great, strong, powerful Spirit?"

"Oh, sweet little mistress mine, 'tis by your fault I am so small, and I cannot grow bigger. . . . And besides, if I were big, you would never have liked me, never have allowed me near you, and your husband even less. You would have had me driven off by your priests and their holy water. . . . I will be big and strong if you wish. . . . Mistress mine, Spirits are neither big nor little, strong nor weak. At desire, the tiniest can become a giant."

"Why? How?"

"Nothing simpler. To turn your Spirit into a giant, you have but to give him a gift."

"A gift! What gift?"

"A sweet woman's soul."

"Oh, horror! Who are you, say? And what is this you ask?"

"Nay, such gifts are made every day. . . . Would you price yourself higher than the lady yonder of the castle? She has pledged her soul to her husband, to her lover; nevertheless she gives it again all to her page, a child, a little silly lad. I am far more than your page; I am more than any serving-boy. In how many things have I been your little maid and tirewoman? Nay, do not blush, do not be angry. . . . Let me tell you only, I am all about you, and already perhaps within you. For how else should I know your thoughts, even the very thought you hide

from your own self? . . . Who am I? I am your little soul, that
talks unconcernedly to your great, your proper soul. . . . We
are inseparable. Do you rightly know how long I have been with
you? For more than a thousand years. For I was your mother's,
and her mother's, your grandmother's and great-grandmother's.
. . . I am the genius of the hearth and home."

"Tempter! tempter! . . . but what will you do?"

"I will make your husband rich, and you powerful, so that folk
shall fear you."

"What say you? Are you then the demon of hidden treasures?"

"Why call me demon, if I am but doing a just work, a task of
kindness and gentle piety? . . . God cannot be everywhere, He
cannot be always at work. He likes to rest sometimes, and leaves
us, the Spirits, to see to little matters, to correct the inadvertences
of His Providence, the miscarriages of His justice. . . . Your
husband is an instance, poor, hardworking, deserving mortal,
who toils and moils himself to death, and gains the barest living.
God has not had time yet to think of him. . . . Albeit a trifle
jealous, still I love him, my good host,—and pity him. He can no
more, he must give in. He will die like your children, killed
already by dire poverty. Last winter he was ill. What will become
of him next winter?"

Then she put her face between her two hands, and wept for
long hours. At last, when she had no more tears left, though her
sobs still shook her breast, he said, "I ask nothing. . . . Only,
I beseech you, let us save him between us."

She had made no promise, but she belonged to him from that
hour forth.

5

DIABOLICAL POSSESSION

But the terrible age is the age of gold. By this I mean the cruel epoch when gold first got the mastery. The date is 1300, in the reign of Philippe le Bel of France, a king at once of gold and iron, it would appear, a great monarch that never opened his mouth, that seemed to have a dumb spirit, but at the same time a mighty arm,—strong enough to burn down the "Temple," long enough to stretch to Rome and with iron gauntlet to give the first buffet to the astonished Pope.

Henceforth gold is High Pope, and god of all, and not without good reason. The movement began in Europe with the Crusades; wealth is not deemed wealth unless it has wings and is capable of moving freely hither and thither, admits of rapid exchange. The King, to strike his far-off blows, needs gold and gold only. The army of gold, the army of the King's treasury, spreads far and wide over the whole face of the land. The great Baron, who has brought home dreams of splendour from the East, is ever longing, for its marvels,—damascened weapons, oriental carpets and spices, horses of pure Arab blood. For all this he must have gold. When the serf brings in his wheat, his Lord spurns him with his foot, crying, "That is not all I want; I would have gold."

From that day the world is changed. Hitherto, in the midst of many evils, there was at any rate peace and security so far as the levies were concerned. As years were good or bad, the quit-rent followed the course of nature and the quality and quantity of the harvest. If the Lord of the Soil said, " 'Tis a fine tribute you offer," the answer was, "My Lord, God has given no more."

But gold! alas! where to find gold? . . . We have no army to raid it from the rich cities of Flanders. Where are we to dig the earth to win its treasure? Ah! if only we had the Spirit of hidden treasures [1] to be our guide!

While all are in despair, the peasant wife with the elfin ally is already seated on her sacks of wheat in the neighbouring little market town. She is all alone, the rest of her village cronies are still busy making up their minds.

She sells at what price she will. Even when the others do arrive, the cream of the custom goes to her; some mysterious, magic attraction draws all to her, and no one even thinks of beating down her terms. Before the appointed day, her husband carries his quit-rent in good solid coin to the feudal elm. "Astonishing! astonishing!" all the neighbours cry. . . . "For sure the Devil must be in the Dame!"

---

[1] Demons afflict the world throughout the whole period of the Middle Ages. But Satan does not assume his definitive character before the thirteenth century. *"Pacts with the Evil One,"* M. A. Maury observes, "are very rarely found before this epoch." I can quite believe it; for how conclude a covenant with a being that really and truly does not as yet exist? Neither of the two contracting parties, in fact, was ripe for the agreement. For the human will to come to this appalling extremity of selling itself for all eternity, *it must* needs have first *grown desperate.* The merely *unhappy* man is still far from despair; it is the being who is *utterly and hopelessly wretched,* who has complete consciousness of his own wretchedness, and consequently full and complete agony of suffering, without any expectation of relief, it is he and he only who knows what despair is. Desperation in this sense may be predicated of the poor man of the fourteenth century, who is asked to perform the impossible,—to pay quit-rent and taxes in money. In the present chapter and the succeeding one, I have noted the incidence, sentiment and progress of despair, capable of leading up to the horrible covenant of the Pact with Satan, and what is even worse than the pact pure and simple, the appalling condition and profession of Sorcery or Witchcraft. The word is used freely enough, but the thing is still exceptional, being nothing more nor less than a marriage with the powers of Evil and a sort of consecration to the Devil. To make my descriptions more easily comprehensible, I have connected the details of this subtle and difficult piece of analysis by a thin thread of fictitious narrative. However, after all the framework is of small importance; the essential point is to realise that such enormities did not arise (as writers have tried to make us believe) *from mere heedlessness and thoughtlessness, from the weakness of fallen human nature, from the chance temptations of concupiscence.* Their existence implied the fatal overmastering pressure of an age of iron, the irresistible constraint of grim necessities,—required that Hell itself should appear a shelter, an asylum, a relief, as contrasted with the Hell of this world.

They laugh, but she is far from sharing their mirth. She is sad and sore afraid. Pray as she will, strange tingling, creeping sensations disturb her rest, and set her trembling in her bed. She sees grotesque and horrible shapes about her. The Familiar Spirit, once so tiny and so gentle, is grown a wilful tyrant. Terrified at his boldness, she is restless and angry and fain to rise. She submits, but with sighs and groans; she feels her loss of independence, and exclaims, "Alack! I am no longer my own woman now!"

"Well! well!" cries the Baron, in high satisfaction, "here's verily a peasant with some sense at last; he positively pays in advance. I tell you, I like you, man! Can you cast accounts?" "Yes! a little." "Well, then, 'tis you shall settle accounts with all my folk. Every Saturday you shall take your seat under this elm to receive their moneys. On Sunday morning, before Mass, you must bring up the proceeds to the castle."

A mighty change this, truly! The goodwife's heart beats high when, Saturday come, she sees her poor husband, mere labourer and serf that was, sitting like a little lord himself under the shadow of the feudal tree. A trifle dazzled and confused at first, he gets used to the position finally and assumes an air of gravity. Nor is it safe to poke fun at him; the Baron means him to be respected. When he comes up to the castle, and rivals are for laughing at him and playing him some nasty trick or other in their jealousy, "You see yonder embrasure," says the Baron; "the rope you may not see, but it is all ready. The first to lay a hand on him, shall dangle out of the one at the end of the other, and so I tell you, shut and stump."

The saying is repeated, and there settles round them a sort of atmosphere of terror, everyone louts low, very low indeed to them; but they are avoided and shunned when they walk the roads. The neighbours strike into bye-paths with a furtive air and a pretence of not seeing them. The change makes them proud just at first, but soon saddens them, as they realise their isolation in the midst of village society. She with her delicate perception sees plainly enough the hate and scorn the Castle bears her, the hate and fear of her companions of the countryside. She feels herself between two dangers, in a terrible loneliness. No protection but the Baron, or rather the money they provide him with; but to get this money, to stimulate the peasant's reluctance, to overcome the *vis inertiæ* he offers, to drag something even from those who have nothing, what persistent pressure, what threats, what harshness, are required! The goodman was never meant for such a trade; his wife encourages him, urges him, saying, "Be stiff with them, cruel if needs must. Strike hard. Else you will be behindhand with your payments. And then we are indeed undone!"

Such the anxieties of the day,—trifling in comparison with the torments of the night. She has all but lost the power of sleeping. She gets up, and paces up and down, prowling about the house. All is quiet; and yet how changed the house is! It has lost all its old pleasant sense of security and gentle innocence! What is the cat ruminating over as she lies before the fire, feigning to be asleep and blinking her half-shut yellow eyes at me? The goat with her long beard and her wily, sinister looks, knows a deal more than she says. And the cow, half seen in the moonlit stall, why does she gaze at me askance in that mysterious way? . . . How uncanny it all is!

She shudders, and lies down again by her husband's side. "Lucky man, how sound he sleeps! . . . But I have done with sleep; I shall never sleep again!". . . Nevertheless she drops off at last. But then, how she suffers! Her importunate friend is at her ear, eager, tyrannical. He persecutes her without mercy; if she drives him off a moment by the sign of the cross or a prayer, he is back again directly in some other shape. "Behind me, Satan! Beware! I am a Christian soul. . . . No! not that; you must *not* do that."

Then in revenge he assumes a hundred hideous forms. He glides a shining serpent over her bosom, dances a loathly toad on her belly, or with a bat's pointed beak steals horrid kisses from her shuddering mouth. . . . He is trying every art to drive her to extremities, to force her, vanquished and exhausted, to assent at last to his vile propositions. But she is not beaten yet; she will not say, Yes! She prefers to suffer her nightly tortures, the never-ending martyrdom of the awful struggle.

"How far can a Spirit be incarnate too? . . . Are his foul attempts corporeal realities or no? Would she be doing carnal sin if she yielded to her persecutor? Would it be actual and veritable adultery?" . . . Subtle questions these he asks at times to unnerve and undermine her resistance. "If I am nothing but a breath, a vapour, a puff of wind (as many Doctors of the Church teach), why so fearful, little trembling soul? and what has your husband to say in the matter?"

One of the worst torments of pious souls throughout the Middle Ages is that many doubts we should deem frivolous and purely academical were then burning questions, agitating and terrifying men's minds, taking the form of visions, sometimes of fierce arguments with the Devil, or agonising debates with a tortured conscience. The Demon, for all his furious manifestations in the case of demoniacs, nevertheless remains a Spirit down to the very end of the Roman Empire, and up to the time of St. Martin, in the fifth century. On the invasion of the barbarians, he grows barbarian too, and more and more carnal and corporeal, —so much so that he takes to stone-throwing, and amuses himself with pelting to pieces the bell of St. Benedict's cloister. The Church, to frighten off the savage encroachers on ecclesiastical property, makes the Devil more and more frankly incarnate, teaching men to believe he will torment sinners, not merely as soul acting upon soul, but materially in their flesh, that they will suffer actual bodily tortures,—not the flames of an ideal hell, but every exquisite pang of physical pain that blazing brands, the gridiron, and the red-hot spit can inflict.

This conception of diabolic torturers, tormenting the souls of the dead with material agonies, was a perfect gold-mine for the mediæval Church. The survivors, torn with grief and pity, asked eagerly, "Cannot we, from this world to that, redeem these unhappy souls? Cannot we expiate their offences by dint of fines and imposition, as is done in earthly matters?" The bridge between the two worlds was Cluny,—the Cluniacs from their first foundation (about 900) having at once grown into one of the richest of the monastic orders.

So long as God punished in person, *making His hand heavy* on sinners, or at any rate *striking by sword of an angel* (according to the noble antique phrase), it was not so horrible. The hand of the Lord was severe,—a Judge's hand, but still a Father's too. The angel when he struck was still pure and clean as his own sword. But it is by no means so when the ministers of execution are foul demons. They are very far from imitating the angel that burned Sodom,—but only after quitting the city. *They* remain, and their hell is a horrid Sodom, where Damned Souls, more deeply stained with sin than the sinners given into their power, find an odious pleasure in the torments they inflict. This doctrine men saw inculcated in the *artless* sculptures carved around church doors, from which they learned the dreadful lesson how fiends experience a wanton delight in causing pain. Under pretext of punishment, the devils work out on their victims the most revolting caprices. A profoundly immoral conception, and a truly damnable, this,—of justice, falsely so-called, favouring the coarser part, making its perversity yet more perverse by handing it over a plaything to torment, corrupting the very demons themselves!

A cruel, cruel time! Think how black and lowering was the sky; how it weighed on the heads of mankind! Think of the poor little children, their minds filled with these dreadful notions, trembling with terror in the very cradle! Think of the pure, innocent girl, shuddering lest Damnation lurk in the pleasure she involuntarily finds in the workings of the Spirit; of the wife, as she lies in the marriage-bed, tortured by the same assaults, resisting yet ever and anon feeling the stir within her! . . . A horrid experience, known to those who have the tapeworm. To be conscious of a twofold life, to feel the horrid thing moving within one, now violently, now with a silky, undulatory creeping that is even worse, and recalls the sensations of seasickness,— till a man dashes away in frenzy, horror-struck at himself and his own body, longing only to escape, to die. . . .

Even at such times as the Demon was not actively tormenting her, the woman subjected to his assaults might be seen gloomily roaming around, a prey to melancholy thoughts. For there is no hope left of cure. His entry is irresistible; he penetrates everywhere like a foul miasma. Is he not the Prince of the Air, the Prince of Storms,—of internal no less than of external storm? We find this coarsely, but vigorously, portrayed under the arch of the great doors of Strasburg Cathedral. At the head of the company of *Foolish Virgins,* their leader, the woman of sin who is enticing them down to the abyss, is full, swollen out, with the Demon, who hideously distends her body and escapes from beneath her skirts in a black cloud of dense, stifling smoke.

This distension is one cruel mark of Diabolical Possession,— at once a punishment and a boast. She carries her belly thrust forward, the proud wanton of Strasburg, and her head well thrown back, triumphing in her hideous grossness, rejoicing in her monstrous deformity.

She is not like this yet, the woman we are describing. But she is already puffed out with the Devil, and with evil pride in her new fortunes. Sleek and fair, she walks the street, her head high, her face expressing pitiless disdain and scorn of the very earth she treads on. Her neighbours are afraid, and both hate and admire her.

Our village dame says plainly by mien and look: " 'Tis I

should be the Lady of the Castle! . . . What is *she* at, I would
know, in the high tower yonder, wanton, idle jade, among all
those men, and her husband so far away?" A rivalry springs up;
and the village, which hates her, is proud of her none the less.
"The Lady of the Castle is Baroness; but ours is Queen . . .
more than Queen, something none dare name. . . ." Terrible
and fantastic her beauty, a cruel beauty, compact at once of pride
and pain. The Foul Fiend in person glares out of her eyes.

She is his in a sense, but only in a sense as yet. She is herself
still, and steadfastly refuses to surrender her personality. For
the moment she is neither the Devil's nor God's. True the demon
may enter into her, permeate her whole being in subtle vapours;
but so far he has really won nothing, for her *will* is still unsub-
dued. She is possessed, bedevilled; but Satan is still very far
from having got her in his power. At times he will practise on her
atrocious, but quite unavailing, torments. He will kindle a flame
of fire in bosom and belly and bowels; she writhes and struggles
in agony, but nevertheless defies him.
    "No! vile torturer, I will not yield up my identity, I will not!"
    "Beware! I will lash you with a whip of scorpions; I will tear
your flesh so savagely, you will thenceforth go in tears, piercing
the shuddering air with your screams."
    The succeeding night he does not come. Next morning (it is
Sunday morning) her husband went up to the castle, and returned a picture of desperation. The Baron had told him: "A
stream that trickles drop by drop will never turn the mill. . . .
You bring me a farthing at a time,—what use is that? . . . I
must be starting in a fortnight. The King is marching on Flanders, and I have not so much as a war-horse ready, for my old
charger goes lame since the tourney. See to it; I must have a
hundred silver pounds." "But—but where to find them, my
Lord?" "Sack the whole village as you will. I will give you men
enough. . . . Tell your oafs they are ruined men unless the

money comes—and yourself shall be the first to die. . . . I am sick of you. You have a woman's heart; you are a craven and a sluggard. You shall pay dear for your cowardice and slackness. Look you! only a straw turns the scale that I don't keep you here, that you never see your home again. . . . 'Tis Sunday; they would have a good laugh down yonder to see you dancing in the air over my battlements."

The unhappy wight repeats this to his wife. In sheer despair he prepares for death, and recommends his poor soul to God. She is as terrified as he, and can neither rest nor sleep. But what can she do? She is deeply sorry now she sent the Spirit away. If only he would come back again! . . . Next morning at her husband's rising, she falls back exhausted on the bed. In an instant she feels a ponderous weight on her breast; she pants and almost chokes. The incubus slips lower, presses the woman's belly, while simultaneously she feels her arms gripped by a pair of hands that are like steel. "You wished for me. . . . Well! here I am. Ha! cruel recreant, at last, at last your soul is mine?" "Nay! but, great sir, is it mine to give? My poor husband! You used to love him. . . . You said so. . . . You promised. . . ." "Your husband! come, have you forgotten? . . . are you so sure you have always kept your will steadfast for him? . . . For your soul, I *ask* you for it out of mere complacence, for indeed 'tis mine already. . . ."

"Not so, great sir," she answers back, her pride rekindling spite of her sore strait. "Not so! my soul is mine, my husband's, consecrated by my marriage vow. . . ."

"Little fool, little fool! you are incorrigible! Even now, under the goad, you persist in struggling! . . . I have seen it, your soul, I know it by heart, every hour of the day and night,—and better than you do yourself. Day by day I have watched your first essays at resistance, your times of grief and of despair! I have noted your hours of discouragement, when you murmured to yourself, 'Who can resist the irresistible?' I have been present at your periods of yielding too. You have suffered something, and cried a little, but never very loud. . . . If I have claimed your soul of you, 'tis because it is a lost soul already. . . .

"Now your husband is on the verge of ruin. . . . How save him? I will take compassion on you. . . . You are mine; but I would have more,—I would have you give yourself to me, avowedly and of your own free will. If not, his ruin will be consummated."

She answered soft and low, through her sleep: "Alackaday! my body and my miserable flesh, take them, take them, to save my husband. . . . But my heart, never. None has ever had it yet, and I cannot give it."

So said, she lay waiting her fate, resigned. . . . Then he threw her two words, saying: "Remember, in them is your only safety." Then she shuddered from head to foot, rigid with horror to feel herself empaled by a fiery bolt, inundated by an icecold flood. . . . A piercing scream,—and she found herself lying in her astonished husband's arms, drenching him with her tears.

She tore herself violently away, and sprang from the bed, trembling at the thought of forgetting the two indispensable words. Her husband was terrified; for she did not so much as see him, but kept throwing the savage looks of a Medea at the chamber walls around her. Never was her beauty more resplendent. In the dark pupil and the yellow-tinctured white of her fierce eyes flashed a gleam no man would dare encounter, the sulphurous lava glow of a volcano.

She marched straight to the town. The first of the two words was *green*. She saw hanging at the door of a shop a green robe,—green, colour of the Prince of this World. It was old and worn, but once on her shoulders shone forth new and dazzling. She marched, without a word of inquiry, straight to the house of a Jew, and knocked loudly. The door is opened cautiously, and the poor Jew discovered sitting on the ground, half smothered in the

ashes. "Good sir, I must have a hundred silver pounds!" "Why!
lady, how should I lend such a sum? The Prince Bishop of this
city, to force me tell where my gold lies hid, has had my teeth
drawn one by one.[2] . . . Look, see my bleeding gums." "I know,
I know; but it is just the means to destroy your Prince Bishop I
come to you for. When the Pope is buffeted, the Bishop will
scarce stand firm. Who says so? It is the word of Toledo." [3]

The Jew hung his head. She stooped over him and breathed
softly in his ear. . . . She was in deadly earnest, and the Devil
to back her to boot. A strange wave of heat filled the room; even
the old man felt as if a fountain of fire had shot up before his
eyes. "Lady," he cried, gazing at her from under his brows,
"Lady, poor, ruined as I am, I had a few pence in reserve to buy
meat for my unhappy children." "You will never repent it, Jew.
. . . I will swear you *the great oath*, the oath that kills. . . .
What you lend me you shall have back in one week, in good time,
at earliest morn. . . . I swear it by your *great oath*, and mine,
a mightier watchword still, *Toledo*."

A year passed. She was grown stout and rosy, resplendent like
fine gold. Men marvelled at her fascination, and admired and
obeyed her with one consent. By a miracle of Satan, the Jew was
become open-handed, ready to lend money at the smallest sign.
She it was, and she alone, kept up the castle as well by her credit
in the city as by the terror her harsh exactions inspired in the village. The triumphant green robe was everywhere, coming and
going, every day seeming newer and more splendid. Her own per-

---

[2] This was a method in high favour for compelling the Jews to disgorge. John
Lackland, King of England, had frequent recourse to it.

[3] Toledo would seem to have been the Holy City of the Sorcerers and
Sorceresses, a countless host in Spain. Their relations with the Moors, highly
civilised as was this people, and with the Jews, a wise folk and in those days
masters of all Spain (as agents of the Royal Exchequer), had given the
Sorcerers a high culture, and they formed at Toledo a sort of university of
their own. By the sixteenth century they had been Christianised, changed
and modified, reduced to mere *white magic*. See the *Déposition du sorcier
Achard, sieur de Beaumont, médecin en Poitou* (Evidence of the Wizard Achard,
Sieur de Beaumont, a leech in Poitou), in Lancre, *Incrédulité*, p. 781.

son assumed an almost superhuman beauty, instinct with victory and haughty insolence. One prodigy there was that startled beholders, and each said wonderingly, "A grown woman,—and she grows taller, more stately, day by day!"

Meantime a new development; the Seigneur is returned. The Lady of the Castle, who for long durst not come down for fear of confronting the lady of the plain, has mounted her milk-white palfrey. She comes to meet her husband, with all her folk about her, draws rein and gravely greets him.

First and foremost she exclaims, "Ah! how wearily have I waited you! how could you leave your faithful bride to languish so long in lonesome widowhood? . . . And yet, and yet, I cannot give you place by my side this night, an you grant me not one boon." "Ask it, ask it, fairest lady!" returned the knight, laughing gaily. "But ask quickly. . . . Verily I am in haste to have you in my arms, lady mine. . . . I wot you are grown more beautiful than ever!"

Then she spoke low in his ear, and none knows what it was she said. But before climbing to the castle, the good Baron set foot to earth before the village church, and went in. Under the porch, standing at the head of the village grandees, he sees a lady he fails to recognise, though he louts low before her. Proud as Lucifer, she wore towering above the heads of the men the lofty two-peaked coif of the period,—the Devil's bonnet as it was often called on account of the double horns that formed its ornament. The great lady blushed hotly, and passed on eclipsed and looking small and homely by comparison. Then furious she hissed under her breath. "Yes! there she stands,—your vassal, your serf all the while! 'Tis the last straw; all rank and order is overset, and asses bray insult at horses!"

Coming out, the bold-faced page, the favourite, draws a poniard from his girdle, and dextrously, with a single slash of the keen blade, slits the fine green robe from waist to feet.[4] She came

---

[4] Such is the monstrous and cruel outrage we find quite commonly employed in those rough times. In the Gallic and Anglo-Saxon laws it is laid down as the

near fainting at the cruel outrage, while the crowd stood staring and amazed. But they soon understood, when they saw the Baron's retainers one and all dash forward to hunt the prey. . . . Swift and pitiless fell the whistling lashes. . . . She flies, but feebly; she is already a trifle unwieldy. Barely ten paces, and she stumbles. Her best friend and gossip has thrown a stone in her path to trip her feet. . . . At this a shout of brutal laughter; but she lies cowering, screaming shrilly. . . . But the pages are remorseless, and whip her to her feet again with their lashes. The noble, gallant pack join in, and pick out the tenderest spots for biting. At long last, a haggard figure in the dreadful procession that welters round her, she reaches her own house-door,—to find it shut! With hand and foot she knocks and kicks, shrieking, "Good husband, quick! oh, quick! open, open!" But yet she hung there, spread-eagled, like the wretched barn-door owl you see nailed to a farmer's door, while the blows continued to rain down on her unceasingly. Not a sound within the house. Was the husband within? or was it that, scared for his riches, he dared not face the crowd, dared not risk the pillage of his goods?

Under all these outrages and blows and sounding buffets she fell swooning at last. Then she sat crouching on the chill stones of the threshold, naked, half-dead, her long hair barely covering her bleeding flesh. Then one of the castle party cries enough; "We have no wish to kill her."

So they leave her, and she runs to hiding. But in spirit she sees

penalty for immodesty (Grimm, 679, 711; Sternhook, 19, 325; Ducange, iii. 52; Michelet, *Origines,* 386, 389). Later on, the same affront is shamefully and unjustly inflicted on honest women, tradesmen's wives beginning to show overmuch spirit, whom the nobles wish to humiliate. The snare is familiar into which the tryant Hagenbach enticed the honourable dames of the superior bourgeoisie of Alsace, probably in mockery of their rich and royal costume, all of silk and cloth of gold. Again, I have mentioned in my *Origines* (p. 250), the extraordinary right which the Sire de Pacé, in Anjou, claimed over the *fair* (honest) women of the neighbouring lands. These were bound to bring him to his castle four deniers and a rose wreath, and to dance with his officers. A perilous enterprise for them, one in which they had much reason to fear meeting with some such dire insult as that of Hagenbach. To force them to come, the threat is added that the recalcitrant will be stripped and branded with the Baron's arms on their naked flesh.

the gay doings in the Castle Hall. The Baron, giddy-headed as he is, could not help exclaiming, "Nay! I am half sorry for it all." But the chaplain says smoothly, "If the woman is *possessed,* as they say she is, my Lord, your duty to your good vassals, your duty to all the countryside, is to deliver her up to Holy Church. It is awful to see, since these scandals of the Templars and of the Pope, the progress the Devil is a-making. Against him one thing only avails, the stake. . . ." A Dominican interrupts, "Excellent well, your Reverence, you have spoke excellent well. Deviltry—deviltry is heresy of the first degree. Like the heretic, the devil-possessed must be burned alive. Still sundry of our good Fathers do not trust now even to the stake itself entirely. Wisely and well they would fain before all have the erring soul slowly and surely purged, tried, tamed by fastings, lest it be burned in its unrepentant pride and go triumphing to the stake. If you, my Lady, in your piety and sweet charity, if yourself would take the task of working in this our sister's stubborn heart, setting her for some years or so *in pace* in a brave dungeon of which you only should hold the key, you might indeed by firm discipline and proper torments, save her poor soul, shame the Foul Fiend, and at last yield her up, chastened and humbled, into the hands of Mother Church."

The PACT with SATAN

ONLY the victim lacked. All knew the most acceptable gift they could offer the châtelaine was to deliver the unhappy creature into her power. Right tender the gratitude she would have shown the man who had given her this proof of devotion, handed over to her mercy the poor bleeding limbs of her rival.

But the prey was on the alert. A few moments more and she would have been spirited away, imprisoned for good and all within the stone walls of a dungeon. She snatched up a tattered cloak lying in the cattle-shed to cover her nakedness, took wings, so to speak, and before midnight struck, found herself leagues away, far from any thoroughfare, on a desert heath all thistles and brambles. The heath skirted a wood, where, under the glimpses of an uncertain moon, she was able to scrape together a few acorns, which she munched and bolted like a wild beast. Centuries seemed to have passed since yesterday; she was another woman altogether. The proud beauty, the queen of the village, was no more; her very soul and its every outward manifestation was utterly changed. She pounced on the acorns like a famished wild boar, sat squatted at her food like an ape. Thoughts, scarcely human, were crowding through her brain, when she hears, or thinks she hears, a screech-owl's hoot, followed by a shrill peal of laughter. She is startled; but there! 'tis perhaps only the mocking jay that can imitate every sound, and delights in these deceptions.

The weird laugh is heard again. Where it comes from she cannot tell. It seems to issue from an old hollow oak.

But now she hears words plainly articulated, "Ah, ha! so you are come at last. . . . Very unwilling you were to come; you never would have come at all had you not found yourself in the extremity of direst straits. . . . You must needs, proud lady, be whipped to the enterprise, and cry and whine for mercy, mocked, scorned, an outcast and a byword to your own husband. Where would you be this night, if I had not pitied you and shown you the *in pace,* the dungeon they were making ready for you in the castle crypts? . . . Late, late in the day, you come to me,— old woman, old witch, they call you now. . . . You were young once, and you treated me ill then, me your little Robin Goodfellow that was so eager to serve you. . . . Your turn now (if I will have you) to serve me, and kiss my feet.

"You were mine from your birth up; the roguery you hid so well, the diabolic charm you could not hide, made you mine. I was your lover, your husband. Your own has shut the door in your face. But I will be kinder; I welcome you to my domains, my free and open plains and spreading forests. . . . What do I gain, you ask? Have I not long had you in my power at propitious seasons? Have I not overwhelmed, possessed you, filled you with the flame of my desire? I have changed, renewed the very blood in your veins. There is not an artery in your whole body I do not circulate through. You cannot tell yourself how completely and entirely you are my bride. But your wedlock has not yet been solemnised with all the formalities due. I am a stickler for propriety, a gentleman of scruples. . . . We must be made one for all eternity."

"Great sir, situated as I am, what can I, what should I say? Oh, indeed I have felt, I have felt only too plainly, since many a day, that you are my destiny, my only and inevitable destiny. Artfully have you caressed and favoured and enriched me, to bring me to ruin at the last. Yesterday, when the black hound bit my poor naked limbs, his teeth burned in my flesh . . . and I cried, 'It is he!' The same evening, in the Castle Hall, when that Herodias debauched and overawed the board, someone was there ready to pander to her hate and promise her my blood . . . and it was you again!"

"True enough! but 'tis I likewise that saved you, and led you hither. And why did I so? Because I would fain have you all my own, with none to interfere between us. Frankly, your husband was an offence to me. And you, you would be for ever bargaining, making terms. Quite other is my way; my maxim is, all or nothing! That is why I have tormented you a trifle, disciplined, chastened you, to ripen you for my embraces. . . . I am particular, and pick and choose; I do not, as folk think, accept every silly soul that may be ready to give itself to my power. I am for select souls, at the right toothsome crisis of fury and despair. Look you! I must needs tell you, I like you well, as you are to-day; you are more desirable than ever before, you are a delectable soul for Satan. . . . Ah! how long, how long I have loved you! . . . But to-day I am hungry, hungry for you! . . .

"I will deal largely and liberally with you. I am not one of those husbands who make bargains with their future bride. If you would merely be rich, rich you should be on the instant. If you would merely be a queen, step into the place of Queen Jeanne of Navarre, it should be done, and none should say me nay—and verily the King would lose little in the pride and wilfulness of his spouse. 'Tis a greater destiny to be my wife. But there, say what you would have yourself."

"Great sir, I want nothing but the power of working ill."

"Ah, a charming, a right charming answer! . . . How well you merit my love! . . . Truly that comprehends everything, both the Law and the Prophets. . . . Seeing you have chosen so wisely, you shall be given into the bargain all the rest to boot. You shall know all my secrets. You shall see the foundations of the earth. The world shall come to you, and pour out gold at your feet. . . . More, here I give you the true diamond, my bride, the brilliant of first water, *Revenge*. . . . I know, you gipsy, I know your most hidden wish; our two hearts beat as one in this. . . .

That is the thing will ensure me final and certain possession of you. *You shall see your lady enemy on her knees before you,* asking mercy and beseeching, happy if only you would hold her pardoned, doing the same she did once to you. Yes, she shall weep . . . and you shall say No! with a condescending smile, and hear her cry in her agony, 'Death and damnation, ah me!' . . . Then comes my turn to act."

"Great sir, I am your servant. . . . I was ungrateful once, I confess. For indeed you have always been over good to me. I am yours, I am yours, my master and my god! I want no other. Gracious is the light of your countenance, and your service a sweet service of delight."

With this she falls grovelling, and adores him from the ground! . . . First she does him homage according to the Templars' rite, symbolising the utter abnegation of self and self-will. Her master, the Prince of this World, the Prince of the Gales of Heaven, breathes himself into her being like a rushing mighty wind. She receives at once and together the three sacraments, reversed and desecrate,—Baptism, Priesthood, and Marriage. In this new church, the exact opposite of its counterpart, the Church of God, everything is reversed. Patient and submissive, she bore the cruel initiation,[1] her spirit borne up and comforted by the one word, "Revenge!" Far from the infernal levin exhausting her energies, making her weak and ailing, it made her more strong and terrible, and brought fire from her eyes. The moon, that had modestly veiled her face an instant, shuddered to see her now. Swollen out horribly with the hellish vapour, with fire and fury, and (a new circumstance) with an unholy longing of desire, she showed for a moment enormous in her excessive proportions, and of an awe-inspiring beauty. She gazed around her, . . . and nature itself seemed changed. The trees had found a language of their own, and told her tales of ages long ago. The

---

[1] This will be found explained later. We must beware of the pedantic additions of the moderns in the seventeenth century. The tinsel ornaments fools tack on to so awful a reality only serve to lower Satan to their own poor level.

herbs were simples now. Plants that yesterday she kicked away contemptuously like hay, were become beings that spoke to her of healing.

Next day she woke in full security, far, far out of her enemies' reach. They had sought her fruitlessly, finding only a few fluttering rags of the fatal green robe. Had she in her despair leapt into the torrent? Had she been carried off bodily and alive by the Demon? None knew. In either case she was damned, there could be never a doubt of that. The Lady of the Castle was comforted not a little they had not found her.

Had they met her, they would hardly have known her, so mightily was she changed. Her eyes alone remained the same, not bright and flashing, but filled with a strange, appalling, sombre glow. She was afraid, herself, of terrifying others; she did not drop them, but she looked askance, to mask their sinister effect by the obliquity of her gaze. Suddenly grown dark of skin, she might to all appearance have passed through the flames. But such as gazed more heedfully, felt that the flame was rather an internal one—that an unclean and consuming fire glowed in her bosom. The flaming bolt Satan had driven through her, still glowed within, and threw, as if from a sinister, half-veiled lamp, a grim, but still perilously enticing, reflection. Men drew back shuddering, but did not quit her, and their senses were stirred and troubled.

She found herself at the entrance of one of those caves of the troglodytes that occur in such numbers in certain hills of the centre and west of France. It was the border marches, then a wild stretch, between the land of Merlin and the land of the Faery Queen. Open heaths, stretching limitless on every side, bore present witness to old-time wars and everlasting forays, the terrors of plunder and violence that kept the countryside yet unpeopled. There the Devil was at home; of the scattered inhabitants, the most part were his fervent disciples, his devotees. For all the fascination the rugged brushwoods of Lorraine, the dark pine forests of the Jura, the salty wastes of the Burgos, may have exercised over him, his favourite haunt was perhaps these western borderlands of France. It was not merely the home of the dreamy shepherd, of the satanic accoupling of she-goat and goat-herd, but the scene of a close conspiracy with Nature deeper than elsewhere, of a more intimate comprehension of healing drugs and noxious poisons, of mysterious relations, the connecting link of which has never been fathomed, with Toledo the learned, that university of diabolic arts.

It was the beginning of winter. His cold breath, stripping the trees, had piled up heaps of leaves and twigs of dead wood. All this she found ready at the mouth of her gloomy shelter. Traversing a stretch of forest and a quarter of a league of heathy waste, one came down within hail of a group of hamlets a runlet of water had brought into existence. "Behold your kingdom," the voice within her whispered. "A beggar-woman to-day, to-morrow you shall be queen of all this countryside."

7

KING of the DEAD

A<small>T</small> first she was not greatly touched by these promises of future greatness. A hermitage without God, torturing memories that assail her in the deep solitude, the losses she had borne and the insults she had endured, her sudden, cruel widowhood, her husband who had left her alone to her shame and humiliation, all this saddened and overwhelmed her. A plaything of destiny, she saw herself like the wretched weeds of the waste, without root, beaten and buffeted by the north wind, tormented, cruelly battered this way and that; she seemed a poor fragment of coral, dull, grey, and angular, that possesses only coherence enough to be the better shattered. Children stamp on it, and men in mockery call it "The wind's wife."

She laughs wildly and bitterly, as she likens herself to these things. But from the recesses of the darkling cave comes a voice, "Ignorant and foolish, you know not what you are saying. . . . This weed that thus goes fluttering down the wind has good right to scorn all the fat, common herbs of the field. It has no abiding place or root, but 'tis complete, sufficient to itself, bearing everything, flower and seed within itself. Be you like it; be your own root, and in the very face of the whirlwind, you shall yet blossom and bear flowers, our own flowers, such as spring from the dust of tombs and the ashes of volcanoes.

"The first flower of Satan, I give it you this day, that you know my earliest name, the token of my antique might. I was, I am *the King of the Dead*. . . . How have I been traduced! . . . 'Tis I alone (an infinite boon that should have won me altars of

61

thanksgiving), I alone, that bring the Lost Ones back to earth. . . ."

To penetrate the future, to call up the past, to anticipate or to resuscitate the days that fly so fast, to enlarge the present by what has been or what will be, two things these sternly proscribed in the Middle Ages. In vain; in this Nature is irresistible and prohibition unavailing. To offend against such law is to be a man. He would be none, who should stay for ever bound to his furrow, with downcast eyes and gaze confined to the next pace he takes behind his plodding oxen. No! we men must always, as we go, be looking inquiringly higher, and farther, and deeper. This earth, yes! we measure it painfully and meticulously, but we spurn it too and cry constantly, "What have you in your bowels? What secrets? What mysteries? You give us back duly the grain we entrusted to you; but you never return us that human harvest, the dead loved ones we have lent you. Shall they not germinate too, our friends, our lovers, that we have planted there? If only for one hour, one instant, they might come back to us!"

Ourselves too shall soon be of that *terra incognita,* whither they have already gone. But shall we see them again? Shall we be with them? Where are they? What is their life yonder?— They must indeed, my dead dear ones, be close captives not to vouchsafe even a sign! And what shall *I* do to make them hear? My father, whose only joy I was and who loved me so exceedingly, why, why does he never come to me? . . . On this side and on that, only sore constraint, and bitter captivity and mutual ignorance! A gloomy night where we look for one ray of light in vain! [1]

These never-ceasing ponderings of human nature, which in Antiquity were merely sad, became in the Middle Ages cruel, bitter, demoralising, making men's hearts to grow faint within

---

[1] This ray does shine to some extent in the *Immortalité* and the *Foi Nouvelle* of Dumesnil; *Ciel et Terre* by Reynaud, Henri Martin, and others.

them. It would seem as though the world had set itself deliberately to degrade the soul and render it "cribbed, cabined, and confined" to the measure of a coffin. The servile mode of burial between four planks of deal is well adapted to accomplish this, suggesting as it does an uneasy sense of suffocation. The dear one who has been coffined thus, if he comes back in dreams, is now no light, radiant shadow, centred in the aureole of a better and lighter place, but a tortured slave, the unhappy prey of a horrid, clawed hell-cat,—*bestiis,* the text itself says, *Ne tradus bestiis,* etc. ("Deliver us not to the *beasts*"). Hateful and impious thought, that my father, so good and so lovable; my mother, so looked up to by all, should be the playthings of this horror! . . . You laugh at this to-day. But for a thousand years it was no laughing matter, but one for bitter burning tears. To this day one cannot write of these blasphemies without the heart swelling, and the very pen and paper grating a protest of fierce indignation!

Another truly cruel innovation was to have displaced the Feast of the Dead from Spring-time, to which Antiquity assigned it, to fix it in November. In May, where it stood originally, the dead were buried in flowers. In March, where it was put later, it marked, with the commencement of ploughing, the first awaking of the lark; the dead man and the living seed were put in the earth simultaneously, with the same hope of revivification. But, alas! in November, when all field work is ended for the year, the weather overclouded and gloomy for months to come, when mourners returned to the house, and a man sat down by his fireside and saw the place opposite for ever empty . . . what an aggravation of sadness was here! . . . Plainly by choosing this period already mournful enough in itself, this period of the obsequies of dying nature, the fear was that else man would not have grief enough of his own to make him properly mournful! . . .

The calmest of us, the busiest, however much distracted by

the activities and anxieties of life, have strange moments at times. In the twilight of dark winter mornings, at nightfall, coming down so fast to engulf us in its gloom, ten years, twenty years afterwards, feeble, mysterious voices sound in your heart of hearts, "Greeting, dear one; 'tis we! . . . So you are still living and working on, as always. . . . It is well! You are not bowed down with the grief of losing us; you can do well without us. . . . But we, we can never forget you. . . . The ranks are closed up again, the vacant place obliterated. The house that was ours is full of life, and we bless its prosperity. All goes well,—better than in those far-off days when your father carried you in his arms, when your little girl in her turn asked you, 'Carry me, father, carry me!' . . . But there, you are weeping. . . . Enough,—farewell to meet again."

Woe is me! they are gone, after uttering this gentle, heart-breaking plaint. But is it a just one? Not so! a thousand times rather would I forget myself than forget them! And yet, cost what it may to say it, we must allow that certain characteristics escape us, are already less perceptible; certain features of the dear face are, not effaced indeed, but darkened, faded. A hard thing, a bitter and a humiliating, to feel oneself so fugitive and feeble, as quick to lose impressions as the unremembering waters; to realise that at long last we are losing that treasured grief it was our hope to keep intact for ever! Give it back, give it back, I implore; I value so fondly that gracious source of tears. . . . Restore, I beseech you, those cherished images. . . . If nothing else, make me at least dream of them by night!

Many a one says so in drear November. . . . And, while the bells are tolling, and the dead leaves raining down, they disperse from the church door, whispering low to each other, "Do you know this, neighbour? There lives up yonder on the moors a woman they speak both good and ill of. For my own part, I dare not say; but she has strange powers over the under-world. She calls up the dead, and they answer her summons. Ah! if only she could (innocently, mind you, without offending God), if only she could bring back my loved ones that are dead! . . . I am all alone, you know; I have lost all I had to live for in this world. But who is this woman? Who knows her? Whence she is, from heaven or from hell? I will never visit her,"—yet all the while he is dying to go. "I will never risk my immortal soul by going near her. Those woods, besides, are haunted; many a time men have seen in the heath things that were not there to see. . . . Remember poor Jacqueline, who wandered there one night to search for a strayed sheep of hers. She came back a mad woman. I will never go."

Nevertheless, hiding the fact one from the other, many of the men do go. Scarce as yet do the women dare to confront the risk. They think of the dangerous road, ask many questions of such as have been there already. The pythoness is not like the Witch of Endor, who called up Samuel at Saul's bidding; she shows no shadowy forms, but she gives the cabalistic words and beverages of might that will compel the dead to come back once more in dreams. How many sorrows come to her. Even the old grandmother of eighty, frail and tottering, would fain see her little grandson once again. By a supreme effort, not without remorse for committing such a sin when so near the tomb, she drags herself to the witch's hut. The savage-looking place, rough with its yews and briars, the bold, dark beauty of the implacable Proserpine she finds there, all frightens her. Prostrate and trembling on the earth, the poor old woman weeps and prays. No answer is vouchsafed; but when at length she dare raise her head a little, she sees hell itself has been weeping in sympathy.

This simple impulse of pure natural feeling set poor Proserpine blushing. Indignant at her own weakness, "Degenerate creature, weakling soul," she ejaculates, "you that came hither in the fixed design of working ill and only ill. . . . Is *this* the result of your master's teaching? Ah! how he will laugh me to scorn!"

"Nay, not so. Am I not the great shepherd of shades, to bid

them come and go, to open them the gate of dreams? Your Dante, when he paints my portrait, forgets my true attributes. Adding a grotesque and superfluous tail, he never sees how I hold in very deed the shepherd's rod of Osiris, and have inherited his caduceus from Mercury. They thought to build an impassable wall to block absolutely the road from one world to the other; but my feet are winged, and I flew lightly over the obstacle. Vilely calumniated, called a ruthless monster, I have yet felt the prick of pity, succoured the afflicted, and consoled sorrowing lovers and mothers bereaved of their little ones. Spirit of evil, I have yet felt compassion and pitiful revolt against the harshness of the new God."

The Middle Ages and its chroniclers, Churchmen to a man, have been careful not to avow the hidden, but profound, changes taking place in popular sentiment. It is plain that Pity now appears ranged on the side of Satan. Even the Virgin, the ideal of grace, makes no appeal to this need of every feeling heart, nor the Church either. Evocation of the Dead is indeed expressly forbidden. While all the books go on dilating glibly either of the swinish Satan of the earliest conceptions or else of the clawed demon, king of torments, of a later age, the Devil has taken quite another aspect for the unlearned, who write no books. He has something of the classical Pluto, but pale and majestic, by no means deaf to prayers, granting to the dead return and to the living to see their dead once more, he approximates closer and closer to his sire or grandsire, Osiris, the shepherd of souls.

This change involves many others. Men confess with their lips the official hell of the Churches, the fiery furnaces and boiling cauldrons; but in their hearts do they really believe it all? Is it possible to reconcile a hell thus complacent towards sorrowing hearts with the awful traditions of a place of torment? One conception neutralises the other, without entirely obliterating it, the resultant being a compound picture, vague and shadowy, destined to assimilate more and more nearly to the Virgilian idea of the infernal regions. An incalculable relief this to the over-burdened spirit; above all a sweet alleviation for unhappy women, whom this terrible dogma of the torture of their loved ones kept for ever weeping and uncomforted,—their whole life one long-drawn moan of horror.

The Sibyl was pondering the master's words when a small, light step makes itself heard. The day is barely dawning yet,—after Christmas Day, getting on for the New Year. Tripping over the crackling, frosty grass, a small woman, with fair face and yellow hair, draws near with trembling limbs; reaching the door, she sinks fainting on the threshold, scarce able to breathe. Her black dress proclaims plainly enough she is a widow. Medea's piercing look strikes her nerveless and speechless; yet is her story manifest, no mystery left unrevealed in all her shrinking form. Then the Sorceress in confident tones, "Dumb, little one? Yet, what need to speak,—and you would never find words to tell. I will say it for you. . . . Well, then, you are dying for love!" Recovering some little presence of mind, clasping her hands, all but falling to her knees, she makes her confession, avowing everything. She had suffered and wept and prayed,—and all without a word. But those Christmas merry-makings, those family reunions at the festive season, the ill-concealed satisfaction of happy wives pitilessly flaunting a sanctioned love, brought back the old cruel smart to her heart. . . . Alack! what should she do? . . . If only he could come back to comfort her for an instant! "I would give my life for the boon . . . let me die, if I may but see him once again!"

"Go back to your house, and shut the door close. Draw the shutter too against prying neighbours. Quit your mourning weeds and put on your wedding dress. Lay his place at table; yet he will not come. Sing the song he made for you, and sang so often; yet he will not come. Draw from the chest the coat he wore last and kiss it, and say, 'The worse for you, the worse for you, if you refuse to come!' And without an instant's tarrying, drink this wine ('tis bitter, but a sovran sleeping-draught) and lay you down in the bridal bed. Then, have no fear, he will come."

She would not have been a woman, if she had not next morning, glowing with soft happiness, whispered the miracle softly in the ear of her bosom friend. "Not a word of it to any, I beseech you. . . . But he told me himself, if I wear this dress, and sleep without once waking, every Sunday night he will come back to me."

A happiness not without sore risk! What would happen the venturesome woman, if the Church found out she was a widow no longer? that, raised up by love, the spirit of her mate comes back to comfort his forlorn wife?

A most unusual thing, the secret is well kept! The word goes round among her friends and neighbours never to betray a mystery so tender. Indeed, it concerns them one and all; for who is there has not suffered, who is there has not wept tears of bereavement? Who but sees with joy unspeakable this bridge built to connect the two worlds of life and death?

"Oh, good, kind Sorceress! . . . Good Spirit of the Depths! blessings, blessings on you both!"

8

PRINCE of NATURE

THE winter is hard, long, and dismal in the gloomy north-west. Even after it seems well ended, it suffers relapses, like a pain that has been stifled, yet stings afresh and rages intermittently. One morning, and all Nature awakes bedecked with sparkling ice-needles. In this bitter, ironical beauty of a day that sets all living things a-shivering, the vegetable world seems turned to stone, losing all the soft charm of its mobile variety and stiffening in rigid crystals.

Our poor Sibyl, sitting benumbed at her wretched fire of dead leaves, buffeted by the cutting wind, feels her very heart cower under the cruel lash of the weather. Her loneliness oppresses her, but is a tonic too. Her pride is roused, and with it comes a strength that warms her heart and kindles her spirit. Alert, bright, eager, her sight grows keen as the ice-needles themselves; and the world, that world that makes her suffer so, is as transparent to her as glass. She triumphs over it as over a conquered province.

Is she not its queen? Has she not courtiers in plenty to pay her reverence? The ravens are manifestly obedient to her service. In solemn, dignified array they come, like augurs of old times, to tell her the news of the day. The wolves slink by timidly, greeting her with furtive, sidelong looks. The bear (not so uncommon then) will now and then take his seat ponderously, with his heavy, good-natured mien, at the threshold of the cave, like a hermit paying visit to a brother hermit, as we see so often pictured in the Lives of the Thebaïd Fathers.

All, birds and beasts that man scarce knows except in connec-

tion with killing and the chase, all are outlaws like herself. There
is a mutual understanding. Is not Satan the outlaw of outlaws?
and he gives his followers the joy and wild liberty of all free
things of Nature, the rude delight of being a world apart, all-
sufficient unto itself.

Fierce, keen joys of solitude, all hail! . . . The whole earth
seems shrouded in a white winding-sheet, imprisoned under a
load of ice, chained down by relentless icicles, all alike, and all
sharp and cruel. Especially after 1200 the world was close shut
like a transparent sepulchre, where everything stands horribly
motionless and, as it were, petrified with cold.

It has been said that "a Gothic church is a complex crystalli-
sation,"—and it is true. About 1300, architecture, sacrificing
all it possessed of living variety and graceful caprice, enters into
rivalry with the monotonous prisms of the Spitzberg. 'Tis a true
and terrible image of the dead city of adamantine crystal, within
which a dreadful dogma thinks it has succeeded in burying
human life.

But, no matter how strong the supports and buttresses and
abutments that sustain the edifice, one thing sets it tottering. Not
the noisy batterings from without, but a something soft and
yielding in the foundations, something that affects the seemingly
unyielding crystal with a gradual, almost imperceptible, thaw.
What is it?—the flood of warm human tears a lowly, pitiful world
has shed, a sea of weeping? What?—a breath of the future, a
mighty, invincible resurrection of the natural life. The fantastic
pile, crumbling already in many a joint, groans to itself in tones
not devoid of terror, " 'Tis the breath of Satan, the breath of
Satan."

Picture a glacier on the flank of Hecla, and we shall see a like
process. The ice lies over a volcano, not one receding to make
sudden and fierce eruption, but for all that a centre of slow heat,
gradual, gentle, stealthy in its operation, which warms the icy

mass caressingly from beneath, whispers it softly to come down, —and down it comes.

The Sorceress has good cause for laughter, if from her shade she sees yonder, in the full light of day, how profoundly ignorant of the true facts are Dante and St. Thomas Aquinas. They make out that Satan progresses by dint of terror or cunning. They represent him a grotesque and coarse-minded being, such as he was in his earliest days, when Jesus could still drive him to enter into the herd of swine. Or else, as an alternative, they show him a subtle reasoner, a scholastic logician, a phrase-mongering jurist. If he had been nothing else, only a beast, or else a rhetorician, if his only alternatives had been the mire of the sty, or the vain distinctions of empty logic, he would soon have perished of sheer hunger.

The triumph is too easy a one when they show him us in Bentolo, pleading against the Virgin, who soon has him nonplussed, condemned, and cast in costs. It is presently discovered that here on this earth precisely the opposite is what really happens. By a supreme effort and final success he wins over his adversary herself—his fair adversary, woman—seducing her by an argument that is no mere play of words, but a living reality, entrancing and irresistible. He lays in her hand the precious fruit of Science and of Nature.

No call for so much disputation, no need for special pleading; he has only to show himself, the embodiment of the "gorgeous East," a veritable Paradise Regained. From Asia, that men thought they had abolished, rises a new dawn of incomparable splendour, whose rays strike far, very far, till they pierce the heavy mists of the West. Here is a world of nature and art that brute ignorance had called accursed, but which now starts forth to conquer its conquerors in a peaceful war of love and maternal charm. All men yield to the spell; all are fascinated, and will have nothing that is not from Asia. The Orient showers her wealth upon us; the webs, and shawls, and carpets of exquisite softness and cunningly blended colours of her looms, the keen, flashing steel of her damascened blades, convince us of our own barbarism. But far more than this, the accursed lands of the infidel, where Satan holds domain, possess, in sign manifest of Heaven's blessing, the best products of all Nature, the very elixir of the creative powers of God, *the first of vegetables* and *the first of beasts,*—coffee and the Arab steed. Nay! beside this, a whole world of treasures,—silk, and sugar, and all the best of wonder-working herbs that cheer men's hearts, and console and soften their woes.

Towards the year 1300 all this comes to a head. Spain herself, won back by the barbarous Goths, yet ever dreaming of the Moors and Jews of old, testifies for her heathen conquerors of an earlier day. Wherever the Mussulmans, those sons of Satan, are at work, all is prosperity, water-springs bursting from the soil, and the earth all carpeted with flowers. Under the stimulus of good, honest, happy work, the land is glorified with those wondrous vines that make men forget their griefs and recover their serenity, seeming to drink in with the noble liquor happiness itself and Heaven's sweet compassion.

When Satan offers the brimming cup of life and happiness, in all this world of fasting mankind, is there one being of sanity strong enough, where sanity is so rare, to receive all this without giddiness, without intoxication, without a risk of losing self-control?

Is there a brain, that not being petrified, crystallised in the barren dogmas of Aquinas, is still free to receive life, and the vigorous sap of life? Three Wizards [1] essay the task; by innate vigour of mind, they force their way to Nature's source; but bold and intrepid as their genius is, it has not, it cannot have, the adaptability, the power, of the popular spirit. So Satan has re-

[1] Albertus Magnus, Roger Bacon, Arnold of Villeneuve—the last-named discoverer of the art of distilling spirit from the grape.

course to his old ally, Eve. Woman is the one thing left in the world most replete with nature. She has never lost certain aspects of roguish innocence that mark the kitten and the precocious child. In virtue of this side of her character, she is better adapted, more congruous, to the comedy of human life here below, more fitted for the great game the universal Proteus is about to play.

But how light-minded, how fickle-hearted is woman, so long as she is not struck serious, steadied by grief! Our lady of the heath, outlaw from society, rooted in her savage waste, at any rate gives us something to take hold of. Remains to be seen whether chafed and embittered, her heart full of hate and venom, she will back to nature and the soft pleasant ways of life? If she does, it will for sure be harshly and inharmoniously, often by round-about ways of ill. She is wild and fierce and rough, from the very fact of her utter helplessness amid the welter of the storm.

When from the genial warmth of springtide, from the air, from the depths of earth, from flowers and their voiceless tongues, the new revelation rises round her on every side, she is at first seized with giddiness. Her bosom swells nigh to bursting; the Sibyl of knowledge has her ordeal, as her sisters had, the Cumæan, the Delphic Sibyl. Pedants may declare, "It is the *Aura,* the air merely that fills her to bursting, and that is all. Her lover, the Prince of the Air, puffs her out with fancies and lies, wind, smoke, and infinite emptiness," but they are wrong and their simile absurdly mistaken. The truth is just the opposite; the cause of her intoxication is that no emptiness at all, but reality, actuality, definite form and substance, have taken shape over-suddenly in her bosom.

Have you ever seen the Agave, that rude, harsh native of the African plains, spiky, bitter, sharp-thorned, with pointed spears instead of leaves? This Aloe loves and dies every ten years. One morning, the wondrous flower-shoot, so long growing silently and voluptuously within the rude exterior of the plant, bursts forth with a sound like a gunshot and soars heavenward,—a veritable tree in itself, full thirty feet high, encrusted with sad-looking blossoms.

Something analogous is experienced by the gloomy Sibyl, when one morning of spring, a late, and for that very reason a more vigorously fecundating spring, all round her burst the infinite explosion of new life.

And all this reacts on her, is done for her sake. For each creature whispers low, "I am for that being that has comprehended me."

The contrast! . . . She, bride of the desert and black despair, fed on hate and vengeance, lo! she finds all these innocent creatures inviting her to smile. The trees, bending before the south wind, do her gentle reverence. All the grasses of the field, with their divers virtues, perfumes, healing drugs or poisons (more often than not one and the same thing), offer themselves, murmuring, "Gather me, gather me!"

Everything speaks manifestly and by invisible signs of love. " 'Tis all a mockery surely! . . . I had been ready prepared for Hell, but not for this strange festival. . . . Spirit, dread Spirit, are you indeed the Spirit of terror I have known, the cruel trace of whose passage I can still feel (though I scarce know what it is I really feel), the wound that burns still within me? . . .

"Nay! it is no more the Spirit I longed for in my frenzied rage, *'He that pronounces the everlasting No.'* Here I find him cooing a soft Yes of love and sweet intoxication and giddy joy. . . . What means it? Can he be the wild, the reckless, startled soul of life and its delights?

"They said great Pan was dead. But lo! he is here, living in Bacchus, in Priapus, grown impatient at the long tarrying of desire,—menacing, burning, fecundating. . . . No! no! away with the cup from my lips. Mayhap I should but be drinking the troubled dregs therein; mayhap but a bitter despair the more to add to my fixed despair!"

Meanwhile, wherever the woman appears, she is the sole and only object of love. All follow her, all for her sake scorn the females of their own kind. Why speak in particular of the black he-goat, her so-called favourite? The feeling is universal, common to one and all. The stallion neighs for her, breaks from all restraint, imperils her safety. The dreaded lord of the plains, the black bull, if she passes him, bellows his right to see her vanish in the distance. Nay, the very birds of the air swoop to her feet, and deserting their kind, with fluttering wings make her overtures of their love.

Her grim lord and master's domination has taken a new and unexpected form. By a fantastic transformation he is changed of a sudden from King of the Dead, as men deemed him, to King of Life.

"Nay!" she cries; "leave me my hate. I asked this, and nothing more. Let me be feared, an object of dread. . . . Fear is the stigma of my beauty—the beauty that accords best with the snaky blackness of my elf-locks, with my features furrowed by anguish and blasted by the lightning flash. . . ." But here sovereign Evil hisses in her ear in low, insidious whispers, "Ah! but you are more beautiful than ever, more moving in your frenzied passion! . . . Shout, curse! 'Tis a spur to desire. Deep calls to deep. Steep and slippery and swift is the path from rage to voluptuous delight!"

Neither anger nor pride were to save her from these seductions. Her safety came from the immensity, the infinitude of her desire. No single passion would suffice. Each single life is limited, weak and impotent. Away, courser of the plains! away, bull of the prairies! away, ardours of the feathered tribe! Away, feeble creatures! of what avail are ye to one that craves the infinite?

She feels a woman's overmastering caprice. And what is the object of her caprice? Why, the All, the great, the illimitable All of the universe at large.

Satan had failed to foresee this prodigious longing, a longing that could find appeasement with no single living creature.

This was something beyond even his powers, a mysterious impulse without a name, without a possibility of realisation. Yielding to these vast, unbounded aspirations, deep and limitless as the ocean, she falls softly asleep; losing all memory of past wrongs and suffering, all thoughts of hate and vengeance, in involuntary, as it were reluctant, innocence, she lies wrapt in slumber on the herbage, as any other tender creature—a lamb, a dove—might have done, her limbs relaxed, her bosom open to the heaven,—loved, but I cannot, I dare not, say loving.

So she slept and dreamed . . . a beautiful, a wonderful dream. She dreamed—'tis a thing hard to set down in words— how a wondrous monster, the genius incarnate of life universal, was absorbed in her; she dreamed that henceforth Life and Death and all Nature were shut within her body, that at the cost of, oh! what infinite travail, she had conceived in her womb great Nature's self.

9

SATAN the HEALER

THE silent, sombre drama of the Bride of Corinth is repeated literally and exactly from the thirteenth to the fifteenth centuries. In the gloom of night which still broods over the world, the two lovers, Man and Nature, meet again and embrace with transports of joy; and lo! at the self-same instant, to their horror, see themselves smitten with appalling scourges! Still, as of old, we seem to hear the bride telling her lover, "All is over. . . . Your locks shall be white to-morrow. . . . I am a dead woman, and you shall die."

Three horrid afflictions in three successive centuries. In the first, the loathsome disfigurement of the outward form,—skin diseases, leprosy. In the second, an inward curse,—weird nervous excitations, epileptic dances. These die down, but the blood grows tainted, chronic ulcerations pave the way to syphilis, that scourge of the sixteenth century.

The diseases of the Middle Ages, so far as we can get vague and unsatisfactory glimpses of them, were predominantly hunger, languor, and poverty of blood, the emaciation men admire in mediæval sculpture. The blood was thin as water, and scrofulous complaints were bound to be all but universal. With the exception of Arab or Jewish physicians, hired at great cost by the rich, medical treatment was unknown,—the people could only crowd to the church doors for aspersion with holy water. On Sundays, after Mass, the sick came in scores, crying for help,—and words were all they got: "You have sinned, and God is afflicting you. Thank Him; you will suffer so much the less torment in the life to come. Endure, suffer, die. Has not the Church its prayers for the dead?" Feeble, fainting, neither hoping nor caring to live, they followed this advice to the letter, and dropped into the grave in sheer indifference to life.

A fatal despair, a wretched death in life, that could not but prolong indefinitely these times of lead, and constitute a fatal bar to all progress. What could be worse than this facile resignation, this docile acceptance of death, this impotence and total absence of energy and aspiration? Better far the new epoch, those last years of the Middle Ages, which at the price of atrocious sufferings, at last inaugurates for mankind the possibility of renewed activity,—the *resurrection of desire*.

The Arab philosopher Avicenna maintains that the prodigious outbreak of diseases of the skin which marks the thirteenth century resulted from the use of those excitants whereby men at that period sought to awake, or to revive, the flagging energies of love. No doubt the hot, inflammatory spices, imported from the East, were not without effect; while the newly discovered art of distillation and various fermented liquors then first coming into use may likewise have exerted an influence in the same direction.

But another and a mightier fermentation, and a much more general one, was taking place. From the bitter internal conflict of two worlds and two spirits a third survived which silenced them both. Waning Faith, nascent Reason were in the death grip; between the two combatants another intervened and mastered mankind,—the unclean, fierce spirit of their eager, passionate appetites, the cruel emanation of their furious ebullition.

Finding no outlet, whether in bodily gratifications or in a free play of mind, the sap of life is dammed back and putrefies. Without light or voice or speech, it yet spoke in pains of body, in foul eruptions of the skin. Then a new and terrible thing follows; baulked desire, unsatisfied and unappeased, sees itself checked

by a cruel spell, a hideous metamorphosis.[1] Love that was drawing nigh, blindly, with arms thrown wide, steps back shuddering.
Yes! love may fly; but the fury of the tainted blood persists, the
flesh burns in agonising, itching torments, while more agonising
still, the inward conflagration rages, fanned by the breath of
despair.

What remedy does Christian Europe find for this double evil?
Death, captivity; nothing else is better. When bitter celibacy,
hopeless love, fierce thwarted passion, bring you to an unhealthy,
morbid state; when your blood grows corrupt, down with you
into an *in pace,* or build your lonely cabin in the desert. You shall
live, warning-bell in hand, that all may flee your presence. "No
human being must see you; no consolation can be yours. If you
approach too near, death is the penalty!"

Leprosy is the last degree, the apogee, of the scourge; but a
thousand other terrible and cruel ills only less hideous abound
everywhere. The purest and the fairest of womankind were
stricken with detestable eruptions that were looked upon as the
visible sign of sin or a direct punishment from God. The men had
recourse to means mere loss of life would never have led them to
adopt; prohibitions were forgotten, and the old consecrated medicines forsaken, and the holy water that had proved so useless.
They visited the Witch, the Sorceress. From force of habit, as

---

[1] Leprosy was supposed due to the Crusades, to be an importation from
Asia; but as a matter of fact Europe had only herself to thank for the scourge.
The war persistently waged by the Middle Ages against the flesh and against
cleanliness was bound to bear fruit. More than one female saint is commended
for having never washed even the hands;—how much less the rest of the body!
An instant's nakedness would have been a mortal sin. The worldling faithfully follows these precepts of the cloister. The society of those days, so
subtle and refined, which makes sacrifice of marriage and appears animated
only by the poetry of adultery, retains singular scruples on this simple point
of personal ablutions, dreading every form of purification as a defilement.
Never a bath known for a thousand years! We may be quite certain not one
of those knights, those fair and ethereal ladies, the Percivals, Tristrams, Iseults,
ever washed. Hence a cruel accident, highly unpoetical in such romantic
surroundings,—the furious itches that tortured our thirteenth-century ancestors.

well as from fear, they still frequented the churches; but the true church was henceforth her hut, her haunt in heath, in forest, and in desert. Thither it was they now carried their prayers.

Prayers for healing, prayers for some joy of life. At the first symptoms that showed the blood corrupted, they would away in great secrecy, at furtive hours, to consult the Sibyl: "What must I do? What is this I feel within me? . . . I am burning; oh! give me something to calm my blood. . . . I am burning; give me something to appease my intolerable longing."

A bold, guilty step they repent them of when evening comes. It must indeed be pressing, this new and fatal constraint; the fire must indeed be agonising, to make all the saints so utterly of no avail. But then the trial of the Knights Templars, the trial of Pope Boniface, have unmasked the Sodom that lurked under the altar stones. A Pope a Sorcerer, a friend of Satan, and finally carried off by the Foul Fiend: this turns all men's notions upside down. Not without the Devil's help surely could the Pope, *who is no longer Pope in Rome,* in his city of Avignon, Pope John XXII., a cobbler's son of Cahors, amass more gold than the Emperor himself and all the kings of the earth! Like Pope, like Bishop; did not Guichard, Bishop of Troyes, win a boon of the Devil, the death of the King of France's daughters? . . . It is not death *we* ask for, but pleasant things, life, health, beauty, pleasure,—things of God, that God refuses us. . . . Well, then, suppose we were to get them by the favour of the *Prince of this World?*

That great and puissant doctor of the Renaissance, Paracelsus, when he burned the wise books of ancient medicine *en masse,* Greek, Jewish, and Arab, declared he had learned nothing at all but from popular medicine, from the *good women,*[2] from shepherds, and hangmen. The latter were often clever surgeons,— setters of broken or dislocated bones, and accomplished farriers.

I have little doubt but that his admirable book, so full of

---

[2] The polite, flattering name fear conferred upon the Sorceresses.

genius, upon the *Diseases of Women,* the first ever written on this important, profound, and touching subject, owed its special merits to the experience of women themselves, those women whose help their sisters were used to appeal to,—I mean the Sorceresses who in every country fulfilled the office of midwives. No woman in those days would ever have consulted a male physician, trusted to him, or told him her secrets. Sorceresses were the only observers in this field, and, for women in particular, were the sole and only practitioners.

The most certain fact we know as to their methods is that they made great use, for the most various purposes, as calmants and as stimulants, of a wide family of herbs, of doubtful repute and perilous properties, which proved of the most decided advantage to their patients. These are appropriately known as the *Solanaceæ* (herbs of consolation).[3]

A profuse and familiar family of plants, the majority of whose species are to be found in extreme abundance, under our feet, in the hedgerows, in every field. So numerous a family, that a single one of its genera embraces eight hundred species.[4] Nothing in the world easier to detect, nothing commoner. Yet these herbs are for the most part very risky to employ. Audacity was required to determine the doses, it may well be the audacity of genius.

To begin at the bottom of the ascending scale of their po-

---

[3] It is cruel to note the ingratitude of mankind. A thousand other plants have usurped their place, a hundred exotic herbs have been preferred by fashion, while these poor, humble *Solanaceæ* that saved so many lives in former days have been clean forgotten with all the benefits they conferred. Who indeed has any memory for such things? Who recognises the time-honoured obligations men owe to innocent nature? The *Asclepias acida,* or *Sarcostemma* (flesh-plant), which for five thousand years was the *consecrated host of Asia,* the palpable god-made flesh of all that continent, which gave five hundred millions of the human race the blessedness of eating their god, the same plant that the Middle Ages knew as the *Poison-killer* (Vincevenenum), has never a word of recognition in our books of botany. Who knows but two thousand years hence mankind will have forgotten the virtues of wheat? See Langlois, on the *soma* of India, and the *horn* of Persia (*Mém. de l'Académie des Inscriptions,* xix. 326).

[4] *Dict. d'Histoire Naturelle* of M. d'Orbigny; article *Morelles* (Nightshades), by M. Duchartre, after Demal, etc.

tency.[5] The first to be named are simply pot-herbs, good to eat, and nothing more,—aubergines, tomatoes, inappropriately called love-apples. Others of these harmless varieties are the quintes-' sence of all that is calming and soothing,—the mulleins (shepherd's club), for instance, so useful for fomentations.

Next in the scale you will find a plant already open to suspicion—one that many believed a poison; a herb honey-sweet at first, afterwards bitter, that seems to say in the words of Jonathan, "I have tasted a little honey, and behold! for this I die." Yet this death is useful—it is the deadening of pain. The bittersweet, that is its name, was bound to be the first essay of a bold homœopathy, which by slow degrees aspired to the most dangerous poisons. The slight irritation, the pricking sensations it produces, sufficed to point it out as a remedy for the predominant maladies of the period, viz. diseases of the skin.

The fair girl, in despair at seeing herself marked with hateful blotches, carbuncles, spreading eruptions, came weeping for succour in her affliction. With married women the scourge was still more cruel. The bosom, the most delicate thing in all nature, and its vessels, which form an interlaced flower of incomparable perfection below the skin,[6] is, by virtue of its liability to congestion and blocking of the veins and arteries, the most exquisite instrument of pain,—pain keen, pitiless, and never ceasing. How willingly would she have welcomed any and every poison to gain relief! No stopping to bargain with the Witch who promised a

---

[5] I have not been able to find this scale detailed in any work I have consulted. It is the more important, inasmuch as the witches who undertook this series of experiments, at the risk of being branded as poisoners, undoubtedly began with the weakest, and advanced little by little to the more powerful. Thus each degree of potency gives a relative date, and allows us to establish in this very obscure subject an approximative chronology. I propose to say more of this in the following chapters, when I come to speak of the Mandragora and the Datura. I have followed particularly Pouchet, *Solanées et Botanique générale* (Solanaceæ and General Botany). In this important monograph M. Pouchet has not disdained to draw from the ancient writers, Matthiole, Porta, Gessner, Sauvages, Gmelin, etc.

[6] See plate in that excellent and quite inoffensive work, the *Cours de Physiologie* of M. Auzouz.

cure, and between whose hands she was ready at once to place the poor painful, swollen organ.

After the bitter-sweet, too feeble a medicament for such a case, came the black mulleins, possessing a somewhat greater activity. This would afford relief for a day or two. But at the end of that time the poor woman would be back again with tears and supplications. "Well, well! you must return once more this evening. . . . I will find you something. You decide to have it; but 'tis a deadly poison."

The Sorceress was running a terrible risk. Nobody at that time had a suspicion that, applied externally or taken in very small doses, poisons are remedies. All the plants which were confounded together under the name of *Witches' herbs* were supposed ministers of death. Found in a woman's hands, they would have led to her being adjudged a poisoner or fabricator of accursed spells. A blind mob, as cruel as it was timid, might any morning stone her to death, or force her to undergo the ordeal by water or *noyade*. Or, worst and most dreadful fate of all, they might drag her with ropes to the church square, where the clergy would make a pious festival of it, and edify the people by burning her at the stake.

She makes the venture for all that, and starts in search of the fearsome herb, slipping out late at night or early in the morning, when she is less afraid of being observed. But a little shepherd lad was there, who tells the village, "If you had seen her as I did, gliding among the fallen stones of the old ruin, glancing from side to side, muttering some unintelligible gibberish to herself the while! . . . Oh, I was rarely frightened, I tell you. . . . If she had caught me, I should have been done for. . . . She might have turned me into a lizard, or a toad, or a bat. . . . She gathered a villainous-looking herb, the ugliest I ever saw,—a pale, sickly yellow, with stripes of black and red, like flames of hell-fire. The dreadful thing was that all the stem was hairy, like a man's hair,—long, black, snaky hair. She tore it up roughly, with a groan,—and in an instant I lost sight of her. She could not have run so fast, she must have flown away! . . . What an awful woman! What a danger for all the countryside!"

Doubtless the plant looks terrifying. It is the henbane (*hyoscyamus*), a cruel and deadly poison, but at the same time an excellent emollient, a soothing, sedative plaster, that relaxes and softens the tissues, relieves the pain, and often cures the patient.

Another of these poisons, the *belladonna*, doubtless so named out of gratitude, was sovran for calming the convulsions that sometimes occur in childbirth, superadding peril to peril and terror to terror at this supreme crisis. But there! a motherly hand would slip in this soothing poison,[7] lull the mother to sleep, and lay a spell on the door of life; the infant, just as at the present day when chloroform is administered, worked out its own freedom by its own efforts, and forced its way to the world of living men.

This belladonna cures the convulsive dancing of the limbs by setting up another dance,—a venturesome homœopathy that could not but be terrifying at the first blush. In fact it was *Medicine spelt backwards,* as a rule the exact opposite of that which the Christians knew and thought the only efficacious kind, the medicine of the Jews and Arabs.

How came the great discovery? No doubt by simple application of the great satanic principle *that everything should be done backwards,* precisely in the reverse way to that employed by the world of religion. The Church had a holy horror of all poisons; Satan utilises them as curative agents. The Priest thinks by spiritual means (Sacraments, prayers) to act even upon the body. Satan, acting by contraries, employs material means for acting even on the soul; he gives potions to secure forgetfulness, love, reverie, any and every state of mind. To priestly benedictions he

---

[7] Madame La Chapelle and M. Chaussier have returned to these practices of old-fashioned popular medicine with great advantage to their patients (Pouchet, *Solanées,* p. 64).

opposes magnetic passes by dainty female hands that lull pain and anguish to sleep.

Through change of treatment, and still more of clothing (no doubt by the substitution of linen for wool), skin diseases lost much of their virulence. Leprosy diminished, but at the same time seemed to strike inwards and produce more deep-seated mischief. The fourteenth century oscillated between three scourges, epileptic convulsions, the plague, and those ulcerations which, if we are to believe Paracelsus, paved the way for syphilis.

The first named was by no means the least formidable danger. It broke out about the year 1350, under the appalling form of *St. Guy's dance* (St. Vitus's dance, *chorea*), having this strange peculiarity, that the complaint was not, so to speak, individual; those suffering from it, as if carried away by one and the same galvanic current, would grasp each other by the hand, group themselves in huge, endless chains, and whirl, and whirl, like Dervishes, till they died of exhaustion. The spectators would roar with laughter at first, then presently caught by the contagion, would give in and join the mighty stream, and swell the awful band of dancing maniacs.

What would have happened if the malady had persisted in the same way as leprosy did for a long period, even in its decline?

The answer is, it was a first step, an approximation, towards epilepsy; and if this first generation of sufferers had not been cured, it would have produced a second definitely and distinctly epileptic. The imagination shudders at the thought! all Europe packed with madmen, maniacs, idiots! We are not told how the complaint was treated, and finally arrested. The particular remedy recommended at the time, the expedient of falling on the dancers with kicks and fisticuffs, was infinitely well adapted to aggravate the cerebral disturbance and lead to actual epilepsy.

We cannot doubt there was another treatment practised that was never voluntarily mentioned. At the period when Sorcery and Witchcraft were at their point of highest activity and repute, the very extensive employment of the *Solanaceæ,* and especially of belladonna, was the most marked general characteristic of the remedial measures taken to combat this class of disease. At the great popular gatherings, the Witches' Sabbaths, we shall describe later, the *Witches' herb,* infused in hydromel, beer, as well as in cider [8] and perry, the strong drinks of the West, set the crowd dancing,—but in wanton, luxurious measures, showing no trace of epileptic violence.

But the greatest revolution the Sorceress brought about, the chief movement of all *in contradiction,* in direct contradiction to the spirit of the Middle Ages, is what we might well call a rehabilitation of the belly and its digestive functions. They boldly proclaimed the doctrine that "nothing is impure and nothing unclean." From that moment the study of physical science was enfranchised, its shackles loosed, and true medicine became a possibility.

That they carried the principle to mischievous lengths no one can deny; indeed, the fact is self-evident. Nothing is impure but moral evil. Everything physical is pure; nothing physical can properly be excepted from examination and study, prohibited in deference to an empty idealism, or worse still a silly feeling of repulsion.

Here above all had the Middle Ages displayed their most essential characteristic, what we may call *anti-Nature,* splitting up the unity of created things, and drawing distinctions, constituting castes, classes, hierarchies. Not only according to this is the spirit *noble,* the body *not noble,*—but there are actually particular parts of the body which are *noble,* and others not,— plebeian it would appear. Similarly, Heaven is noble, the Abyss not. Why? "Because heaven is high." But heaven is neither high nor low; it is above us and beneath us at once. And the Abyss, what is *it?* Nothing; a figment of the imagination. The same

---

[8] Then quite a new beverage. It first began to be manufactured in the twelfth century.

foolish conceptions as to the macrocosm of the universe and the microcosm of the individual human being.

All is of a piece; solidarity rules throughout. The belly is the servant of the brain, and feeds it; but it is no less true that the brain, working ceaselessly to make the sugar required in the processes of digestion,[9] is no less active to assist the belly.

Abuse was lavished upon them; filthy, indecent, shameless, immoral, were only some of the epithets levelled at the Sorceress. For all that it can confidently be affirmed her first steps in the direction indicated were a happy revolution in all that is most moral, in kindness and human charity. By a monstrous perversion of ideas, the Middle Ages regarded the flesh, in its representative, woman (accursed since Eve), as radically impure. The Virgin, *exalted as virgin, and not as Our Lady,* far from raising actual womanhood to a higher level, had degraded it, starting men on the path of a barren, scholastic ideal of purity that only led to ever greater and greater absurdities of verbal subtlety and false logic.

Woman herself even came eventually to share the odious prejudice and to believe herself unclean. So she lurked in hiding at the hour of childbirth, blushed to love and give happiness to men. Woman, so sober as a rule in comparison with the opposite sex, who in almost every land is a vegetarian and an eater of fruits, who sacrifices so sparingly to the natural appetites, and by her milk and vegetable diet wins the purity of the innocent substances that are her food, she of all others was fain to ask pardon almost for existing at all, for living and fulfilling the conditions of life. A submissive martyr to false modesty, she was for ever torturing herself, actually endeavouring to conceal, abolish, and annul the adorable sign of her womanhood, that thrice holy thing, the belly of her pregnancy, whence man is born in the image of God everlastingly from generation to generation.

[9] This is the great discovery that makes Claude Bernard's name immortal.

Mediæval medicine concerns itself exclusively with the superior, the pure being (to wit, man), who alone can be ordained priest, and incarnate the living God upon the altar.

Animals, too, occupy some of its attention; indeed, it begins with them. But does it ever think of children? Very seldom. Does it pay any heed to women? Never!

The Romances of those days, with their subtle refinements, represent the exact opposite of the everyday world. Apart from the courts of kings, and high-born adultery, the main subject-matter of these tales, woman is always the poor, patient Griselda, born to exhaust every sort of pain and humiliation, often beaten, never properly cared for.

The Devil only, woman's ally of old and her confidant in the Garden, and the Witch, the perverse creature who does everything *backwards and upside down,* in direct contradiction to the world of religion, ever thought of unhappy womanhood, ever dared to tread custom underfoot and care for her health in spite of her own prejudices. The poor creature held herself in such lowly estimation! She could only draw back blushing shyly, and refuse to speak. But the Sorceress, adroit and cunning, guessed her secrets and penetrated her inmost being. She found means to make her speak out at last, drew her little secret from her and overcame all her refusals and timid, shamefaced hesitations. Submit to treatment! She would sooner die, she said. But the *barbarous Witch* knew better, and saved her life.

CHARMS and LOVE POTIONS

Do not conclude too hastily from what I have said in the preceding chapter that my purpose is to whitewash, to clear of all blame whatever, the gloomy bride of the Evil One. She often effected good, but was equally capable of grievous mischief. Great and irresponsible power is always liable to abuse; and in this case she queened it in a very true sense for three long centuries during the interregnum between two worlds, the old dying world and the new one whose dawn was still faint on the horizon. The Church, destined later on to recover something of its vigour (at any rate as a fighting force) in the struggles of the sixteenth century, is still wallowing in the mire in the fourteenth. Read the convincing picture of its condition given us by Clémangis. The nobility, swaggering in novel and sumptuous forms of defensive armour, meets only the more dismal disaster at Crécy and Poitiers and Agincourt. The French nobles prisoners in England! What an opportunity for the scoffers! Bourgeoisie, even peasantry, are dissolved in mocking laughter, and shrug contemptuous shoulders. This general and compulsory absenteeism of the seigneurs afforded no small encouragement, in my opinion, to the Witches' Sabbaths. These had always existed, but under the new conditions they grew into huge popular festivals.

Think of the power wielded by Satan's Chosen Bride! She can heal, prophesy, predict, conjure up the spirits of the dead, can spell-bind you, turn you into a hare or a wolf, make you find a treasure, and most fatal gift of all, cast a love charm over you there is no escaping! Awful attribute, more terrible than all the rest put together! How should a headstrong spirit, more often than not a wounded spirit, sometimes one altogether soured by disappointment, fail to use such a weapon for the satisfaction of hatred and revenge, and sometimes for the indulgence of perverse and foul proclivities?

The secrets of the Confessional were no secrets to her,—secrets of sins committed and of sins to come. Every man is her slave by her knowledge of some shameful incident of his past, and his still viler aspirations for the future. She is the confidante of deformities of body and of mind, and of the lascivious ardours of a poisoned and heated blood, of morbid, overmastering longings that fiercely torment the flesh with a thousand needle-pricks of concupiscence.

All come to her and make her their shameful avowals with a reckless and brutal candour. They seek the boon of life, of death, of healing medicines and poisonous drugs. To her comes the poor weeping girl who has been betrayed, to ask means for procuring abortion. To her the stepmother (an incident of the commonest in the Middle Ages) to complain how her first husband's brat eats and eats and will not die. To her the woe-begone matron, worn out year after year with children that are only born to die. Appealing to her compassion, she is told the way to paralyse pleasure at the supreme instant and make it barren. On the other hand, there comes a stripling, ready at any cost to buy the sovran brew that will trouble a high-born lady's heart, and making her forget distinctions of rank and place, turn her gentle looks towards her little page.

The marriage of the period has only two types or forms, both of them extravagant and *outré*.

The proud "heiress of broad lands," who brings a dowry, a throne, or a rich fief, an Eleanor of Guyenne, will maintain under her very husband's nose, her court of lovers, and will do very much what she pleases. Leaving on one side romance and poetry, let us look the facts in the face. The reality is terrible enough, culminating in the wild orgies of the daughters of Philippe le Bel, and the excesses of the cruel Isabella, who had her husband, Edward II., impaled by her lovers' hands. The effrontery of the feudal dame comes out in a devilish fashion in the two-horned headdress of state occasions, and other shameless modes of dress.

But in this century when the classes begin to intermix to some degree, the woman of inferior origin who wedded a baron had good reason to fear harsh treatment. This is shown in the story, perfectly true and authentic, of Griselda, the lowly, gentle, patient Griselda. The tale, quite serious and historical in my own belief, of "Blue Beard" gives the popular form of the same legend. The wife he kills so often and so often replaces can only have been a vassal. There would have been a different tale to tell with the daughter or sister of a baron, in a position to avenge her wrongs. If I am not mistaken in this highly probable conjecture, we must conclude this story to be of the fourteenth century rather than to belong to an earlier period, when a great lord would never have stooped to take a wife beneath him in consequence.

One very remarkable thing in the touching story of Griselda is that under all her trials she appears not to have the consolation either of religion or of another lover. She is manifestly faithful, chaste, and unsullied. It never occurs to her to find comfort in fixing her love elsewhere.

Of these two types of mediæval women—the Great Heiress on the one hand, Griselda on the other—it is exclusively the former that has her *cavalieri servente,* that presides at Courts of Love, that favours the humblest of lovers, and (like Eleanor) pronounces the famous dictum, regarded as undisputable in those days: "No love possible betwixt married folk."

Hence a secret hope,—secret, yet ardent and masterful, that springs in many a young heart. End as it may, even in his giving his soul to the Evil One, the young lover will rush head down into the bold emprise. Be the keep guarded ever so well, there will always be a loophole for Satan to creep in. The game is perilous indeed; is there the shadow of a chance? Why, no! says Prudence. Ah! but if Satan says "Yes"?

Nor should we forget how great the distance feudal pride set between noble and noble. Words are deceptive; *knights* were very far from being all alike.

The Knight *Banneret*, who led a whole army of vassals to join the King in the field, looking down his long table, saw with unmitigated contempt the poor lackland knights who sat at its lower end. This epithet of "lackland" was a mortal insult in mediæval times, as in the instance of John *Sans Terre*, John Lackland, of England. How much more so the common varlets, squires, pages, etc., who fattened on the leavings from the high table! Seated at the lower end of the Great Hall, close to the door, they scraped the platters the great folks, sitting by the warm hearth, sent down to them,—often empty. It never even entered the head of the lordly Seigneur that these humble inferiors could have the hardihood to lift their eyes to the fair lady mistress, the proud heiress, sitting there on the daïs by her mother's side, "under a chaplet of white roses." While surprisingly ready to condone the advances of some stranger lover, who was the fair châtelaine's avowed champion and wore her colours, he would have punished cruelly one of his own dependants who should have had the audacity to aim so high. This is the explanation of the savage jealousy shown by the Sire de Fayel, angered beyond all bounds, not because his wife had a lover, but because the said lover was one of his own domestics, the seneschal (common caretaker) of his castle of Coucy.

The deeper, the more impassable the gulf fixed between the Lady of the Fief, the great heiress, and squire or page, who had only a shirt to call his own, for his very coat he received from his lord and master,—the stronger, it would seem, was the temptation for Love to overleap the abyss.

The gallant's imagination was fired by the seeming impossibility of success. At length, one day he found himself free to leave the fortress; he hurried to the Witch's dwelling to ask her advice and aid. Would a philter avail,—a *charm* to fascinate the senses? If not, must he make an express *pact* with the Devil? The awful thought of selling himself to Satan had no terrors for him. "It shall have our best consideration, young sir. Meantime return; you will find there is some change come about already."

The change is in himself. A vague, mysterious hope stirs within him; everything shows it in his own despite, the deep glances of his lowered eyes that flash with an uneasy flame. Someone—easy to guess who—is quick to note the symptoms before others; her gentle heart is touched, she throws him a passing word of pity. . . . Oh, joy ineffable! Oh, kind-hearted Satan! charming, adorable Witch-wife! . . .

He cannot eat or sleep till he has been to see her again. He kisses her hand with deepest respect, almost grovels at her feet. Let her ask him what she will, order him what she please, he will obey. Would she have his gold chain, the ring he wears on his finger—his dying mother's gift,—he will give them without an instant's hesitation. But she is naturally spiteful, full of malicious hate for the Baron, and finds it only too delightful to stab him in the dark.

An undefined feeling of impending trouble haunts the castle. A voiceless tempest, without lightning or thunder, broods over it, like an electric cloud on the surface of a swamp. Not a sound to break the silence; but the Lady Châtelaine is overwrought, she is sure some supernatural power has been at work. Why this youth more than another, perhaps handsomer and better bred, and already renowned for noble exploits? There is something surely underneath all this. Has he thrown a spell over her, used a love-charm? . . . The question only stirs her heart to wilder emotion.

The Sorceress's spite finds good stuff to feed on. She was always queen of the village; now the castle comes and puts itself in her power,—and that just where its pride runs the direst risk of humiliation. For us, the interest of such an intrigue is the gallant effort of a generous heart to attain its ideal, its protest against social barriers and Fate's injustice. For the Sorceress it is the pleasure, deep and keen, of degrading her proud neighbour, perhaps avenging slights of her own, the pleasure of paying back to the Seigneur in the same coin the wrongs he has inflicted on her sister vassals, to indemnify herself, by a lad's audacity, for the outrageous right the Lord of the Soil possesses,—the *jus primæ noctis*. There can be no doubt whatever, in these intrigues where the Sorceress played her part, that she was many a time actuated by an underlying grudge, natural enough to the peasant, who is invariably a leveller at heart.

It was always something gained, and something considerable, to have humiliated the great lady to the love of a *domestic*. Jean de Saintré and Cherubino must not mislead us. The youthful dependant in a mediæval castle performed the basest offices of the household. The chamber servant or valet, properly so called, did not yet exist, while on the other hand few serving-women, or none at all, were to be found in fortified places. Every office is performed by these young hands, which are in nowise degraded thereby; service, particularly corporal service, rendered their liege lord and lady only honours and exalts. Nevertheless it could not but place a young nobleman at times in situations decidedly melancholy, prosaic, and we may go as far as to say ridiculous. Little recked the Lord of the Castle. His good lady must verily and indeed have been bewitched by the Devil not to see what her eyes rested on day after day,—her favourite engaged in filthy and menial offices.

It is characteristic of the Middle Ages, this bringing face to face of the sublime and the ridiculous. Where poetry is reticent we may glimpse the truth from other quarters. Mingled with these ethereal passions much coarseness of circumstance is very plainly to be seen.

Everything we learn about the charms and love-potions employed by Witches and Sorceresses shows how fantastic these were,—often wilfully fantastic, shamelessly compounded of substances one would suppose least likely to awake the sentiment of love. These women went to extraordinary lengths, without the infatuated being they were making a plaything of ever having his eyes opened to the truth.

Philters were of many and very different sorts. Some were intended to excite and trouble the senses, like the aphrodisiacs so freely abused to the present day by Eastern peoples. Others were dangerous, and often treacherous, drugs administered to cloud the wits and deprive the victim of all power of self-control. Some, again, were tests or proofs of passion, defiances to try how far the greediness of desire was capable of carrying the senses, making lovers accept as the most supreme of favours, as a sort of mystic communion, the least agreeable of matters coming from the loved one's person.

The rude structure of mediæval castles, made up as these were of great halls and little else, made a public function of domestic life. It was only reluctantly, as it were, and at a much later date that privacy was consulted by the contrivance of bower and oratory in some tower of the vast pile. It was easy to watch the châtelaine's daily habits; then, on some day chosen for the purpose, after careful observation, the bold pretender, acting on the Witch's suggestion, could strike his blow with every hope of success, drugging the posset and slipping the love-potion in the cup.

Still, it was at best a rare and perilous undertaking. A far easier course was to filch some trifle the fair lady would never miss or give a thought to,—to gather with scrupulous care the almost invisible parings of a nail, to collect reverently the combings of her hair, a strand or two from her lovely head. These were carried to the Sorceress, who would often demand (as do somnambulists of the present day) such and such an article of the most intimate nature, imbued, as it were, with the wearer's personality, but which she would never have given of her own free will; for instance, a fragment torn from a garment long worn and soiled which she had moistened with the sweat of her body. All this, remember, smothered with adoring kisses and wistfully regretted. But it must be ruthlessly burned and reduced to ashes to serve the required purpose. One day or another, looking at the garment again, the keen-sighted fair one would notice the tiny rent, would guess its meaning with a tender sigh, but say never a word to betray her knowledge. . . . The charm had taken effect!

One thing is certain, that if the lady hesitated, felt some lingering respect for her marriage vow, this life lived within such narrow bounds, where each saw the other so continually, and dividing distances were so short, though so all-important, must soon have grown into a veritable torture. Even where she had yielded, still, in presence of so many observers, her husband and others not less jealous, happiness was doubtless rarely secured. Hence many a piece of frenzied folly, the result of unsatisfied desire. The less actual intercourse was possible, the more profound the longing for a symbolic union. This a morbid fancy sought to find in all sorts of extravagances, equally unnatural and unreasonable. Thus, to create a means of secret intercommunication between two lovers, the Witch would prick out on the arm of each the shapes of the letters of the alphabet. When one wished to transmit a thought to the other, all he had to do was to revive, restore, by sucking the blood to them, the letters forming the word desired. Simultaneously the corresponding letters, so it was believed, on the other's arm were suffused with blood.

Sometimes in these outbursts of mad folly lovers would drink each other's blood, to effect a mystic communion which, it was supposed, made their two souls one. Coucy's heart, devoured by his widow, and which she "found so good, she never ate more in her life," is the most tragic instance of these monstrous sacraments of cannibal affection. But when the absent lover did not die, but it was love died within him, then the lady would away to consult a Witch and beseech her for means to bring him back and bind him to her.

The magic incantations of Theocritus and Virgil continued to be used even in the Middle Ages, but were rarely efficacious. The attempt was tried to bring back the recreant lover by another charm, also apparently imitated from an Antique model. Recourse was had to the magic cake, the *confarreatio*, which from furthest Asia to furthest Europe was ever the sacrament of love. But the aim here was to bind more than the soul,—to bind the flesh, to create an identity of substance, so that, dead to all other women, he should live and breathe for one and one alone. The ordeal was no trifle. "Take it or leave it," was the Witch-wife's answer to all remonstrances; and her proud client grew instantly submissive, and suffered her to strip her to the skin, this being an indispensable condition in all these ceremonies.

What a triumph for the Sorceress! And above all, if the lady was one who had treated her despitefully in former days, what a fine piece of revenge and retaliation! The woman has her lying stark naked under her hands. Nor is this all. On her loins she lays a board, and on it a miniature oven, in which she bakes the magic cake. . . . "Sweet friend, I can bear no more. Quick, quick, I cannot stay like this!" "Nay, madam, 'twas bound to be so; you must needs burn. The cake is a-baking; 'twill be heated of your very body, the hot flame of your passion!"

The rite is ended, and we have the magic cake of antiquity, of Hindoo and Roman marriage, seasoned and hotly spiced with the lewd spirit of Satan. She does not say, like Virgil's sorceress: "Come back, Daphnis, come back to me! Oh, bring him back to me, my songs!" But she sends him the cake, all impregnated with her pain, and heated with her love. . . . Scarce has he bitten it when a strange tumult, a giddiness, confuses his senses. . . . His heart beats wildly, his blood boils, his face is suffused with blushes, his whole body burns. Love's madness seizes him once more, and inextinguishable desire.

COMMUNION of REVOLT

WITCHES' SABBATHS

The BLACK MASS

WITCHES' *Sabbaths*. We must use the plural, for it is obvious the word has denoted very different things at different epochs. Unfortunately, we possess detailed accounts of such scenes only of quite late date,—reign of Henri IV.[1] By that time it had degenerated into little more than a huge carnival of lust, under pretence of magic rites. But even in these descriptions of an institution so far gone in decay are to be found certain marks of extreme antiquity that bear witness to the successive periods and divers forms through which it had already passed.

We may start with one fact that admits of no doubt, that for many centuries the serf lived the furtive life of the wolf and the fox, that he was a *nocturnal animal,* meaning by this, exhibiting the least activity possible by day, being really alive only at night.

Still, up to the year 1000, when the people is still busy canonising its saints and framing its legends, the life of daylight continues to be of interest to him. His nocturnal Sabbaths are merely

---

[1] The least unsatisfactory is that given by Lancre. He is a man of wit and perspicacity, and being manifestly in relations with certain young witches, was in a position to know the whole truth. Unfortunately, his Sabbath is confused and overloaded with the grotesque ornaments of the age. The descriptions of the Jesuit Del Rio and of the Dominican Michaëlis are ridiculous, impossible portraits of a pair of silly, credulous pedants. In that of Del Rio are found an incredible number of platitudes and absurdities. Still, taking the thing as a whole, it contains some interesting and valuable traces of antiquity, which I have been able to turn to account.

an unimportant relic of Paganism. He honours and fears the moon, exerting as she does an influence over the productions of the soil. Old women are her devotees, and burn little candles in honour of *Dianom* (Diana-Luna-Hecaté). Goat-footed Pan still chases women and children, under a mask, it is true, the black face of the ghostly Hallequin (Harlequin). The festival of the *Pervigilium Veneris* is scrupulously observed on May 1st. On St. John's day the he-goat of Priapus-Bacchus-Sabasius is slaughtered in celebration of the Sabasia. All this without a thought of mockery. It is the serf's harmless carnival.

But, as we approach the year 1000, the Church is all but closed against him by difference of language. In 1100 her officers become unintelligible to him. Of the mysteries performed at the church doors, what he remembers best is the comic side, the ox and the ass, etc. He makes carols out of this material, but with an ever-increasing spice of mockery in them—true "Sabbatic" literature.

We may well believe the great and terrible revolts of the twelfth century were not without influence on these mysteries and this nocturnal life of Werewolf and Moonrakes, of the Wild Game of the Woods, as the cruel barons style it. These revolts may likely enough have often begun in such moonlight festivals. The Holy Sacraments of insurrection among serfs—drinking each other's blood, or eating earth by way of host [2]—were doubtless often celebrated at the Witches' Sabbath. The *Marseillaise* of the period, sung more by night than by day, is perhaps a "Sabbatic chant:—

> Nous sommes hommes comme ils sont
> Tout aussi grand cœur nous avons!
> Tout autant souffrir nous pouvons! [3]

---

[2] At the battle of Courtrai. See also Grimm, and Michelet's *Origines.*

[3] "We are men as much as they!
We have a heart as big as they!
We can suffer no less than they!"

But the ponderous coffin lid falls back again in 1200. The Pope
sits atop, and the King, both exerting enormous pressure, and
poor mankind is immured within without hope of escape. Does
the old nocturnal life survive? Undoubtedly, and more vigorous
than ever. The old Pagan dances are revived, more fast and furious than ever. The Negroes of the Antilles, after an intolerable
day of heat and exhausting labour, forgot all their sorrows in
moonlight dances. The serf did likewise; but with his revelry
were inevitably mingled fierce anticipations of the delights of
vengeance, sarcastic buffooneries, mockeries, and caricatures of
the lord and the priest. A whole literature of the dark side of nature, that knew never a word of that of its brighter aspects, and
little even of the *fabliaux* of the intermediate bourgeois classes.

Such was the essence of the "Sabbath" before 1300. For it to
assume, as it did later, the astounding character of an open war
against the god of those times, much more was needed, two things
in fact, that the lowest depths of despair should be sounded, and
that *all sense of revenge should disappear.*

This consummation is only reached in the fourteenth century,
during the Great Schism when the Papacy had migrated to
Avignon, and the two-headed Church seemed no longer a Church
at all, when all the nobility of France and the King himself are
crestfallen prisoners in England, squeezing the uttermost farthing out of their vassals to provide their ransom. Then it is the
Sabbaths adopt the imposing and grimly terrible ceremonial of
the *Black Mass,* the Holy Sacrament turned inside out, so to
speak, when Jesus Christ is defied, called up to strike his impious
worshippers dead—if he can. This devilish piece of play-acting
would have been impossible in the thirteenth century, when it
would have raised a shudder of pious horror. Later again, in the
fifteenth, when every sentiment was outworn, even that of suffering, an outburst of the sort could never have taken place;
men's spirits were unequal to so monstrous a creation. It belongs
essentially to the century of Dante.

It was, I hold, the invention of a moment,—the frenzied out-break of a maddened brain, lifting impiety to the level of popular indignation. To realise what this indignation was, we must re-member how the people, brought up by the clergy themselves in the firm belief of the credibility and possibility of miracles, so far from supposing God's laws immutable, had for centuries ex-pected and hoped for a miracle,—that never came. In vain men called for this miraculous intervention in the day of their despair and utmost need. From that hour forth Heaven seemed but the ally of their savage tyrants and oppressors, itself a tyrant as blood-thirsty as any.

Hence the *Black Mass* and the *Jacquerie*.

The original framework of the Black Mass was elastic and could find room for a thousand variations of detail; neverthe-less it was strongly put together, and in my opinion all of a piece.

I was enabled to retrace the course of this grim drama in 1857 in the *Histoire de France,* where I recomposed its four successive Acts,—an easy enough task. Only, at that date, I was too lavish in leaving it a superfluity of those grotesque ornaments and after-growths the primitive Witches' Sabbath borrowed from modern times, and failed sufficiently to indicate how much belongs to the old framework, so gloomy and so terrible in its grim simplicity.

The date of this general framework is fixed beyond a doubt by sundry abominable characteristics of an accursed age,—as also by the dominant place woman holds in it, a marked peculiarity of the fourteenth century.

It is the special note of this century that woman, very far from being enfranchised as she is, yet reigns as its queen, and this in a hundred rude forms. She inherits fiefs in those days, brings a dowry of kingdoms to the Sovereign. She sits enthroned in this world, and still more in the skies. Mary has supplanted Jesus. St. Francis and St. Dominic beheld the three worlds lying in her gracious bosom. In the immensity of her grace she drowns the guilt of sin; what do I say, she abets sin. Read the legend of the nun whose place in choir the Virgin keeps for her, while she goes to see her lover.

In the sublimest heights, in the lowest depths, it is woman, always woman. Beatrice is in heaven, ringed about by the stars, while Jean de Meung, in the *Roman de la Rose,* is preaching the indiscriminate enjoyment of women. Pure, degraded, woman is everywhere. We may say of her what Raymond Lulle says of God: "What part is He of the Universe? The whole."

But in the skies, in the realm of poetry, the woman that is exalted is not the fertile mother, the parent glorified with children. It is the virgin,—Beatrice, sterile, and dying young.

A fair English damsel, they say, visited France about 1300, to preach the redemption of women, who deemed herself the Messiah of that creed.

The *Black Mass,* in its primary aspect, would seem to be this redemption of Eve from the curse Christianity had laid upon her. At the Witches' Sabbath woman fulfils every office. She is priest, and altar, and consecrated host, whereof all the people communicate. In the last resort, is she not the very God of the Sacrifice as well?

There are many popular elements in it all, and yet it does not come solely and entirely from the people. Your peasant respects force and force alone; he holds women in light esteem. This is seen only too plainly in all the old French "Coutumes" (see Michelet's *Origines*). He would never have given woman the dominant place she here occupies, had she not taken it of her own initiative.

I should be quite ready to believe the Sabbath, in its contemporary shape, was the creation of woman's efforts, of a woman driven to desperation, such as was the Sorceress of those days. In the fourteenth century she sees opening before her a long and terrible career of punishment and torments—three hundred, four hundred years lighted up with blazing faggots! Subsequently to the year 1300 her medicines are adjudged to be mischievous, her remedies condemned as poisons. The harmless spells where-by the lepers of that time thought to alleviate their lot lead to the massacre of these unhappy beings. Pope John XXII. has a bishop flayed alive on suspicion of sorcery. Under such a system of blind and indiscriminate repression, to venture little, to venture much and far, is all one, and the risk the same. The very danger incurred increased the Sorceresses' recklessness, and led them to do and dare everything.

Fraternity of man with man, defiance of the Christians' heaven, worship of Nature's God under unnatural and perverted forms,—such the inner significance of the *Black Mass.*

The altar was raised to the Spirit of the revolted serf, *"to Him who has suffered wrong,* the Proscribed of ancient days, unjustly driven out of Heaven, the Great Creator of the earth, the Master that makes the plants germinate from the soil." Under such titles as these the *Luciferians,* his adorers, did him honour, and, if we are to credit a not improbable conjecture, the Knights of the Temple likewise.

The great marvel of all, in those times of utter poverty, is that means were forthcoming for the nocturnal feast of fraternity which could never have been provided by day. The Sorceress, at her own sore peril, induced those in better circumstances to contribute, and collected the offerings they made. Charity, as a satanic virtue, being at once crime and conspiracy, and assuming the aspect of revolt, exercised a mighty influence. Men stinted their meals by day to contribute to the nocturnal feast where rich and poor met at a common table.

Imagine the scene,—a wide heath, often in the neighbourhood of an old Celtic dolmen, at the edge of a wood. The picture is twofold,—on one side the heath brightly lighted up, and the crowds of people feasting; on the other, towards the wood, the

choir of this church whose vault is the open heaven. The choir
I speak of is a knoll rising somewhat above the surrounding
country. Midway between the two, resinous fires burn with yellow tongues of flame and ruddy embers, making a vague, fantastic veil of smoke.

In the background the Sorceress set up her Satan, a great
wooden Satan, black and shaggy. In virtue of his horns and the
he-goat that stood by his side, he might have passed for Bacchus;
but his virile attributes unmistakably proclaimed him Pan and
Priapus. A darkling countenance, that each saw under a different
aspect. While some beheld only an incarnate terror, others were
moved by the haughty melancholy that seemed to enfold the
Exile of Eternity.[4]

Act the First. The superb *Introit* Christianity borrowed of
antiquity,—usual at all ceremonies where the people wound in
and out in long-drawn file under the temple colonnades, before
entering the sanctuary,—this the ancient god, come back to his
own again, appropriated for his services. Similarly, the *lavabo*
was copied from the old Pagan rites of purification. All this
Satan claimed as his own by right of ancient use.

His Priestess is always *The Aged,* this being a title of honour,
but she may as an actual fact be quite young. Lancre speaks of
a Sorceress of only seventeen, a pretty woman and atrociously
cruel.

The Devil's Bride must not be a mere child; she should be full
thirty years of age, with the face of a Medea and the beauty of
Our Lady of Sorrows; her eye deep-set, tragic, and restless, her
hair a dark untamable torrent, falling round her shoulders wildly
like writhing snakes. Perhaps to crown all, the vervain crown
above her brow, the funereal ivy, and the violets of death.

She bids the children stand aloof,—till the feast. The office
begins.

---

[4] This comes from Del Rio, but is not, I should suppose, exclusively Spanish.
It is an antique trait and characteristic of primitive inspiration. Farcicalities
come later.

"I will enter in, to this altar. . . . But, Lord, preserve me from the Traitorous and the Overbearing" (the Priest and the Seigneur).

Then comes the denial of Jesus, homage to the new Master and the feudal kiss, as at the receptions of neophytes by the Templars, where all and everything is yielded without reserve, shame, dignity, or choice,—with this outrageous aggravation of insult added to the repudiation of their God "that they love Satan's backside better."

It is his turn now to consecrate his priestess. The wooden god welcomes her as of old Pan and Priapus did their female adorers. Agreeably to the Pagan ceremonial, she gives herself to him, sits a moment on him, like the Pythia on the tripod of the Delphic Apollo. She thus absorbs breath, soul, life from him by way of this mimic impregnation. This done, with equal solemnity she purifies her person. Henceforth she is the living altar of the shrine.

The *Introit* is ended, and the office interrupted for the banquet. In contrast with the nobles' merrymakings, where they sit sword by side, here at the feast of brothers not a weapon is to be seen, not so much as a knife.

To safeguard the peace, each has a woman with him. Without a woman no guest is admitted. Relation or no, wife or no, old, young, makes no matter; but a woman each must have.

What liquors went round the board? Mead? beer? wine? heady cider, or perry? Who can say? The last two, at any rate, first came into use in the twelfth century.

Beverages to delude the mind, with their dangerous admixture of belladonna, did these appear at the board as yet? The answer is undoubtedly No! Children were present. Besides, excessive disorder of the faculties would have hindered the dance that was to follow.

This dance, this whirling frenzy, the notorious "Witches' Round," was amply sufficient by itself to complete the first stage of intoxication. The performers danced back to back, arms behind the back, without seeing their partner, though back often came in contact with back. Little by little each man lost all knowledge both of self and of her he had beside him. Old age and ugliness were abolished by a veritable satanic miracle; she was still a woman, still lovable and confusedly loved.

Act the Second. At the moment when the crowd, united in one and the same giddy madness, felt itself drawn into a single personality as well by the subtle influence of the feminine element as by a vague, undefinable emotion of fraternity, the service was resumed at the *Gloria.* Altar and host came on the scene. Under what form? That of woman incarnate. By her prostrate body and humiliated person, by the vast silken net of her hair, draggled in the dust, she (that proud Proserpine) offered up herself a sacrifice. On her loins a demon performed Mass, pronounced the *Credo,* deposited the offertory of the faithful.[5]

In later times all this was an exhibition of indecency. But in the fourteenth century, that period of calamity, the dread epoch of the *Black Death,* and famine after famine, the days of the Jacquerie, and the robberies and cruelties of the *Great Companies,*—for a people exposed to so many perils, the effect was nothing if not serious. The whole assemblage had the worst to fear in case of surprise. The Sorceress herself ran the extremest risk, and in this act of defiant daring was in a very true sense giving away her life. Nay! worse, she was facing a perfect hell of possible torments,—tortures one dares scarcely so much as speak of. Torn with pincers and broken on the wheel, the breasts amputated, the skin flayed off little by little (as was done to the

---

[5] This highly important point, that woman was herself the altar, and that the office was performed on her, we know from the trial of La Voisin, published by M. Ravaisson, senior, among the other *Bastille Papers.* In these imitations, of recent date, it is true, of the Witches' Sabbath, carried out for the amusement of the great nobles of the Court of Louis XIV., there is no doubt that the antique and classical forms of the primitive Sabbath were reproduced, even in respect of a point such as this, where the ancient ceremonial may very likely have been discontinued during the intermediate period.

Sorcerer Bishop of Cahors), roasted before a slow fire and limb
by limb, she might have to endure an eternity of agony.

All present must indeed have been deeply stirred, when over
the body of the devoted being thus submitting to voluntary self-
humiliation, prayer and offering were made for the harvest.
Wheat was presented to the *Spirit of the Earth,* who makes the
crops grow. Birds let loose—no doubt from the woman's bosom
—bore the *God of Liberty* the signs and supplications of the
unhappy serfs. What was the boon they craved? That we, we
their far-away descendants, might win enfranchisement.[6]

What was distributed by way of host at this strange eucharist?
Not the burlesque and abominable stuff we shall find so used in
Henri IV.'s day; but most probably the same *confarreatio* we
have met with in philters, the sacrament of love, a cake baked on
her body, on the victim who to-morrow might as likely as not
pass through the fire herself. It was her life, her death, they ate.
The morsel was impregnated already with the savour of her
burning flesh.

Last of all, they laid on her two offerings apparently of human
flesh, representations of the *last dead* and the *last born* respectively of the community. They shared the merit of the woman
who was at once altar and sacrifice, and the assemblage (sym-
bolically) communicated in both these novel elements. Triple
the sacrifice, and human in all three; in Satan's dim and gloomy
rites the people was the sole object of adoration to the people.

Here was the true sacrifice, and it was accomplished at last.
Woman, having given her very flesh to the crowd to eat, had
ended her task. She rose to her feet again, but did not leave the
spot till she had firmly established and as it were ratified the
authenticity of it all by appeal to the lightning, a defiance cast in
the face of the God whose empire she had usurped.

---

[6] This charming offering of wheat and birds is peculiar to France (Jaquier,
Flagellans, 57; Soldan, 225). In Lorraine, and no doubt in Germany also, black
animals were offered up,—black cats, black goats, black bulls.

In ribald mockery of the words: *Agnus Dei,* etc., and the breaking of the wafer in the Christian Eucharist, she had a skinned toad brought to her which she then tore in pieces. With eyes rolling horribly and looks upturned to heaven, she decapitated the toad, repeating these strange words: "Ah! *Philip,*[7] if only I had you between my hands, I would treat you the same!"

Jesus making no reply to her defiance, no lightning stroke ensuing, He was deemed vanquished. The nimble troop of demons would seize this moment for astonishing the crowd with small miracles that impressed and terrified the credulous. Toads —perfectly harmless creatures, but which were believed to be deadly poisonous—were bitten and freely mangled between their teeth. Unharmed they would leap over blazing fires and red-hot embers, to amuse the populace and set them laughing at the fires of hell.

Laughing? was the people moved to laughter, the ceremonial so tragic, so bold, and reckless as it was? Impossible to say; but there can be no doubt whatever hers was no laughing mood who first did and dared it all. The bonfires could not fail but call up the image of those that might ere long blaze round the stake of her own doom. Hers, too, the weighty responsibility of safeguarding the succession of satanic sovereigns, of training up the Sorceresses of the future.

---

[7] Lancre, 136. Why the name *Philip,* I have no idea. It is as impossible to give a reason as to say why Satan, when he names Jesus, calls him little John, or *Janicot.* Can it be she says *Philip* here, from the odious name of the King who gave France a hundred years of English wars, who inaugurated at Crécy the series of national defeats and cost the country the first invasion of her soil? The long, almost uninterrupted, period of peace that had gone before made war all the more horrible to the masses. Philippe de Valois, author of this interminable war, was held accursed, and perhaps left behind him in this popular ritual a never-forgotten word of malediction.

BLACK MASS Continued

LOVE and DEATH

SATAN DISAPPEARS

THE people is enfranchised and emboldened. The poor serf, free for once, is king for a few hours' space. But his time is short; already the night is passing, the stars verging to their setting. Very soon the cruel dawn will send him back to slavery, set him once more, under the malignant eye of his taskmaster, under the shadow of his lord's castle and that of the Church, to the monotonous labour, the everlasting weary round regulated by the two bells, whereof the one says *Ever* and the other says *Never*. Each peasant among them, with glum, submissive looks and an air of jog-trot habit, will be seen sallying forth to his day's work.

At least let them enjoy their momentary respite! Let each one of earth's disinherited sons be fully happy for once, and find his utmost dreams fulfilled! . . . What heart so miserable, so dead and withered, as not to have some day-dreams, some wild aspirations,—to say sometimes, "Ah! if only such or such a thing could happen"?

The only detailed descriptions we possess are comparatively modern, as I have already mentioned, dating from a period of peace and prosperity, viz. the last years of the reign of Henri IV. when France was once more flourishing. These were years of luxury and plenty, altogether different from the black days when the Witches' Sabbath was first organised.

If we were to trust implicitly to M. Lancre and his fellows, we should picture this Third Act to our mind's eye as a sort of Rubens' kermesse, a wild, confused orgy, a vast masked ball, giving licence to every sort of illicit intercourse, and particularly to incest between closely connected relatives. According to these authors, whose only wish is to inspire horror and make their readers shudder, the chief end of the whole festival, its main lesson and express doctrine, was incest; they would have us believe that at these huge gatherings (sometimes as many as twelve thousand souls were present) the most monstrous acts were openly committed before the assembled spectators.

This is hard to believe. The very same writers tell us other facts which seem diametrically opposed to such cynicism. They say the folk only came there in couples, that they only sat at the feast two by two, that supposing an individual arrived unaccompanied, a young demon was actually told off on purpose to shepherd the lonely visitor and do the honours of the festival. They inform us that jealous lovers were not afraid to attend and bring with them their fair companions, curious to see the strange sight.

Again we have seen how the great majority attended by families, their children accompanying them. These they sent away only for the First Act, not for the banquet or the religious (or rather anti-religious) ceremonial, and not even for the Third Act here in question. This proves the existence of a certain degree of decency. Besides, the performance was twofold. The family groups remained on the brilliantly lighted heath. It was only beyond the fantastic curtain of pitchy smoke clouds that a darkling outer region began, to which those who wished could slip away.

Judges and inquisitors, bitterly hostile as these were are forced to admit that a noble spirit of gentleness and peace prevailed generally. Of the three things that shocked decorum so much at the feasts of the nobles nothing was found here. No brawling, no duels, no tables stained with blood. No vile treachery in the name of gallantry to outrage the *brother in arms*. Lastly, the foul promiscuity of the Templars, for all that has been said to the contrary, was unknown, indeed unneeded; at the Sabbath woman was everything.

With regard to incest, we must distinguish. Then every connexion with relations, even such as are held the most legitimate in our days, was reckoned a crime. Modern law, which is charity personified, understands the human heart and the good of families. It permits the widower to marry his wife's sister,—in other words, to give his children the best and kindest of new mothers. It permits the uncle to afford his niece necessary protection by making her his wife. Above all, it permits marriage with a female cousin, a trusty and familiar bride, often the object of affection since childhood, companion of youthful sport, and an acceptable daughter-in-law to the mother, who has long ago taken her to her heart. In the Middle Ages all this was incest!

The peasant, whose affections never go beyond his own family circle, was driven to sheer desperation. In the sixth degree even, it would have been held monstrous to wed his cousin. Impossible to marry in his own village, where the ties of relationship imposed so many barriers; he was bound to look elsewhere, further away. But in those days intercommunication was of the slightest, mutual knowledge non-existent, and neighbours cordially detested. Different villages, on fête days, would fight each other without a notion why they did so,—as is the case to this hour in countries ever so little removed from each other. A man would hardly dare to go look for a wife at the very spot where the battle had occurred, and the peril of wounds and death confronted.

Another difficulty. The feudal lord of a young serf would not allow him, if he wished, to marry in the fief of a neighbouring baron. He would have become the serf of the wife's over-lord, and so been lost to his own.

Thus while *the priest barred the cousin, the feudal forbade the stranger;* and so many men never married at all.

The result was precisely what they most wished to guard against. At the Witches' Sabbath the natural affections had their way in double force. There the young man encountered once more the girl he knew and loved already, who when he was a lad of ten had been called his *little wife*. Be sure he liked her best, and treated the canonical objections with supreme indifference.

A thorough study of mediæval family life throws entire discredit on all those rhetorical declamations we hear about a wide general promiscuity affecting crowds of human beings. The exact opposite is perceived to be the case,—that each separate little group, constituted on the narrowest basis and in the most concentrated form, is to the last degree averse to admit any foreign element whatever.

The serf, anything but jealous—towards his own kinsfolk, but miserably poor and wretched in his circumstances, is excessively apprehensive of worsening his lot yet further by multiplying a long family he cannot possibly feed. The priest and the baron both would have him augment the number of their serfs, would like to see his wife everlastingly with child; and the strangest sermons were preached on this subject,[1]—occasionally savage recriminations and murderous threats indulged in. All this only made the husband more obstinate in his precautions. As for the wife, who poor creature could never hope to rear children under such conditions, and found only cause for tears in their arrival, she dreaded nothing so much as pregnancy. She only ventured to attend the nocturnal festival on the express assurance repeated again and again that "no woman ever returned therefrom heavier than she came."[2]

---

[1] It is only a very short while ago that my witty and accomplished friend, M. Génin, brought together a mass of most curious information on the point in question.

[2] Boguet, Lancre, all the authorities are at one on this point. A flat contradiction on Satan's part, but a state of things entirely agreeable to the serf, the peasant, the poor man. The Devil makes the harvest sprout, but renders woman barren; wheat in abundance, but never a child.

They came no doubt, but drawn to the ceremony by the banquet, the dance, the gay lights, and the love of amusement; in no way by the incitements of the flesh. Some indeed found only pain and suffering there; while others abhorred the icy purification that followed instantly on the act of love to nullify its effects. No matter; they were ready to undergo anything rather than increase their poverty, bring another unfortunate into the world, give the over-lord another serf.

Strong was the common determination, trusty the mutual agreement that limited love to the family and excluded the stranger from all participation. No reliance was felt but in kinsfolk united in the same serfdom, who, sharing the same burdens, were duly careful not to increase these.

Hence no general movement of population, no mixing and mingling confusedly of divers elements; but, on the contrary, only a series of narrow and mutually exclusive family groups. This very fact was bound to render the Witches' Sabbath powerless as an instrument of revolt, ineffectual as a means of stirring and combining the masses. The family, careful above all things to avoid a prolific offspring, secured its object by strict limitation in matters of love to very near relations, in other words, to those pledged to the same interest. A sad, depressing, unhallowed state of things, darkening and degrading the sweetest moments of life. Alas, alas! even in love and marriage all was mere squalid wretchedness and revolt against untoward circumstance.

Society was very cruel. Authority kept on saying, "Marry"; but it made marriage next door to impossible, as well by excess of abject poverty as by the senseless rigour of canonical prohibitions.

The result was the exact opposite of the purity the Church was for ever preaching. Under a Christian disguise, the old patriarchal system of Asia was the only existing reality.

The eldest son only could marry. The younger brothers and

the sisters all worked under him and for him.[3] In the isolated
mountain farmsteads of the south, far removed from all intercourse with neighbours or other women, the brothers lived with
their sisters, who were their servants and belonged to them body
and soul,—a state of morals corresponding to that described in
the Book of Genesis, and analogous to the marriage customs of
the Parsees and the usages subsisting to this day among some of
the pastoral tribes of the Himalayas.

What was even more shocking was the lot of the mother of the
family. She found herself unable to marry off her son; she could
not unite him with a kinswoman and so make sure of a daughter-
in-law who would have some consideration and respect for her.
Her son would marry, if marry he could, a girl from a distant
village, often a hostile one; then her arrival was a veritable and
terrible invasion, whether to the children of the first bed or to
the poor mother, who often found herself turned out of doors by
the stranger. It will scarce be credited, but there is no doubt
about the fact. At best she was ill treated,—driven ignominiously
from the fireside and the domestic board.

A Swiss law expressly forbids depriving the mother of her
place at the chimney corner.

She dreaded above all things the event of her son's marrying.
Yet her lot was not much more tolerable supposing he did not.
She was just as much an inferior—servant of the young *master
of the house,* who succeeded to all his father's rights, even to that
of beating her. I have myself seen instances at the present day in
the south of France of this horror,—a son of twenty-five chastis-
ing his own mother when she got drunk.

How much more in these ruder times! . . . It was more likely
to be the son that would return from village merrymakings in a
condition of semi-intoxication, scarcely knowing what he was
after. Same bedchamber, same bed—for two was an absolutely
unknown luxury. The mother was far from feeling secure. He

---

[3] A very common condition of things in France, I have often been told by
the learned and accurate M. Monteil.

had seen his friends married, and the sight had roused his evil passions. Hence floods of tears, extreme prostration, the most deplorable self-abandonment. The unhappy woman, thus threatened with violence by her only god, her son, wounded in her fondest affections, reduced to such a hideous, unnatural plight, was in despair. She would try to sleep, to feign unconsciousness. Then there happened, without either quite realising the enormity, what so often happens to this day in the poor quarters of great cities, where some poor creature, constrained by terror or perhaps by blows, submits to the last indignity. Submissive henceforth, and spite all her scruples, far too readily resigned, the mother became the victim of a piteous servitude. A shameful and an agonising, anxious life, for year by year the discrepancy of age would increase, and more and more tend to separate them. A woman of thirty-six could still hold the affections of a boy of twenty; but at fifty, alas! and at a more advanced age still, what then? From the Great Sabbath, when distant villages met together, he might any day bring home a strange woman to be the young mistress of the house—an unfamiliar, hard outsider, without heart or pity, who would rob her of her son, her fireside, her bed, all the household gods she had got together by her own labour.

By what Lancre and others tell us, Satan held it a great merit on the son's part to remain faithful to his mother, made this particular crime into a virtue. If this is true, we may easily guess the reason how one woman naturally stood up for another, how the Sorceress was a ready partisan on the mother's side, to help her hearth against the son's wife, who, stick in hand, would have turned her out to beg her bread.

Lancre goes further and declares, "never was thoroughpaced Witch yet but was the child of incest, born of mother and son." The same rule held good in Persia for the birth of the genuine Mage, who must be the offspring, so men said, of this odious mystery of iniquity. In this way the lore of the Wise Men, the magic of the East, was confined to the narrowest limits, within a family that was renewed perpetually from its own blood.

By an impious misreading of Nature, they believed themselves to be copying in this hateful ritual the innocent mystery of the rustic year, the ever-renewed cycle of vegetation growth, whereby the corn, reaped and again sown in the furrow, comes up once again as corn.

Less monstrous forms of union (of brother and sister), common among the Jews and Greeks, were unloving and very seldom fruitful. Very wisely they were abandoned before long, and would never have been resorted to again, but for the spirit of revolt which, exasperated by ridiculous prohibitions, drove men recklessly into every extreme most violently contrasted with use and wont.

In this way unnatural laws, acting on the evil passions, the hate, of mankind, produced unnatural crimes.

A hard, an accursed time! and the inevitable mother of despair!

So far so good,—or rather so bad; but lo! the dawn of a brighter day is all but come. In a moment, the hour strikes that puts all evil spirits to flight. The Sorceress feels the gloomy flowers of sin withering on her brow. Farewell her royal state! her very life, it may be! . . . What would happen if the dayspring found her still exposed to its beams?

What will she make of Satan? a flame of fire? a heap of ashes? He asks nothing better. He knows very well, the wily schemer, that to live, to be born again, the only way is to die.

Shall he die, the mighty evoker of the dead, he who gave weeping friends the only joy they knew in this world, the dream, the image of their vanished dear ones? Nay! he is very sure to live.

Shall he die, the mighty spirit who finding Creation accursed and Nature lying rejected in the mire, that Nature which the Church had tossed disdainfully from her lap like an unlovely, unloved foster-child, took her up again and laid her softly in his bosom? Nay! the thing cannot be.

Shall he die, the sole and only healer of the Middle Ages, that age of sore disease, who saved the people by his poisons and told them to "Live on, foolish folk, love on"?

As he is assured of life, the sturdy rogue, he dies quietly and comfortably enough. He "slips off this mortal coil" like a conjuring trick, dexterously burns his fine black goat-skin, and vanishes in a flash of fire and the brilliant light of the coming dawn.

But she, she who made Satan, who made everything, good and ill alike, who fostered and favoured so many causes,—love, self-devotion, crime! . . . What is her fate? Behold her all alone on the deserted heath!

She is far, very far, from being, as represented, the horror of all mankind. Many will bless her name.[4] More than one has found her fair, more than one would sell his share of Paradise if he dared but approach her. . . . But round about her is a great gulf,—the admiration she excites passes all bounds, and the terror is excessive of this all-puissant Medea, of her wondrous deep-set eyes and the voluptuous snaky ringlets of coal-black hair that flood her shoulders.

Alone for ever; for ever loveless and alone! Who and what is left her? Naught but the dread Spirit who stole away from her side but now.

"Well, then, good Satan, let us away. . . . I am in haste to be in those regions down below. Hell is better than earth. Farewell this world and all its shows!"

She who first invented, first played the awful drama, could hardly survive her companion long. Satan, submissive to her behest, had near by and ready saddled a gigantic black horse, whose eyes and nostrils shot fire. She sprang to his back with one bound,—and away. . . .

---

[4] Lancre speaks of Sorceresses who won both love and adoration.

118   *Satanism and Witchcraft*

The eyes of the bystanders followed her vanishing form. . . .
The good folks asked in terror, "Oh, what, what will become of
her?" As she went she laughed, a horrid peal of fiendish mirth,
and disappeared from sight like an arrow from a bow. Men fain
would know, but know they never shall, what was the unhappy
creature's final doom.[5]

---

[5] This is almost exactly the end of an English Witch whose history is told
by Wyer.

PART TWO

The SORCERESS
in HER DECADENCE

SATAN MULTIPLIED
and VULGARISED

Now we have another type altogether,—a delicate Devil's plaything, the little Witch-wife, child of the Black Mass; she has quite superseded the grim Sorceress of an earlier day, blossoming into being, with all the wily ways and sportive grace of a kitten. The very opposite of her predecessor, she is soft and silky, stealthy of approach and shy, treading so softly, softly, and loving, above all things, to be caressed. Nothing Titanic about *her*, that is very clear; on the contrary, she is a low-minded, tricky creature, a wanton from her very cradle, bursting with every naughty, dainty caprice. Her whole life will be but the expression of a certain midnight hour, a dark and evil moment, when a vile reverie that would have excited a mere horror of disgust by daylight, took form in the licence of dreams.

Born with such a secret in her very blood, possessing an instinctive knowledge of evil, with looks that pierce so far and so low, she will respect neither thing nor person in this world, and barely so much as think of religion. Satan himself will not move her hugely, for after all he is a Spirit, and her tastes are pronounced, confined exclusively to material pleasures.

As a child, she loved dirt. Grown a big girl and a pretty, she was a wonder of nastiness. In her Sorcery will become the strange laboratory of a strange, mysterious alchemy. From a very early period she handles, by predilection, repulsive matters, drugs and medicaments to-day, to-morrow nauseous intrigues. This is her element, love and disease; she will turn out an apt go-between, a clever, bold experimenter. She will be persecuted for alleged murders, for the concoction of poisonous brews; but unjustly. Her instinct by no means lies in that direction; she has no hankering after death. Malevolent as she is, she yet loves life, prefers to heal the sick, and prolong existence. She is dangerous in another way,—in two other ways. She will sell recipes to produce sterility, perhaps abortion. On the other hand, with her wild, reckless wantonness of fancy, she will be only too ready to help women to their ruin by her accursed potions, and find a cruel joy in crimes of the sort.

What a contrast to the other! She is a mere trafficker after all; while the other was Antichrist, the Demon, the Spirit of Revolt, the wife of Satan, and, in a sense, his mother. For did he not wax great from her and her inward might? But the latter Witch is, at most, the Devil's daughter, inheriting two attributes from him—her uncleanness and her love of handling life. Such is her lot; she is an artist in this line, and a successful one —and mankind is her raw material!

They say of her she will perpetuate her race by incest, whereof she sprang herself. But there is no need; without intervention of any male, she will bear an innumerable breed. In less than fifty years, by the beginning of the fifteenth century, under Charles VI., a prodigious contagion spreads far and wide. Whoever believes himself to possess secret remedies, mysterious recipes; whoever thinks he can divine the future, whoever has dreams and waking reveries, dubs himself the favourite of Satan. Every light-headed, silly woman adopts as her own the imposing name of Witch.

A dangerous title, but a lucrative one, readily enough given by the hatred of the populace, which assails with alternate insults and prayers her unknown powers. It is no less readily accepted, often actually claimed. When children pursue her in the streets with gibes, and women shake their fists at her, and hurl the word at her as if it were a stone, she turns upon them and says proudly, "Yes! you say true; a Sorceress I am!"

The trade is improving, and men are taking it up,—a new comedown for the art and mystery. The humblest of Witchwives still retains something of the Sibyl. But these self-styled Wizards, sordid charlatans, commonplace jugglers, mole and rat catchers, casting spells over cattle, selling secrets they do not possess, infect the age with a foul, black, smothering smoke of fear and foolish terror. Satan becomes common, his vogue enormously increased, but in what low, sordid conditions! A poor triumph indeed, for he only grows dull and tiresome. Yet the people flock to him, will scarce endure any God but him; but his old self, his old dignity, are gone for ever.

The fifteenth century, for all its two or three great discoveries, is yet, I take it, a tired, outworn, exhausted century, lacking in ideas.

It starts grandly enough with the Royal *Sabbath* of St. Denis, the mad, wild, gloomy festival Charles VI. gave in the Abbey of St. Denis to celebrate the reinterment of Duguesclin, who had been in his grave many a long year. For three days and three nights Sodom caroused over the tombs of the dead. The mad King, not yet the imbecile he afterwards became, forced all the kings, his ancestors, their dry bones dancing in their coffins, to share his revel. Grim Death, whether he would or no, was made a pandar and added a horrid spur to the wanton pleasures of the Court. There in all their effrontery flaunted the base fashions of the period, when great ladies, their height exaggerated by the "devil's coif," or double-horned headdress of the day, threw the belly into unnatural prominence, so that one and all seemed pregnant—an admirable device, by-the-by, for concealing the fact if it were really so.[1] The mode was dear to women, and lasted a good forty years. The young nobles on their side were just as shameless, and exposed their persons in an equally disgusting fashion. Whilst women wore Satan on their brows in the twin-peaked cap, knights and pages displayed his symbol on their feet in those pointed shoes that turned up like so many angry scorpions. Under the guise of animals, they disported themselves in brazen travesty of the basest lusts of beasts. It was there Gilles de Retz, the infamous kidnapper of children, himself a page at the time, first learned his monstrous vices. These great ladies and mistresses of broad fiefs were bold-faced Jezebels every one, more shameless even than the men; they would not so much as deign to wear a mask, but exposed their bold faces quite unveiled. Their sensual rage, their mad ostentation of debauch, their outrageous defiance of all decency, were for King, for all,—for reason, life, body, soul, the sheer abyss and bottomless pit of hell.

And what was the result? The whipped curs of Agincourt, that poor etiolated generation of nobles who in miniatures make us shiver to this day to see beneath their tight-laced doublets their wretched, thin, shrunken limbs.[2]

I commiserate the Sorceress from the bottom of my heart, who on the Great Dame's return from the King's feast will have to be her confidante and the minister of her pleasures, for be sure she will demand mere impossibilities of her.

In her castle, it is very true, she is alone, the only, or almost

---

[1] Even in a painting representing the most mystical of subjects, in a work of genius, the *Holy Lamb* of Van Eyck (known as John of Bruges), all the virgins look as if they were in child. Such was the grotesque mode of the fifteenth century.

[2] This excessive thinness of persons worn out and enervated by excesses is enough to spoil, in my eyes, all the superb miniatures of the Court of Burgundy, the Duc de Berry, etc. The subjects are such deplorable creatures that no beauty of execution can make these pictures really pleasing and successful works of art.

the only woman there, in a whole houseful of unmarried men.

By what the romances tell us, the Lady Châtelaine would seem to have delighted in collecting round her a court of pretty girls; but history and our own common sense say just the contrary. Queen Eleanor was not so silly as to set the Fair Rosamond as a counterfoil to her own beauty. These queens and great ladies were as abominably jealous as they were licentious —instance the story related by Henri Martin of one who had a maid her husband admired overmuch, outraged to death by the common soldiery. The high-born dame's power over men, we repeat, depended on her being alone and without rivals. Let her be as old and ugly as you please, she is the dream of one and all. The Sorceress enjoys fine sport in rousing her to abuse this divinity of hers, to make mock of this herd of besotted and submissive males. She makes her dare every extreme, and treat them like brute beasts. Her will lays a spell on them; down they go on all fours, cringing apes, lumbering bears, nasty dogs, swine, ready to obey every caprice, to welcome every outrage of their mistress Circé.

All this only moves her to pity—and sick disgust! She spurns away the crawling animals with her foot; they are base and foul enough, but too innocent for her. Then she finds a grotesque remedy for her satiety; as they are all so impotent to please her, she chooses a lover more impotent still, a little lad to lavish her caresses upon. The idea is worthy of the Witch who suggested it,—to blow into precocious flame the spark of naughtiness lurking in the innocent child slumbering in the pure sleep of boyhood. This is the ugly story of Jehan de Saintré, type of the Cherubinos and other miserable dolls and playthings that women have corrupted in times of decadence.

Under so many pedantic ornaments and trappings of sentimental morality, the sordid cruelty that underlies the proceeding is evident enough. It is killing the fruit by nipping the flower in the bud. It is, in a sense, the very thing often cast up against the Sorceresses, that "they ate children." At any rate, it is drinking

their life blood. With all her tender ways and motherly affecta-
tions, the fair lady whose caresses are so soft is a vampire to
drain the blood of her weakling victim,—nothing more nor less!
The result of the horrid process the romancer tells us himself.
Saintré, the story says, grows up a very perfect knight, yes! perfectly frail and feeble, so that eventually he is braved and defied
by the lout of a peasant abbé, in whom the fair lady, coming at
length to a better mind, finds what suits her wishes best.

These vain caprices serve only to augment her ennui, to set an
edge to the empty feeling of satiety. Circé, surrounded by her
beasts, utterly bored, utterly jaded, would fain be a beast herself. She feels wild impulses working, and shuts herself up in a
lonely tower of the castle keep. Thence she throws sinister,
questioning looks over the gloomy forest. She is a prisoner, and
knows all the savage fury of a she-wolf kept chained. "Hither
instantly, the Witch-wife! I want her, I want her. Come, quick!"
and before two minutes have gone by, "What! is she not here
yet?"

Ah! here she is. "Now listen carefully. . . . I have a caprice
(an irresistible hankering, you understand), a hankering to
strangle you, to drown you, or deliver you up to the bishop, who
has long been wanting you. . . . You have one way of escape,
and one only—to satisfy another hankering of mine, to change
me into a she-wolf. I am so tired of my life. I cannot sit still any
longer; I long, at any rate o' nights, to gallop free in the forest.
I would be done with submissive fools that wait on me, and dogs
that deafen me, and blundering horses that jib and refuse the
woodland paths."

"But, dear lady, suppose they caught you?" . . . "Insolent
woman! I tell you, you shall die the death." "But surely you
know the history of the werewolf woman whose paw was cut
off.[3] . . . I should be so grieved to see such an accident!"

---

[3] This dreadful idea was not unfamiliar to the great ladies of those days, the
high-born prisoners in mediæval castles. They were hungry and thirsty

" 'Tis my affair, I tell you; and I will listen to no excuses.
. . . Come, time presses; I have begun to yelp and howl already.
. . . Oh! the joy of it, to go hunting all alone, by the light of
the moon, and all alone to pull down the hind with my strong
jaws—yes! and men too, if they come across my path; to bite
little tender children,—and women too, women best of all! to
make my teeth meet in their flesh! . . . How I hate them all.
. . . But none of them as bitterly as you. Never start back, I
won't bite you; you move my disgust too sorely, and besides,
you have no blood in your veins. . . . Blood, blood! I must
have blood!"

No way of refusal is open, "Nothing easier, my lady. Tonight,
at nine o'clock, you shall drink the brew. Then lock yourself up
in your chamber. While they think you there, you will be
another creature, flying through the woods."

So said, so done; and next day the lady finds herself worn out
and utterly exhausted, at the very end of her powers. She must
have covered, last night, a full thirty leagues. She has hunted and
killed. She is all covered with blood; but perhaps this only
comes from the brambles she has torn herself against.

A great source of pride, and no less of danger, to her who has
done this miracle. Nevertheless her mistress, who demanded it,
receives her very gloomily. "Sorceress! Sorceress! what an awful power you possess! I should never have thought as much!

---

after freedom, and the cruelties of absolute freedom. Boguet relates how, in
the mountains of Auvergne, a hunter one night fired at a she-wolf, missing
a vital spot, but cutting off one of the animal's paws. The beast made off,
limping on three legs. Presently the hunter went to a neighbouring castle to
ask hospitality of the nobleman who lived there. The latter, on seeing him,
asked if he had enjoyed good sport. In answer to the question he was for
drawing from his game-bag the wolf's pad he had just shot off; but what was
his astonishment to find, instead of an animal's foot, a human hand, and on
one of the fingers a ring, which the nobleman instantly recognised as his
wife's! He went to her immediately, and found her wounded and concealing her forearm. It was handless; the one the hunter had brought in was
fitted to it, and the lady was forced to confess it was indeed she who, under
the form of a she-wolf, had attacked the hunter, and afterwards escaped,
leaving a paw behind on the field of battle. The husband had the cruelty to
give her up to justice, and she was burned at the stake.

But now I am terrified and horror-struck. . . . Ah! they do well to hate you! 'Twill be a good day when you are burned. I will be your death, when so I please. My peasants this very evening would whet their scythes on you if I said one word of the night's doings. . . . Away with you, you vile, black, ugly wretch."

She is hurried by the great folks, her patrons, into strange adventures. Having only the castle to rely on to guard her from the priest, and be some surety against the stake, how can she refuse aught her formidable protectors ask? Suppose, for instance, the Baron, just back from the Crusades and from Nicopolis, and an amateur of Turkish ways, calls her to him, and entrusts her with the charge of kidnapping children for him, what is she to do? These razzias, carried out on such a large scale in Greek lands, where on occasion two thousand pages would enter the seraglio at one time, were by no means unknown to the Christians,—to the English barons from the twelfth century onwards, at a later date to the knights of Rhodes and of Malta. The infamous Gilles de Retz, the only one who was brought to trial, was punished not for having carried off his serfs' little boys to his castle (not an uncommon occurrence in those days), but for having sacrificed them to Satan. The Sorceress who acted as agent in these crimes, though she could hardly know the fate reserved for the victims, found herself between two dangers. On one side the peasants' pitchfork and scythe, on the other the tortures of the Baron's tower, which a refusal would inevitably have brought down on her head. De Retz's myrmidon, that terrible Italian of his,[4] was as likely as not to have pounded her to death in his mortar.

---

[4] See my *History of France,* and above all the learned and precise little book by our lamented Armand Guéraud, *Notice sur Gilles de Rais,* Nantes, 1855—reprinted in the *Biographie Bretonne* of M. Levot. From it we see that the purveyors of this horrid supply of children to the monster were more often than not men. There was a La Meffraye mixed up in the business as well,— was this a Sorceress? We are not told. M. Guéraud was to have published the

On all sides danger, and gain to compensate the danger. No situation could well be more full of temptations. The Sorceresses themselves often did not deny the ridiculous powers the populace credited them with. They admitted that by means of a doll or mannikin pierced with needles, they could *bewitch* anyone they pleased, making them get thinner and thinner till they pined away and died. They confessed that with the mandragora, torn up by the roots at the gibbet's foot (by the tooth of a dog, they declared, which invariably died of the effects), they could overthrow the reason, change men into beasts, turn women lightheaded and insane. Even more terrible was the frenzied delirium produced by the thorn-apple or *Datura,* which sets men dancing till they die,[5] makes them unhesitatingly submit to a thousand shameful horrors, of which they have no present consciousness, and no subsequent recollection.

Hence savage excesses of hate on the one hand, and no less violent extremities of terror on the other. The author of the *Marteau des Sorcières* (Hammer of the Sorceresses), Sprenger, records with horror how he saw, at a season of heavy snow, when the roads were all broken up, a whole population of wretched beings, frantic with fear and cursed with calamities only too real, crowding all the outskirts of a small German town. You never saw, he says, pilgrimages nearly so numerous to Our Lady of Grace, or Our Lady of Eremites. All these poor folks, foundered in the deep ruts, stumbling, blundering and falling, were on their way to the Witch's hut, to implore pity of the

---

trial. Such a publication is much to be desired, but printed *in extenso,* in its genuine form and unmutilated. The MSS. are at Nantes and at Paris. My learned friend, M. Dugast-Matifeux, informs me a copy is in existence *more complete* than these originals in the archives of Thouars.

[5] Pouchet, *Solanées et Botanique Générale;* Nysten, *Dict. de Médecine* (edit. Littré and Robin), article *Datura.* Thieves are only too ready to make use of these decoctions. One day they made the hangman of Aix and his wife, whom they wished to rob of their money, take a dose of this nature. The two victims fell into so extraordinary a state of delirium that they passed the whole of one night dancing absolutely naked in a graveyard.

Devil. What feelings of pride and transport must have filled the Witch-wife's heart to behold all this multitude grovelling at her feet! [6]

[6] This pride and exultation sometimes led her into the most reckless dissoluteness. Hence the German saying, "The Witch in her garret showed her comrade fifteen fine lads in green coats, and bade her 'Choose; they are all for you.'" Her triumph was to exchange the respective parts, and inflict as tests of love the most disgusting outrages on the nobles and grandees she thus degraded. It is well known that queens, as well as kings, and high-born ladies (in Italy as late as in the eighteenth century. *Collection Maurepas,* xxx. 111) used to receive in audience and hold court at the moment of performing the most repulsive of nature's functions, and made their favourites undertake the most unpleasant offices for them. In a spirit of fantastic worship, these latter adored everything that came from their idol, and fought for the vilest duty about her person. If only she were young and pretty, and disdainful, there was no mark of attachment so humiliating and abominable her domestic pets (her *cicisbeo,* her chaplain, a love-sick page) were not ready to submit to, under the absurd notion that a philter possessed the more virtue in proportion to its disgusting quality. This is humiliating enough for poor humanity, but what are we to say to the astounding fact that the Sorceress, without being either well-born or pretty or young, a pauper rather, and very likely a serf, dressed in mere filthy rags, by sheer downright cunning and some inexplicable charm of abandoned wantonness and unholy fascination, debauched and degraded so low the gravest personages of the time? Certain monks of a monastery on the Rhine, one of those proud German houses where none could enter without four hundred years of nobility behind him, make this dismal admission to Sprenger: "We have seen her bewitch three of our Abbots one after the other, and kill the fourth, avowing with brazen effrontery, 'I have done it, and I will do it again, and they shall never escape me, because they have eaten . . .'" etc. (*Comederunt meam*—"they have eaten my . . ." Sprenger, *Malleus Maleficarum,* Hammer of the Sorceresses, *quæstio* vii. p. 84). The worst of it all for Sprenger and what most made him despair, is the fact of her being so well protected, no doubt by these infatuated devotees, that he could not burn her. "Fateor quia nobis non aderat ulciscendi aut inquirendi super eam facultas; *ideo adhuc superest.*" —"I confess we had no means of insisting on her punishment, or a proper inquiry into her crimes, *wherefore the woman is still alive.*"

PERSECUTIONS

THE Sorceresses took small pains to hide their proceedings. They rather boasted of their powers; and it is out of their own mouths Sprenger gathered a large proportion of the strange stories which adorn his Manual. The said Manual is a highly pedantic work, following with grotesque servility the formal divisions and subdivisions in use among the Thomist logicians, —yet at the same time the single-minded, earnest and serious production of a man quite genuinely frightened, a man who in the awful duel between God and the Devil, in which the former generally *allows* the Evil One to get the best of it, sees no other possible remedy but to pursue the latter firebrand in hand, burning with all practicable speed those mortal frames wherein he chooses to take up his abode.

Sprenger's sole merit is to have compiled a work more complete than any of his predecessors, the compendium of a vast and elaborate system, the crown of a whole literature. The old *Penitentiaries,* or manuals for the use of confessors in their inquisition into various sins, were succeeded by the *Directories* for the inquisition of heresy, the greatest of all sins. But for the chiefest heresy of all, which is Witchcraft or Sorcery, special *Directoria* or manuals were compiled, the so-called *Hammers* (*Mallei*) for the detection and punishment of Witches and Sorceresses. These manuals, continually enriched by the zeal of the Dominicans, reached their highest perfection in the *Malleus* of Sprenger, a work which governed the author himself in the conduct of his great mission to Germany, and for a century remained the guide and beacon-star of the tribunals of the Inquisition.

What was it led Sprenger to study these questions? He relates how being at Rome, in the refectory where the monks lodged pilgrims, he saw two such from Bohemia,—a young priest namely and his father. The old man was sighing and supplicating for a successful issue to his journey. Sprenger, moved to pity, asks him the cause of his distress. The reason he says is this: his son is possessed by the Devil, and at great trouble and expense he has brought him to Rome, to the tombs of the saints and martyrs. "And this son, where is he?" demands the monk. "There, beside you." "I was startled at the answer, and shrank back. I examined the young priest and was surprised to see him eating his dinner with a quiet, unassuming air and answering very gently any remarks addressed to him. He informed me that having spoken somewhat roughly to an old woman, this latter had cast a spell upon him. The spell was under a tree; but under what tree the Witch absolutely refused to say." Sprenger, still in a spirit of pity and good will, proceeded to lead the patient from church to church and from relic to relic. At each shrine visited, exorcism, frenzy, loud cries and wild convulsions, gibberish in every language under heaven and many uncouth gambols,—all this before the eyes of the public, which followed the pair, wondering, admiring, and shuddering. Devils, common enough in Germany, were less familiar in Italy, and in a few days' time Rome was talking of nothing else. This affair, which caused no small sensation, no doubt drew the general attention upon the Dominican Father concerned in it. He studied the subject, compiled all the various *Mallei* and other manuscript manuals, and became the great authority on questions of Demonology. His great work, the *Malleus Maleficarum,* would seem to have been composed during the twenty years intervening between this adventure and the important mission entrusted to Sprenger by Pope Innocent VIII. in 1484.

It was highly important to select an adroit personage for this mission to Germany, a man of intelligence and tact, who should prevail over the repugnance felt by Teutonic honesty towards the dark, subterranean system he was endeavouring to introduce. Rome had met with a rude check in the Low Countries, which put the Inquisition on its mettle in those regions, and resulted in its being altogether excluded from France. Toulouse, as a former stronghold of the Albigensians, was the only exception, being subjected to all the rigours of the Holy Office. About the year 1460 a Penitentiary of Rome, who had become Dean of Arras, determined to strike terror among the *Chambres de Rhétorique* (Chambers of Rhetoric), or Literary Unions, which were beginning to discuss matters of religion. He burned one of these *Rhetoricians* as a Sorcerer, and with him sundry rich citizens, and even knights. The nobility was furious at this attack on its privileges, while the voice of public opinion spoke out loudly and plainly. The Inquisition was scouted, abominated, held accursed, particularly in France. The *Parlement* of Paris shut the door rudely in its face; and Rome, by her bad management, threw away this opportunity of introducing into the north of Europe the reign of terror inseparable from the methods of the Inquisition.

The moment seemed better chosen in 1484. The Holy Office, which in Spain had assumed such terrible proportions, and overshadowed royalty itself, seemed by this time to have become a conquering institution, well capable of walking alone and bound to penetrate everywhere and subjugate everything to itself. True, it encountered an obstacle in Germany in the jealous opposition of the ecclesiastical princes, who, possessing tribunals of their own, had never shown themselves very ready to revive the Roman Inquisition. But the present situation of these princes, the very grave anxiety which the popular movements of the time occasioned them, made them less recalcitrant. All the Rhine country and Suabia, even the eastern parts towards Salzburg, seemed undermined with sedition. Every instant insurrections of the peasantry were breaking out. Everywhere beneath the surface there seemed to lurk a vast subterranean volcano, an unseen lake of fire, which, now here, now there, betrayed its existence by outbursts of fire and flame. The foreign Inquisition, far more dreaded than the native variety, came very opportunely on the spot to terrorise the country and break down rebellious spirits, burning as Sorcerers to-day the very men who would likely enough to-morrow have been insurgents. It formed an excellent popular weapon to overawe the people, an admirable device for drawing off dangerous humours. This time the storm was to be diverted upon the Sorcerers, just as in 1349 and on so many other occasions its fury had been directed against the Jews.

Only a *man* was indispensable. The inquisitor who was to bell the cat, who before the jealous courts of Mayence and Cologne, before the scoffing populace of Frankfort or Strassburg, was to set up his tribunal, was bound to be a person of intelligence and good sense. His personal tact and dexterity had to counterbalance, to make men forget in some measure, the odious nature of his office. Moreover, Rome has always piqued herself in choosing her men well. Indifferent to abstract questions, anything but indifferent to concrete individualities, she has always believed, and she was justified in believing, that success in practical affairs depended on the particular and special character of the agents accredited to each country. Was Sprenger the right man in the right place? To begin with, he was a German, and a Dominican, assured beforehand, therefore, of the support of that formidable order and all its monastic houses and schools. A worthy son of the schools was indispensable, a good Schoolman, a master of the *Summa Theologiæ*, soundly trained in his Aquinas, never at a loss for a text to clinch the argument. Sprenger was all this,—and more than this, to wit a pedantic fool.

"It is often stated, both in speech and writing, that *dia-bolus* is derived from *dia,* two, and *bolus,* a bolus or pill, because swallowing body and soul at one gulp, the Devil makes of the two only one pill, one single mouthful. But (he continues with all the gravity of Sganarelle), according to the Greek etymology, *diabolus* signifies *clausus ergastulo* (imprisoned in a dungeon), or else *defluens* (whence Devil?), that is to say falling, because he fell from heaven."

What is the derivation of *maléfice* (sorcery)? "It comes from *maleficiendo* (ill-doing), which signifies *malè de fide sentiendo* (ill-thinking on matters of faith)." A remarkable piece of etymology, but one of far-reaching consequences. If sorcery is the same thing as heresy, why! every sorcerer is a heretic, and every freethinker a sorcerer; and the Church is justified in burning as sorcerers any and every body who should dare to hold unorthodox opinions. This is precisely what they had done at Arras, and they were for establishing little by little the same good custom everywhere.

Here lies Sprenger's real merit, which is beyond dispute. He is a fool, but an intrepid fool; boldly and unflinchingly he lays down the least acceptable doctrines. Another man would have tried to elude, attenuate, soften objections,—but this is not his way. Beginning on the first page, he sets down openly and displays one by one the natural, self-evident reasons there are for disbelieving the satanic miracles. This done, he adds coldly, "Merely so many heretic mistakes." And never pausing to refute the reasons given, he copies out the texts on the other side, St. Thomas Aquinas, the Bible, legends, canonists, and commentators. First he shows you what common sense has to say, then pulverises it by weight of authority.

His duty accomplished, he sits down calm, serene, triumphant, and seems to say, "Well! what have you to say now? Would you be so daring now as to use your reason? . . . Can you doubt, for instance, that the Devil amuses himself by interfering between man and wife, when never a day passes but the Church and the canonists allow this as a ground for separation?"

There is no reply to this, and nobody will so much as whisper an objection. Sprenger in the first line of this Manual for the use of Judges, formally declaring the smallest doubt as an *act of heresy,* the judge's hands are tied. He feels there must be no trifling; that supposing he were so unfortunate as to experience some temptation in the way of compunction or tenderheartedness, it would be his bounden duty to begin by condemning himself to a death at the stake.

The method is everywhere identical. Good common sense first of all, followed by a direct frontal attack, a downright, unhesitating negation of common sense. It would seem natural enough, for instance, to say that, love being in the soul already, it is hardly necessary to assume the mysterious intervention of the Evil One to be required. Is not this fairly self-evident? Not so, says Sprenger,—*distinguo.* "The man who splits the wood is not the cause of its burning,—but only an indirect cause. The wood-splitter is love (on this point see Dionysius the Areopagite, Origen, John of Damascus, etc., etc.). Love therefore is only the indirect cause of love."

This it is to be a scholar. It is no second-rate school that could produce such a pupil. Cologne only, Louvain and Paris owned machinery fully adapted to mould the human brain. The School of Paris was strong indeed; for culinary Latin, what could rival Gargantua's *Janotus?* But even mightier was Cologne, famed queen of darkness that supplied Ulrich von Hütten with the type of the *Obscuri Viri* of his world-famous satire, the reactionaries and ignoramuses that have always been so fortunate and so fertile a tribe.

This solid, stolid Schoolman, so full of words and so void of sense, sworn foe of Nature no less than of human reason, takes his seat with superb confidence in his books and his learned gown, in the dust and dirt and litter of his gloomy court. On the desk before him he has on one side the *Summa Theologiæ,* on the other the *Directorium.* This is his library, and he laughs at anything outside its limits. He is not the sort of man to be im-

posed upon, or to waste his time upon Astrology or Alchemy,
—follies not so foolish after all, destined in time to lead to genuine observation of Nature's laws. Why, Sprenger is actually
a sceptic, and has doubts about the old recipes. Albertus Magnus declares positively that sage in a fountain is sufficient to
bring about a great storm; he shakes his head. Sage? don't tell
me; I beg you have me excused. It needs only a little experience
to see in this a trick of Him who would fain deceive and cajole
us all, the wily Lord of the Air; but he will get the worst of it,
he has to deal with a Doctor of the Church more cunning than
the Prince of Cunning himself.

Would I could have seen in the flesh this typical specimen of
the judge and the prisoners brought before his tribunal! Were
God to take creatures from two different planets and set them
face to face, they could not be more sharply contrasted, more
unknown one to the other, more completely lacking in a common language. The old Witch-wife, a ragged skeleton of a
woman, with haggard eyes alight with malice, a creature thrice
tempered in the fires of hell, the grim, lonely shepherd of the
Black Forest or the solitudes of the High Alps,—such are the
wild beings presented to the cold, dull eye of the pedant, to be
judged by the light of his school-bred intellect.

Nor will they, be it said, keep him long sweating in his bed of
justice. They will tell all they know without torture. The question will be applied later on, never fear, but only as a comple-
ment and ornament, as it were, to the depositions. They readily
expound and relate in due order whatever they have done. The
Devil is the bosom friend of the shepherd, and the Witch's bed-
fellow. She says as much, with a conscious smile and a glance
of triumph, evidently enjoying the horror of the audience.

The old creature is a mad woman surely, and the shepherd as
mad as she. A couple of besotted fools, you say? Not so,
neither; far from it. On the contrary, they are keen and subtle-
witted, both of them, beings who can hear the grass grow and

see through stone walls. Another thing they can perceive plainer still is the monumental pair of asses' ears that nod over the learned Doctor's cap. His dominant emotion towards them is fear; for, brave as he pretends to be, he is trembling all the while. He himself allows that the priest very often, unless he takes good heed, when he exorcises the Demon, only determines the evil spirit to change its abode and pass into the body of God's minister himself, finding it a more flattering morsel to inhabit the person of one consecrated to Heaven. Who knows but these simple-minded devils of shepherds and sorceresses might be taken with the ambition to enter into an Inquisitor? He is far from feeling so bold as his confident mien would indicate, when in his biggest voice he asks the Witch-wife, "If your master is so all-powerful, why do *I* not feel his assaults?" "As a fact," the poor man confesses in his book, "I felt him only too plainly. When I was at Ratisbon, how often he would come and rap at my window-panes! How often he would stick pins in my cap! Then there were a hundred evil visions, dogs, apes, and so forth, without end."

But the Devil's greatest delight, for he is nothing if not a logician, is to pose the learned Doctor out of the mouth of the false-hearted hag with embarrassing arguments and tricky questions, from which his only escape is by imitating the cuttle-fish, that avoids his pursuers by troubling the water and making all his neighbourhood as black as ink. For instance, "The Devil is active only so far as God suffers him to be so; then why punish his instruments?" Or else, "We are not free agents; God allows the Devil, as with the Patriarch Job, to tempt and drive us into sin, to force us by blows even. Is it just to punish one who is thus constrained?" Sprenger gets out of the difficulty by saying, "You are free beings,"—here follows a long array of texts. "You are bond-servants only by reason of your pact with the Evil One." To which the reply again would be only too easy, "If God allows the Evil One to tempt us to make a pact, it is He makes the said pact possible," and so on, and so on.

"I show over-much good nature," he declares, "in listening to these gentry at all! 'Tis a fool's part to argue with the Devil." The populace agrees with him to a man. All applaud the proceedings; all are eager, excited, impatient for sentence and execution. Hangings are common enough; but this Sorcerer and Sorceress, it will be a tasty treat to see how the pair will sparkle and splutter like brands in the burning.

The judge has the people on his side. There is no sort of difficulty; under the rules of the *Directorium*, three witnesses were sufficient. How fail to get three witnesses, especially to bear false witness? In every tattling town, in every ill-natured village, witnesses are as common as blackberries. Besides, the *Directorium* is an old-fashioned book, a century behind date. In this fifteenth century, an age of such enlightenment, everything is improved. If no witnesses are forthcoming, the *public voice* is enough, the general cry of popular indignation![1]

This sincere cry of suffering and of fear, the lamentable plaint of the unhappy victims of bewitchment, moves Sprenger strongly. Do not for a moment suppose him a mere unfeeling pedant, a man of dry, unsympathetic hardness. He has a heart, and that is the very reason why he is so ready to kill. He is very pitiful and full of lovingkindness. He pities intensely the weeping wife, a pregnant mother but now, whose babe the Witch stifled in her womb with a look of her evil eye. He pities the poor farmer on whose crops she has brought down the blighting

---

[1] Faustin Hélie, in his learned and instructive *Traité de l'instruction criminelle* (vol. i. 398), has explained with perfect lucidity the way in which Innocent III., about 1200, abolished the safeguards of accusation, till then held indispensable,—in particular the liability to a charge of slander on the part of the accuser. These safeguards were superseded by various subterranean modes of procedure, *Denunciation, Inquisition,* etc. See Soldan for instances of the appalling ease with which these latter methods were applied. Verily blood was poured out like water.

nail. He pities the husband who, no Sorcerer himself, is convinced his wife is a Sorceress, and drags her, a rope round her
neck, before Sprenger, who promptly has her burned.

With a cruel man there might be means of escape; but this
good, charitable Sprenger leaves no room for hope. His humanity is so overpowering, you must just be burned, there is no
help for it,—or at any rate an extraordinary degree of address,
a presence of mind of the readiest, is needed. One day a complaint is lodged with him by three good ladies of Strassburg,
who on the same day and at the same moment felt themselves
struck by an invisible assailant. How did it happen? The only
person they can accuse is an ill-looking fellow, who has cast a
spell over them, it would seem. Summoned before the inquisitor,
the man protests, swearing by all the saints he does not even
know the ladies in question, has never so much as set eyes on
them before. The judge refuses to believe him; neither tears
nor oaths are of the slightest avail. His great compassion for the
ladies made him inexorable, and the man's denial only roused
his anger. He was already rising to order the fellow to the
torture-chamber, where he would have confessed no doubt, as
the most innocent constantly did, when he got leave to speak
and said, "I do indeed recollect how yesterday at the hour named,
I struck . . . who was it I struck? . . . no Christian women,
but three cats that ran at me savagely biting my legs." Then the
judge, like a man of sagacity as he was, saw it all. The poor man
was innocent; without a doubt the ladies on such and such days
were changed into cats, while the artful Fiend amused himself
by setting them at good Christians' legs to work the ruin of these
latter and get them taken for Sorcerers.

A less perspicacious judge would never have guessed that.
But you could not always count on having a man of such pene-
tration on the bench. So it was highly necessary there should
lie always ready on the desk of the tribunal a good guide-book
or manual for fools, to make manifest to simpler and less experienced inquisitors the wiles of the Enemy of Mankind and the

means of frustrating them, in fact the same system of deep and artful strategy which the great Sprenger had employed to such good purpose in his Rhenish campaigns. To this end, the *Malleus* was printed in a pocket edition, generally of a size then uncommon, viz. small 18mo. It would not have been seemly for the judge to have been seen fumbling over the leaves of a great folio lying on his desk, while all the court gaped at him; but he could quite well and without any fuss consult out of the corner of his eye and thumb furtively under cover his pocket manual of folly.

The *Malleus*, like all the books of this kind, contains a strange admission, namely that the Devil is gaining ground, in other words that God is losing it; that the human race, saved by Jesus Christ, is becoming the conquest and prey of Satan. The latter, only too manifestly, is making progress, as legend after legend proves. What an advance he has made since the times of the Gospel, when he was too happy to take up his abode in the swine, down to the period of Dante, when a Theologian and a Lawyer, he argues with the saints, and pleads his case, and as final conclusion of a victorious syllogism, says, as he carries off the soul in dispute, with a triumphant laugh, "Ah! ha! you did not know I was a Logician."

During the earlier years of the Middle Ages he still waits for the death agony before taking the soul and carrying it off. St. Hildegard (*circa* 1100) believes *"that he cannot enter into the body of a living man,* if he did, the members would fall to pieces; it is the shadow and vapour of the Devil only that enter in." This last glimmer of common sense disappears in the twelfth century. In the thirteenth we find a prior so terribly afraid of being taken off alive that he has himself guarded day and night by two hundred men-at-arms.

Then begins a period of ever-increasing terrors, when mankind relies continually less and less on Divine protection. No longer is the Demon a stealthy, furtive Spirit, a thief of the night gliding about in the darkness, but an undaunted foe, the bold ape of God, who under God's own sun, in the open light of day, mimics the works of His hands. What authority is there for the statement,—legends, tradition? Not these only, but the gravest Doctors of the Church. The Devil transforms all creatures, Albertus Magnus declares. St. Thomas Aquinas goes further still. "All the changes capable of occurring naturally and by way of genus, these the Devil can imitate." A startling admission truly, which in so grave a mouth amounts to nothing less than the setting up of another Creator in face of the accredited Artificer of the Universe! "But," he goes on, "whatever can come to pass without germination, a changing of man to beast, the raising to life of a dead man, acts like these the Devil cannot perform." This is indeed to reduce God's domain to small proportions; strictly speaking, He has nothing left Him but miracles, events of rare and altogether special occurrence. But that daily miracle, life, is no more his exclusively; the Devil, his imitator, shares the realm of Nature along with Him.

So far as Man is concerned, whose weak vision draws no distinction between Nature as created by God and Nature as created by the Devil, this is a bi-partition of the Universe. Henceforth a dreadful uncertainty must brood over everything. The innocency of Nature is lost. The limpid spring, the white flower, the little bird, are they really of God's making, or merely mocking imitations, so many snares to catch mankind? . . . *Retro* Satanas! All nature comes under suspicion. Both creations, the good no less than the doubtful, are darkened and degraded. The shadow of the Evil One obscures the light of day, and hangs looming over every department of human life. To judge by appearances and men's apprehensions, he not merely shares the world with God, but has usurped it in its entirety.

Such is the state of things in Sprenger's day. His book is full of the most melancholy admissions with regard to the impotency of God. *He allows it,* is his phrase, to be so. *To allow* so complete an illusion, to let it be believed that the Devil is everything, God nothing, is really more than merely to *allow;* it is to pro-

claim the damnation of a world of unhappy souls utterly defenceless against so grave an error. No prayers, no acts of penitence, no pilgrimages are of any avail; no! not even (he admits
the fact) the Sacrament of the Altar. What an admission of
weakness, what a loss of prestige! Nuns, after full and free
confession, *the host actually in their mouths,* are forced to own
that at that very moment they feel the fiendish lover, shameless
and unabashed, troubling their senses and refusing to quit his
hold over them. And, cross-questioned, they added with tears
and sobs that the Foul Fiend has their bodies, because he
possesses their souls already.

The Manichæans of old, the Albigensian heretics of a later
time, were accused of believing in the power of Evil which con-
tended against the Good, making the Devil the equal of God.
But now he is more than the equal; if God, incarnate in the
consecrated host, can avail nothing, why! then the Devil must
be the stronger and more effectual of the two.

I no longer wonder at the extraordinary aspect presented by
the world at that date. Spain with gloomy ferocity, Germany
with the terrified and pedantic rage the *Malleus* bears witness
to, pursue the insolent and victorious usurper in the persons of
the wretched creatures whom he chooses to take up his abode
in; the stake and the rope are ruthlessly employed against the
fleshly tabernacles that have given him shelter. Finding him
over-strong for them in the soul, persecutors are fain to drive
him out of the bodies of men. But where is the use? Burn one
Sorceress, he makes good his hold on another; nay! sometimes
(if we are to believe Sprenger) he seizes the very priest who is
exorcising him, and wins a special triumph in the actual person
of his judge.

The Dominicans, driven almost to despair, recommended
intercessions to the Virgin, unceasing repetitions of the *Ave
Maria.* Still Sprenger admits even this remedy to be ephemeral.
A suppliant may be whipped off between two *Aves.* Hence the

invention of the Rosary, the chaplet of the *Aves,* by the help of which the devotee can mumble on mechanically for an indefinite time, while the mind is occupied elsewhere. Whole nations adopt this first attempt in the art whereby Loyola will essay to lead the world, and of which his *Exercitia* are the ingenious if rudimentary beginnings.

All this might seem to contradict what we said in the preceding chapter as to the decay of Sorcery. The Devil is now popular, and active everywhere; he appears to have won the day. But does he really profit by his victory? Does he gain in actual, substantial influence? Yes! from the new point of view of that scientific revolt that is to give us the bright, light-bringing renaissance. No! from the point of view of the old darksome spirit of Sorcery. The diabolic legends, in the sixteenth century, both more numerous and more widely diffused than ever, show a marked tendency towards the grotesque. Men tremble, but they laugh at one and the same time.[2]

---

[2] See my *Mémoires de Luther,* for the Kilcrops and the like.

A HUNDRED YEARS'
TOLERATION *in* FRANCE

THE Church always granted the judge and the accuser a right to the confiscated property of those condemned for Sorcery. Wherever the Canon Law remains powerful, trials for Witchcraft multiply, and enrich the clergy. Wherever lay tribunals make good their claim to try such cases, the latter grow fewer and fewer and finally diasppear, at any rate for a hundred years in France,—between 1450 and 1550.

A first gleam of light is visible as early as the middle of the fifteenth century, and it emanates from France. The revision of the case against Jeanne d'Arc by the Parlement and her rehabilitation set me thinking about dealings with spirits, good or evil, and the mistakes committed by the ecclesiastical tribunals. A vile Sorceress in the eyes of the English and in those of the wisest Doctors of the Council of Bâle, for the French she is a Saint and a divine Sibyl. The rehabilitation of the Maid of Orleans inaugurates in France an era of toleration. The Parlement of Paris likewise rehabilitates the so-called Vauclois of Arras. In 1498 the same body dismisses as a mere madman a wizard brought before its bar. Not a single condemnation for Sorcery was registered under Charles VIII., Louis XII., or François I.

Just the opposite in Spain; here under the pious Queen Isabella (1506), under Cardinal Ximenes, they begin burning Witches. Geneva, then governed by its Bishop (1515), burned five hundred in three months. The Emperor Charles V., in his Germanic Constitutions, tries in vain to establish the principle that "Sorcery, as causing injury to property and person, is a *civil* matter, not an ecclesiastical." In vain he *abolishes confiscation of goods,*—except in the case of High Treason. The smaller Prince Bishops, of whose revenues Sorcery supplied a principal source, go on savagely burning all the same. The microscopic bishopric of Bamberg sends six hundred individuals to the stake in one batch, and that of Wurzburg nine hundred! The procedure is of the simplest. To begin with, apply torture to the witnesses, and build up a travesty, a caricature of evidence, by dint of pain and terror. Then drag a confession from the accused by excruciating agonies, and believe this confession against the direct evidence of facts. For instance, a Sorceress confesses she had recently dug up a child's dead body from the churchyard, to use it in her magic compounds. Her husband says, "Go to the churchyard and look; the child is there now." The grave is opened, and the body found intact in its coffin. Yet the judge decides, against the testimony of his own eyes, that it is only an *appearance,* an illusion of Satan. He credits the woman's confession in preference to the actual fact,—and the poor creature is burned.[1]

Things reached such a pass among these worthy Prince Bishops that later on the most bigoted emperor there ever was, the Emperor of the Thirty Years' War, Ferdinand II., is forced to interfere and establish at Bamberg an Imperial Commissioner to see the rights of the empire are not infringed and that the episcopal judge shall not open these trials by tortures which made the result a foregone conclusion and led straight to the stake.

The Witches were very easily convicted on their own confessions, sometimes, without any application of torture. Many were really half-witted. They were quite willing to admit transforming themselves into beasts. The Italian Sorceresses often turned into cats—they said so themselves—and, slipping under

---

[1] See Soldan in confirmation of this true story, and for facts about Germany generally.

the doors of houses, would suck children's blood. In the region of great forests, Lorraine and the Jura, women readily became wolves and devoured travellers, if we are to believe their own accounts, even when there were no wayfarers travelling the roads to devour. Anyway they were burned. Young girls would solemnly declare they had sacrificed their maidenhood to the Devil, and on examination be found virgins still. They were burned likewise. Not a few seemed positively to want to go to the stake, and the sooner the better,—the result of insanity, frenzy, sometimes of despair. An English Witch on being led to the stake, tells the crowd not to blame her judges. "I wanted to die. My family shunned me, my husband repudiated me. If I lived, I should only be a disgrace to my friends. . . . I longed for death, and I lied to gain my end."

The first avowed plea for toleration against the dull-witted Sprenger, his horrible Manual and his persecuting Dominicans, was advanced by a lawyer of Constance, Molitor by name. He maintains for one thing with excellent good sense the unreasonableness of taking the confessions of Sorceresses seriously, inasmuch as from the nature of the case it was the Father of Lies, and none other, who spoke by their mouth. He made fun of the pretended miracles of the Devil, and asserted they were mere figments of the imagination. Indirectly again the mockers, Ulrich von Hütten and Erasmus, in the Satires they composed upon the imbecility of the Dominicans, dealt a severe blow to the Inquisition. Cardau says straight out, "In order to succeed to the goods of the victims, identically the same persons acted as accusers and judges, condemned the innocent to death, and to bolster up their case were ready to invent a thousand fables."

The Apostle of Toleration, Châtillon, who maintained, against Catholics and Protestants alike, that we should not burn heretics, to say nothing of sorcerers, started men's minds in a better path. Agrippa, Lavatier, Wyer above all, the illustrious physician of Clèves, said very justly that, if these unhappy beings, the Sorceresses, are the Devil's playthings, as they are said to be, it is first and foremost the Devil we must deal with, that we should try to cure them rather than burn them off-hand. Before long sundry Parisian doctors push their incredulity as far as to maintain that all the devil-possessed, all the Sorceresses, are nothing more nor less than impostors. This was going too far; the great majority were really sufferers from disease, dominated by a morbid hallucination.

The gloomy reign of Henry II. and Diane de Poitiers ended the days of toleration; heretics and Sorcerers alike are sent to the stake under the fair Diane's influence. Catherine de Médicis on the contrary, surrounded as she was by Astrologers and Magicians, was all in favor of shielding these protégés of hers. They multiplied apace; Trois-Echelles, brought to trial under Charles IX., reckons them by the hundred thousand, and declares all France to be bewitched.

Agrippa and others maintain that all Science is contained in Magic—*white* Magic of course, be it understood. But the terror of fools and the rage of fanatics make small distinction between white and black. Against Wyer, against the genuine men of science, against light and toleration, a violent reaction of darkness and obscurantism arises from a quarter one would least of all have expected. The magistracy, which for nearly a whole century had shown itself just and enlightened, now largely involved in the Catholic Bond of Spain and the fiercely bigoted *Ligue,* prove themselves more priestly than the priests. While driving the Inquisition out of France, they match it and would fain eclipse it with their own severities. Indeed, they went so far that on a single occasion and single-handed the Parlement of Toulouse burned *four hundred human bodies* at the stake. Imagine the horror of it; think of the thick, black smoke from all this burning flesh, picture the masses of fat that amid yells and howls melt in horrid deliquescence and pour boiling down the gutters! A vile and sickening sight such as had not been since the broilings and roastings of the Albigensians!

But even this is not enough for Bodin, the Legist of Angers, and the furious antagonist of Wyer. He begins by declaring the Sorcerers are so many they could in Europe alone make another host of Xerxes, an army of eighteen hundred thousand men. Then he expresses a similar wish to Caligula's, that all these two millions of men had one common body, so that he, the redoubtable Bodin, might judge them and burn them all at one fell swoop.

Presently a rivalry springs up. The lawyers begin to complain that the priest is often too closely connected with Sorcery himself to be a trustworthy judge. And there is no doubt the jurists do for a time seem surer even than the clergy. The Jesuit pleader, Del Rio, in Spain, Remy (1596) in Lorraine, Boguet (1602) in the Jura, Leloyer (1605) in Marne, are incomparable persecutors, men to make Torquemada die of envy.

Lorraine was swept by a dreadful contagion, as it were, of Sorcerers and Visionaries. The populace, driven to despair by the everlasting depredations of marching armies and marauding bands, had long ceased to pray to any deity but the Devil. Many villages, in their terror, distracted between two horrors, the Sorcerers on the one side and the judges on the other, longed, if Remy, Judge of Nancy, speaks truth, to quit their lands and all they possessed and fly to another country. In his book dedicated to the Cardinal de Lorraine (1596), he claims positively to have burned within sixteen years eight hundred Sorceresses. "So good is my justice," he says, "that last year there were no less than sixteen killed themselves rather than pass through my hands."

The priests were humiliated. Could they have done any better than this layman themselves? Accordingly the monks, Lords

of Saint-Claude, when they found their subjects addicted to
Sorcery, chose another layman, the worthy Boguet, to act as
their judge. In this dreary Jura country, a poverty-stricken
district of meagre pastures and barren pine-woods, the serfs
were for ever devoting themselves to the Devil out of sheer hope-
lessness. To a man they worshipped the black cat.

Boguet's book (1602) became an authority of the greatest
influence and importance. The lawyers of Parlement studied
this golden book of the little judge of Saint-Claude as the manual
and mainstay of their practice. Boguet is in very deed a typical
Legist, scrupulous even according to his lights. He inveighs
against the bad faith displayed in these trials; he will not have
the advocate betray his client, nor the judge promise the accused
a pardon to lure him on to his death. He disapproves of the very
untrustworthy tests to which Witches were still habitually compelled to submit. "Torture," he says, "is both useless and unnecessary. They never give in under it." Lastly, he possesses
humanity enough to have them strangled before being cast into
the flames, always excepting in the case of the female were-
wolves, "whom we must take every precaution to burn alive."
He refuses to believe Satan willing to make pact with children.
"Satan is cunning, and he knows far too well that under fourteen the bargain with a minor would be liable to forfeiture on
the ground of insufficient age and discretion." Then children are
safe from the stake? Not at all; for he contradicts himself on
this point, declaring elsewhere that this leprosy can only be
cleansed by burning all, even to babes in the cradle. He would
have come to that if he had lived longer. He turned the whole
countryside into a desert. Never was judge more conscientious,
more thorough, more bent on extermination.

But it was in the Parlement of Bordeaux that the pæan of
victory of lay jurisdiction rose loudest in Lancre's book, entitled, *Inconstance des Démons* (1610 and 1613). The author,
a man of intelligence and ability, and a Counsellor of the Parlement named, relates triumphantly the successful battle against

the Devil he had waged in the Basque country, where in less than three months he has worked off I forget how many Witches and, more important still, three priests. He looks with contemptuous pity on the Spanish Inquisition, which at Logroño, on the frontier of Navarre and Castile, not far from his own district, has had a trial dragging on for two years, ending finally with a poor, miserable little auto-da-fé, from which a whole host of women got off scot-free.

THE BASQUE WITCHES
1609

THIS high-handed execution of priests shows plainly enough
that M. de Lancre was a man of an enterprising and independent spirit. The same is true of him in politics. In his book *Du
Prince* ("Of the Prince") 1617, he makes no bones about declaring that "the Law is above the King."

Never have the Basques been better characterised than in his
work *L'Inconstance des Démons,* above mentioned. In France
no less than in Spain, the privileges they enjoyed really constituted them a virtual republic. The French Basques owed nothing
whatever to the King beyond the obligation of serving him
under arms; at the first tuck of drum they were bound to put
two thousand men in the field, under their own Basque captains.
The clergy were of small weight or account, and did little in the
way of punishing Sorcerers, being in the trade themselves. The
priests used to dance, wear swords, and take their mistresses
with them to the "Sabbath." These mistresses were the priests'
sacristanesses or *bénédictes,* the female officials who kept the
church in order. The curé quarrelled with no one, said his White
Mass for God day by day, and a-nights the Black Mass for the
Devil,—sometimes actually in the same church (Lancre).

The Basques of Bayonne and Saint-Jean-de-Luz, a reckless
and fantastic race, and marked by an incredible degree of
audacious daring, accustomed as they were to visit the wildest
seas in pursuit of the whale fishery, made many widows. Moreover, they crowded in numbers to the colonies founded by King
Henri IV., and formed the empire of Canada, leaving their wives

behind in the care of God or the Devil, as the case might be. As for the children, these sailors, a very upright and godfearing set of men, would have made more account of them, if they could only have been more sure on the question of fatherhood. Returning after their long periods of absence, they would reckon up the time and count the months,—and invariably found themselves quite out of their calculations.

The women, pretty, bold-eyed and imaginative creatures, would pass the whole day in the churchyards, sitting on the tombs and gossiping of the Witches' Sabbath, which they were going to attend so soon as night fell. This was the passion, the infatuation of their lives.

Nature makes them Sorceresses from the cradle, these daughters of ocean nurtured on weird and fantastic legends. They swim like fishes, every one of them, and sport boldly amid the Atlantic rollers. Manifestly their master the Prince of the Air, king of winds and wild dreams, the same who inspired the Sibyl and whispered the secrets of the future in her ear.

The very judge that burns them is all the while charmed with their fascinations. "When you see them pass," he writes, "their hair flying in the wind and brushing their shoulders, so well adorned and caparisoned are they, as they go, with their lovely locks, that the sun glancing through them as through a cloud, makes a flashing aureole of dazzling radiance. . . . Hence the dangerous fascination of their eyes, perilous for love no less than for witchery."

This worthy citizen of Bordeaux and amiable magistrate, the earliest type of those polished men of the world who ornamented and enlivened the Bench in the seventeenth century, plays the lute in the intervals of judicial business, and even sets the Sorceresses dancing before having them burned. He writes well and in a style of much greater lucidity than any of his fellows. And yet at the same time we discern in his case a fresh source of obscurity, arising inevitably from the circumstances of his day, viz. that among so great a number of Witches, all of whom the judge cannot of course condemn to the stake, the greater part are quite clever enough to understand he is likely to show indulgence towards such as shall best enter into his preconceived ideas and feed his peculiar passion. What passion was this? First and foremost, a common failing enough, love of the marvellous and horrible for its own sake, the pleasure of being startled and terrified, and added to this, it must be admitted, the fun of indecent revelations. A touch of vanity besides; the more formidable and fierce these women are artful enough to make the Devil appear, the more is the judge flattered and exalted who can master so fell an adversary. He savours the sweets of victory, gloats over his silly success, poses triumphant amid all this foolish cackle.

The finest example is to be found in the Spanish official report of the Auto-da-fé at Logroño (November 9th, 1610), as given in Llorente. Lancre, who quotes it not without envy, and is by way of depreciating the whole thing, yet admits the unspeakable charm of the fête, its magnificence as a spectacle, and the profound effect of the music. On one scaffold stood the condemned Sorceresses, a scanty band, and on another the crowd of the reprieved. The repentant heroine, whose confession was read out, stuck at nothing, however wild and improbable. At the Sabbaths they ate children, hashed; and as second course dead wizards dug up from their graves. Toads dance, talk, complain amorously of their mistresses' unkindnesses, and get the Devil to scold them. This latter sees the Witches home with great politeness, lighting the way with the blazing arm of an unbaptised infant, etc., etc.

Witchcraft among the French Basques showed a less fantastic aspect. It would seem that with them the "Sabbath" was little more than a fête on a large scale, which everybody, including even the nobles of the country, attended in search of amusement. In the front rank appeared a row of veiled and masked figures, believed by some to be Princes. "In former days," Lancre says, "only the simple, dull-witted peasantry of the

Landes were to be seen at these assemblages. Now people of quality are to be found there." By way of compliment to these local notabilities, Satan would frequently, under such circumstances, elect a *Bishop of the Sabbath*. Such is the title the young Seigneur Lancinena received from him, with whom the Devil was graciously pleased personally to open the ball.

Thus influentially supported, the Sorceresses reigned supreme, exercising over the country an almost incredible domination by means of the terrors of the imagination. Numbers of persons came to believe themselves their victims, and actually fell seriously ill. Many were attacked by epilepsy, and started barking like dogs. One small town alone, Acqs, counted among its inhabitants as many as forty of these unhappy creatures. Such was the terrible relationship that bound them under the Witch's influence, that on one occasion a lady, called as a witness, at the mere approach of the Sorceress, whom she could not even see, began barking furiously, and was utterly unable to stop herself.

Those who were accredited with so formidable a power were masters of the situation, and no man durst shut his door against them. A magistrate even, the Criminal Assessor of Bayonne, allowed the "Sabbath" to be held at his house. The Seigneur de Saint-Pé, Urtubi, was constrained to celebrate the festival at his castle. But so much were his wits shaken by the event that he became firmly persuaded a Witch was sucking his blood. Terror lending him courage, he and another baron hastened to Bordeaux and appealed to the Parlement there. The latter body obtained the King's orders that two of its members, Messieurs d'Espagnet and de Lancre, should be despatched to judge the Sorcerers and Sorceresses of the Basque provinces. They were given plenary powers, subject to no appeal; and setting to work with unexampled vigour, in four short months tried from sixty to eighty Witches, besides examining five hundred more equally marked with the Devil's stigmata, but who figured in the courts only as witnesses (May to August, 1609).

It was an enterprise by no means devoid of danger for two men and a few soldiers to proceed to such measures in the midst of a lawless and headstrong population, and a mob of sailors' wives, notoriously a reckless and violent set of women. A second risk came from the priests, numbers of whom were Sorcerers themselves, and whom the lay Commissioners were bound to bring to trial in spite of the fierce opposition of the clergy.

On the judges' arrival many fled with all speed to the mountains. Others put a better face on the matter and remained, declaring it was the judges who would be burned. So undismayed were the Witches, that actually in court they would doze off in the "Sabbatical" sleep, and openly describe on awakening how before the judges' very eyes they had been enjoying the delights of satanic intercourse. Several declared, "Our only regret is that we cannot properly show him how we burn to suffer for his sake."

When questioned they would affirm they could not speak,— that Satan rose in their throats and obstructed their utterance.

The younger of the two Commissioners, Lancre, the same who writes these accounts, was a man of the world, and the Witches were not slow to perceive that with such a judge to deal with there were possible loopholes of escape. The phalanx was broken. A beggar-girl of seventeen, Little Murgin, as she was called (Margarita), who had found in Sorcery a profitable speculation, and who, while scarce more than a child herself, had been in the habit of bringing children and offering them to the Devil, undertook along with her companion—one Lisalda, a girl of the same age—to denounce all the rest. She told everything, and wrote it all down, with all the vivacity, exaggeration, and fiery emphasis of a true daughter of Spain, along with a hundred indecent details, whether true or false. She both terrified and diverted the judges, twisting them round her little finger and leading them whither she pleased like a pair of dummies. They actually entrusted this vicious, irresponsible, passionate girl with the grim task of searching the bodies of young women and boys for signs of the spot where Satan had put his mark. The place was recognised by the fact of its being insensible to pain, so that needles could be driven into it without extracting a cry from the victim. A surgeon tortured the old women, Margarita the younger ones, who were called as witnesses, but who, if she declared them marked in this way, might easily find their way to the bench of the accused. An odious consummation truly,—that this brazen-browed creature, thus made absolute mistress of the fate and fortune of these unhappy beings, should go pricking them with needles at her pleasure, and might adjudge, if such were her caprice, any one of their bleeding bodies to a cruel death!

Such was the empire she had gained over Lancre she actually induced him to believe that while he slept in his house at Saint-Pé, surrounded by his serving-men and escort, the Devil entered his chamber at night, and said the Black Mass there; that the Witches forced their way under his very bed-curtains to poison him, but had found him too securely guarded by God. The Black Mass was served by the Baroness de Lancinena, with whom Satan had casual intercourse in the judge's apartment itself. The object of this pitiful tale is pretty plain; the beggar-girl bears a grudge against the Great Lady, who was likewise a pretty woman, and who, but for this slanderous story, might also have gained some ascendency over the gallant functionary.

Lancre and his colleague were appalled, but continued to advance from sheer dread of the dangers of drawing back. They ordered the royal gallows to be planted on the very spots where Satan had kept Sabbath, a proceeding well calculated to strike terror and convince all men of the tremendous power they derived from being armed with the King's authority. Denunciations came pouring down like hail. All the women of the countryside came filing in unceasingly to lay accusations one against the other. Eventually the very children were brought and made to give incriminating evidence against their own mothers. Lancre decides with all due gravity that a witness of eight years old is capable of affording good, sufficient, and trustworthy evidence.

M. d'Espagnet was unable to give more than a passing moment to the business, being due in a short time in the States of Béarn. Lancre, infected in spite of himself by the fierce energy of the younger Witches who hurried to denounce their elder sisters, and who would have been in sore peril themselves had they failed to get these latter burned, pushed on the trials whip and spur at full gallop. A sufficient number of Sorceresses were condemned to the flames. Finding their fate sealed, they too had spoken out at last, and scattered denunciations right and left. As the first batch were on their way to the stake, a ghastly scene occurred. Executioner, officer, and police all thought their last day was come. The crowd rushed savagely upon the carts, to force the unhappy occupants to withdraw their accusations. Men held daggers at their throats, while many of them almost perished under the nails of their infuriated sisters.

Eventually, however, justice was satisfactorily vindicated. This done, the Commissioners proceeded to a more arduous and delicate task, viz. the trial of eight priests who had been arrested. The revelations of the young Witches had thrown a flood of light on their lives and morals, and Lancre speaks of their dissolute morals as one who has full knowledge at first hand. Not only does he reproach them with their gallant doings at the nocturnal "Sabbaths," but insists particularly upon their relations with their sacristanesses, those church-dames or *bénédictes,* as they were called, mentioned on a previous page. He even condescends to repeat vulgar tales,—how the priests sent the husbands to Newfoundland, and imported from Japan the devils who yielded up the wives into their hands.

The clergy were much exercised, and the Bishop of Bayonne would have resisted, if he had dared. Failing sufficient courage, he kept away, appointing his Vicar-General to watch the case for him. Luckily the Devil helped the accused more efficiently than the Bishop. He can unlock every door; so that it happened one fine morning that five out of the eight escaped. The Commissioners, without further loss of time, burned the three that were left.

All this took place about August, 1609. The Spanish Inquisitors, who were holding their trials at Logroño, did not on their side reach the final Auto-da-fé before November 8th, 1610. They had had far more difficulties to contend with than their French *confrères*, in view of the prodigious, the appalling number of the accused. Impossible to burn a whole population! They consulted the Pope and the greatest Church dignitaries of Spain, and it was decided to beat a retreat. The understanding was that only obstinate criminals should be sent to the stake, such as persisted in their denials, while all who confessed should be let go. The same method, the application of which had hitherto always saved priests brought to trial for incontinence of opinion or of conduct. Their confession was held sufficient, supplemented by a trifling penance (see Llorente).

The Inquisition, of uncompromising severity towards heretics and cruelly hard on the Moors and Jews was much less harsh where the Sorcerers were concerned. These latter, shepherds in a great many cases, were in no way involved in opposition to Mother Church. The degraded, sometimes bestial amusements of goat-herds occasioned little anxiety to the enemies of liberty of conscience.

Lancre's book was composed mainly with the object of demonstrating the vast superiority of the public justice of France, the justice administered by laymen and members of the legal Parlements, to that of the priests. It is written *currente calamo*, in a light, easy, happy style, clearly manifesting the author's satisfaction at having honourably extricated himself from a serious danger. He is something of a Gascon, boastful and vain of his own achievements. He relates with pride how, on the occasion of the "Sabbath" following the first execution of Witches,

the children of the latter came to lay complaint of their treatment before Satan. He replied that their mothers were not
burned at all, but alive and happy. From the depths of the smoky
cloud the children actually thought they heard their mothers'
voices declaring they were now in full and complete happiness.
Nevertheless, Satan was afraid, and kept away for four successive "Sabbaths," sending as his substitute a quite subordinate imp. He did not put in an appearance again until the 22nd
of July. When the Sorcerers asked him the reason of his absence,
he told them, "I have been to plead your cause against Janicot
(Little John, this is the name he bestows on Jesus). I have won
my case; and the Witches still remaining in prison will not be
burned."

The Prince of Lies was once more shown to be a liar; and
the victorious judge assures us that when the last of them was
burned, a swarm of toads was seen to escape from her head.
The assembled people fell upon these with stones so furiously
that the Sorceress was really more stoned than burned to death.
But, in spite of all their efforts, they failed to account for one
great black toad, which avoiding alike flames and sticks and
stones, escaped, like a demon as he was, to a place where he
could never afterwards be discovered.

SATAN TURNS ECCLESIASTIC

1610

WHATEVER the appearance of fanaticism and satanic possession still displayed by the Sorceresses, it is quite plain both from Lancre's account and others of the seventeenth century that by this time the Witches' Sabbath was become primarily a matter of money-making. The levy contributions which are virtually compulsory, demand payment from those present, and fine the absent. At Brussels and in Picardy they pay in accordance with a fixed tariff anyone bringing in a new member to the confraternity.

In the Basque countries there is no attempt made at concealment. Assemblages are held twelve thousand strong, including persons of every class, rich and poor, priests and nobles. Satan, a nobleman himself, over and above his triple horns, wears a laced hat, like a gentleman. By this time he has found his old throne, the Druid stone, too hard a seat, and has given himself a good gilded armchair. Does this mean he is growing old? Nimbler than in his young days, he plays all sorts of pranks and gambols, springs up like a Jack-in-the-box from the depths of a huge crock, officiates, legs kicking in the air and his head downwards.

He is for having everything done decently and in order, and defrays the expenses of the arrangements and decorations. Besides the usual yellow, red, and blue fires that amuse the eyes and alternately reveal and conceal the flying shadows, he entertains the ear with strange music, "in especial certain little bells that tickle" the nerves, like the penetrating vibrations of some particular harmonies. To crown his magnificence, Satan has silver plate brought for use at the feast. His very toads display an affectation of refinement and elegance, and like little lords, come to the festival tricked out in green velvet. The general appearance is that of a huge fair, a vast masked ball, when the disguises are of the thinnest. Satan, who knows his world, opens the dance with the Bishop of the "Sabbath," or else the King and Queen,—dignitaries established on purpose to flatter the bigwigs, the rich or noble personages who honour the assembly by their presence.

All is changed from the old grim festival of revolt, the sinister orgy of serfs, of *Jacques* as they were nicknamed, communicating by night in love, by day in murder. The frenzied *Sabbatical Round* no longer forms the one and only dance. It is supplemented by Moorish dances, lively or languishing, amorous and obscene, in which girls trained for the purpose, such as the Murgin and the Lisalda mentioned above, simulate and parade the most lust-provoking actions. These dances, it is said, were the irresistible attraction which among the Basques inevitably drew to the Witches' Sabbath all the world of women, wives, maids, and widows,—the last especially in great numbers.

Apart from these diversions and the feast to follow, it would be difficult to account for the unbounded popularity the "Sab·bath" enjoyed. Loveless love was the dominant note; the festival was expressly and avowedly a celebration of female sterility. This Boguet establishes beyond a doubt.

True, Lancre tells a different tale in one place, in order to scare women away and make them afraid of being got with child. But as a rule he is more sincere, and agrees with Boguet. The cruel, indecent examination he undertook of the Witches' persons is good and sufficient proof of his belief in their sterility, and that sterile passive love is the foundation-stone of the "Sabbatical" observances.

This could not but have cast a gloom over the festival, if the men had had hearts. It was the mad women who flocked there to dance and feast that paid for all; but they were resigned to their fate, their sole aspiration being not to leave the place pregnant. True enough they bore the burden of wretchedness and poverty far more than men did; and Sprenger tells us the dismal cry that as early as his day would escape them in the very act of love, "May the Devil have the fruit of our embrace!" Yet in his time (1500) living cost but a penny a day, while at the later period here referred to (1600), under Henri IV., it was difficult to keep body and soul together at ten times that expense. Throughout the whole century, the desire, the craving for sterility is for ever on the increase.

This mournful reserve, this fear of mutual love, must have rendered the "Sabbath" a cold, wearisome function, had not the expert mistresses of the ceremonies, who managed the entertainment, exaggerated the burlesque element, and diverted the spectators with many a ludicrous interlude. Accordingly the opening ceremony of the "Sabbath," the world-old scene, coarse and realistic, of the pretended fecundation of the Chief Sorceress by Satan (in former days by Priapus), was followed by another travesty, a *lavabo*,[1] a cold purification (to chill and sterilise), which she received not without grimaces expressive of shuddering and mortal chill, the whole forming a broad farce in which the Sorceress usually substituted an attractive-looking understudy for herself, the Queen of the "Sabbath," some young and pretty married woman.

Another distraction, no less abominable, centred round the black wafer, the *black radish*, the subject of a thousand coarse witticisms in ancient Greek days, when it was used as an instrument of punishment upon the man-woman or puthic and the

---

[1] The instrument employed is thus described by Boguet (p. 69): it is cold, hard, very slender, a little longer than a finger,—evidently a *canula*. In Lancre (pp. 224, 225, 226) it is much improved, less liable to inflict injury; it is an ell long and bent, part is of metal, the other part flexible, and so on. Satan, on the Basque borders, midway between two great monarchies, is well posted in the progress of this art, already very fashionable among the fine ladies of the sixteenth century.

young debauchee who went with other men's wives. Satan sliced it into little discs which he then solemnly swallowed.

The grand finale was, according to Lancre,—which means, no doubt, according to the two hussies who made him believe whatever they pleased,—a very astonishing thing to happen before so numerous an assemblage. Incest would seem to have been publicly, indiscriminately, and ostentatiously indulged in, by way of reproducing the old satanic conditions needed to originate the Sorceress—that is to say, the mother's impregnation by her own son. But this horror was not only unnecessary by this time, when Sorcery had become hereditary in certain fixed and legally descended families, but impossible in fact, a thing altogether too shocking to be endured. Possibly merely a travesty of it was acted, a grotesque kind of miracle-play between a comic Semiramis and a dotard Ninus.

There was another and probably a more serious feature, a comedy of real and actual life, and one that points strongly to the presence of persons of high rank and corrupt morals,—his was an odious sort of practical joke, a cruel and coarse mystification.

They would entice to the festival some ill-advised married man, whom they proceeded to intoxicate with their deadly brews (datura, belladonna, and the like), till he was *spellbound* and lost all power of motion and speech, but not the use of his eyes. His wife, also *spellbound*, but in a different way, with erotic beverages and reduced to a deplorable state of self-abandonment, would then be shown him naked and unashamed, patiently enduring the caresses of another before the indignant eyes of her natural protector, who could not stir a finger to help her.

His manifest despair, his unavailing efforts to speak, his violent struggles to move his torpid limbs, his dumb rage, his rolling eyes, all provided the spectators with a cruel pleasure, not dissimilar, be it said in passing, to that afforded by certain comedies of Molière's. In the present instance the play was all palpitating with actuality, and was easily pushed to the last extremities of sin and shame. Doubtless the shame was followed by no after effects, as was the invariable rule at these Witches' Sabbaths, and next day's recollections were but dim in the brains of the now sobered victims; but the spectators, the actors, were *they* likely to forget?

These criminal doings show plainly the aristocracy is now at work, bearing no resemblance whatever to the old fraternity of serfs, the primitive "Sabbath,"—impious and impure no doubt, but free, open, and aboveboard, where everything was voluntary and done by universal consent.

Satan, always corrupt, is evidently going from bad to worse. The Evil One is growing a polite, adroit, soft-handed gentleman, —and the change only leaves him a more false-hearted and filthy-minded villain than before. What a new and strange departure is this for a Witches' Sabbath, to find him hand and glove with the priests! What of the curé who brings his *bénédicte,* his sacristaness, to the feast, who burlesques the holy offices, says the White Mass in the morning and the Black Mass at night! Satan, Lancre says, recommends him to debauch his penitents, his spiritual daughters. Simple-minded magistrate, who actually seems unaware that for a good century now Satan has well understood and made good profit of the advantages offered by the Church. The Devil has turned Confessor, Director of Consciences; or if you like it better, the Confessor has turned Devil.

Just recall, my worthy Lancre, the series of trials beginning in 1491, which it may well be did something towards teaching the Parlement of Paris toleration. This body discontinues almost entirely the practice of sending the Devil to the stake, realising that he is no more now than a mask, a cloak, to cover priestly offenders.

Not a few nuns fall victims to his new ruse of borrowing the face and figure of a beloved confessor. We may instance the case of Jeanne Pothierre, a nun of Le Quesnoy, a woman of middle age, forty-five years old, but, alas! only too susceptible.

She declares her passion for her father confessor, who takes good care not to listen to her, and runs away to Falempin, a place at some leagues' distance. The Devil, who never sleeps, at once recognises his advantage, and seeing her (in the chronicler's words) "pricked by the thorns of Venus, he cunningly adopts the form of said father, and returning night after night to the convent, enjoys her favours, deceiving her so thoroughly that she declares herself to have been had by him—she had kept count—four hundred and thirty-four times.[2] . . ." Her subsequent repentance met with no little compassion, and she was speedily relieved from the agonies of shame, a good walled dungeon being at once provided for her in the near neighbourhood, at the Castle of Selles, where she expired in a few days, dying a peaceful, edifying death as a good Catholic should.

What could be more touching? . . . But after all the incident was a trifling thing compared with the notable Gauffridi affair, which occurred at Marseilles while Lancre was still busy at Bayonne.

The Parlement of Provence had no occasion to envy the successes of their confrères at Bordeaux. The lay jurisdiction once more seized the opportunity of a trial for Sorcery to institute a systematic reform of ecclesiastical morals, and undertook a searching scrutiny into the cloistered life and mysterious secrets of the nunneries. The opportunity was a rare and exceptional one, involving as it did, and was bound to do, a remarkable concurrence of circumstances, a series of savage jealousies and acts of reprisal between priest and priest. But for this indiscreet and passionate violence, a passion and violence we shall see breaking out again and again on subsequent occasions, we should possess no information whatever as to the real destiny of the vast population who live and die within these gloomy walls, and never hear one word of what takes place behind

---

[2] Massée, *Chronique du Monde* (1540), and the Chroniclers of Hainault, Vinchant, etc.

convent bars and within the portals the father confessor is alone privileged to enter.

The Basque priest Lancre depicts, so volatile and worldly, tripping sword on thigh to dance at the nocturnal "Sabbath," his sacristaness by his side, was not an object of great concern or apprehension to the authorities. He was not of the sort the Spanish Inquisitors took such pains to screen, and for whose peccadilloes that stern conclave showed itself so indulgent. It is clear enough from what Lancre hints, in spite of all his reticence, there is *something else* behind. The States General of 1614, too, when they lay it down that priests ought not to try priests, are likewise thinking of *something else*. Here lies the mystery, the veil of secrecy that is rudely torn asunder by the Parlement of Provence. The father confessor of nuns, their tyrant and the irresponsible disposer of soul and body alike, fascinating them by all sorts of sinister acts—such is the figure revealed at the trial of Gauffridi, and at a later date in the dreadful affairs of Loudun and Louviers and others which Llorentz and Ricci and the rest have made us acquainted with.

The tactics adopted were invariably the same—to extenuate the scandal and mislead the public by concentrating its attention on the accidental form and diverting it from the essential substance. When a priest was tried for Sorcery, every pain was taken to lay stress on his doings as a Wizard, and juggle into the background his priestly character, in such a way as to put all the mischief down to the magic arts employed, and ignore the natural fascination exercised by a man occupying a position of absolute domination over a herd of women abandoned to his good pleasure.

The first of these sad affairs, that of Gauffridi, it was impossible to hush up. The thing had broken out in mid-Provence, in that land of light where the sunshine penetrates every crevice. The principal scene of the events that followed was not only Aix and Marseilles, but the well-known locality of La Sainte-

Baume (The Holy Balm), a much-frequented place of pilgrimage, to which a crowd of curious devotees now resorted from every part of France to look on at the duel to the death to be fought out between two nuns afflicted with diabolical possession and between their respective demons. The Dominicans, who interfered in the matter as Inquisitors, deeply compromised themselves on this occasion through the keen attention they drew to the event by the marked partiality displayed by them in favour of one of the two combatants. For all the pains the Parlement subsequently displayed in order to arrive at an early settlement of the affair, the monks found themselves bound in honour to explain and excuse the attitude they had adopted. Hence the important book of the monk Michaëlis, a strange medley of truth and myth, in which he exalts Gauffridi, the priest he sent to the stake, as the *Prince of Magicians,* not only of all France, but of Spain, Germany, England, Turkey, as well; in fact, of the whole habitable world.

Gauffridi appears to have been a man of agreeable manners and many accomplishments. A native of the mountains of Provence, he had travelled widely in the Low Countries and in the East. He enjoyed the best of reputations at Marseilles, where he served as priest at the Church Des Acoules. His Bishop thought highly of him, and the most pious ladies selected him as their Confessor. He possessed, we are told, a singular aptitude for winning the love of all such.

Nevertheless, he would probably have preserved his good repute intact had not a certain noble Provençal lady, a woman blinded by passion, and whom he had already ruined, pushed her infatuation to such lengths as to confide to his care (with a view, perhaps, to her religious education) a charming child of twelve, named Madeleine de la Palud, a pretty blonde of a gentle and affectionate disposition. Gauffridi lost his head, and failed to respect either her tender age or the sweet innocence and utter confidence of his pupil.

But presently she grew into a woman, and realised her calamity; how, noble as she was, she was bound to an inferior by an unworthy tie and could now never hope for marriage. In order to keep her, Gauffridi said he could wed her before the Devil, if he could not before God. He flattered her pride by telling her he was the *Prince of the Magicians,* and that she should be the Queen. He placed on her finger a silver ring, engraved with cabalistic signs. Did he take her with him to the Witches' Sabbath, or did he merely make her think she had been there, clouding her mind with magic potions and magnetic spells? This much at least is certain, that the poor child, torn between credulity and doubt, tormented by anxiety and terror, became from this time liable to fits of insanity and subject on occasion to epileptic seizures. Her overmastering dread was of being carried off alive by the Devil. She dared not stay longer in her father's house, and took refuge at the Convent of the Ursuline Sisters of Marseilles.

GAUFFRIDI

1610

Of all the Religious Orders, that of the Ursulines seemed the calmest, the least liable to give way to irrational impulses. The Sisters were not idle, employing a portion of their time in the education of little girls. The Catholic reaction, which had started with all the lofty aspirations of the Spanish cloister towards an ecstatic perfection, quite incapable of realisation under existing conditions, and had recklessly built a host of convents—Carmelite, Feuillantine, and Capuchin—had soon found its vigour exhausted. The poor girls they immured so rigorously within monastic walls as a way to get rid of them, died off promptly, and by this rapid mortality showed up the cruelty of families in lurid colours. What killed them was not the mortifications they were called upon to endure, so much as sheer ennui and despair. After the first burst of enthusiasm, that dread disease of the cloister (dscribed as early as the fifteenth century by Cassien), leaden ennui, the gloomy ennui of afternoons, the tenderly melancholy ennui which loses itself in vague languors and dreamy reverie, quickly undermined their health. Others were more like mad women; their blood was so hot and turbulent it seemed to choke them.

A nun, to die decently, without causing her relatives over-much remorse, should take about ten years to the business,—this is the average duration of life in monastic establishments. Some relaxation of discipline thus became a necessity, and men of sense and experience realised that, to prolong their days, occupation must be found for them and they should not be left too much alone. St. François de Sales founded the Visitandines, whose business was to visit the sick, always going in pairs. César de Bus and Romillion, who had brought into existence the Doctrinaire Fathers (Priests of the Doctrine), in connexion with the Oratorians, now founded what might be styled the Sisters of the Doctrine, the Ursulines, teaching nuns to whom these priests acted as Confessors. All were under the general supervision of the Bishops, and to a limited, a very limited degree, monastic, not being as yet confined to the cloister. The Visitandines could go freely abroad, while the Ursulines received visitors,—at any rate their pupils' relatives. Both were in intimate communication with the world outside, under the direction of well-reputed Confessors. The underlying danger of all this was mediocrity. Both Oratorians and Doctrinaires had produced men of conspicuous ability, it is true, but the general spirit of the Order was systematically ordinary, moderate, careful to avoid too lofty a flight. The founder of the Ursulines, Romillion, was a man of ripe age, a convert from Protestantism, who had gone through, and seen through, all phases of religious emotion. He believed his young Provençal Sisters to be already as discreet as himself, and hoped to keep his little flock contentedly browsing on the meagre pasturage of a monotonous and unemotional faith, as understood by the good Oratorians. This was opening the door wide to ennui, and one fine morning the mine exploded.

The Provençal mountaineer, the traveller and mystic, the man of disconcerting energy and passion, Gauffridi, who visited the convent as Madeleine's Director, produced a very unlooked-for effect there. The nuns felt his mastery, his inherent power, and no doubt from hints dropped by the silly love-sick child, discovered it was nothing less than a diabolic power. One and all are terror-stricken, several love-stricken into the bargain. Imaginations are heated, heads turned. Presently we have five or six of the Sisterhood weeping, screaming, howling, convinced they are in the Devil's grip already.

If only the Ursulines had been confined to their cloister, immured within the convent walls, Gauffridi, as their sole Director, would doubtless have found means to bring them to reason. It might have ended, as it did in the Convent of Le Quesnoy in 1491, by the Devil, who is always ready enough to take the shape of the beloved object, constituting himself, under the guise of Gauffridi, lover-general of the nuns. Or else, as happened in the Spanish nunneries Llorente describes, he would have persuaded them that the priest sanctifies by his priesthood those he loves, and that sin with him is a form of consecration. This was a doctrine widespread in France, and prevalent even in Paris, where these priests' mistresses were called "the sanctified." [1]

Did Gauffridi, finding them all in his power, confine himself to Madeleine? Did he not go on from love to licence? Impossible to say,—though the act of accusation certainly mentions a nun who was not brought forward at the trial, but who reappeared at its conclusion, as having given herself to the Devil and to him.

The Ursulines were a house open to all, where anyone could come and scrutinise whatever was doing. Besides, were they not under the safeguard of their spiritual fathers, the Doctrinaire priests, honourable, and what is more, jealous men?

The founder himself was on the spot, indignant and despairing. What a calamity for the rising Order, which at that very moment was prospering so well and making headway in all parts of France! Its special pride and distinction was discreetness, good sense, placidity; and lo! without an instant's warning sheer midsummer madness! Romillion would fain have hushed up the whole scandal. He had the young women privately exorcised by one of the Doctrinaire Fathers; but the devils made small account of exorcists of that feather. The little fair-haired Madeleine was possessed by no less a fiend than Beelzebub, a high-

[1] Lestoile, edit. Michaud, p. 561.

born devil, the demon of pride, who did not deign so much as to open his teeth.

Among the possessed was one girl in particular, the special protégée of Romillion, a young woman of twenty to twenty-five, highly educated and well trained in polemics. Born a Protestant, but having neither father nor mother, she had fallen under the influence of the Father, like herself a converted Protestant. Her name, Louise Capeau, has a bourgeois ring about it. She was gifted, as appeared only too plainly later on, with a remarkable intellect, passionate determination, and, be it added, terrific force of character. For three whole months she sustained, to say nothing of the diabolic storms raging within, a desperate struggle that would have killed the strongest man in a week.

She declared she had three devils,—Verrine, a good-natured Catholic devil, and a volatile, one of the demons of the air; Leviathan, a bad-hearted devil, a freethinker and a Protestant; lastly, one she admits to be the demon of impurity. But there is yet another she forgot to mention, the demon of jealousy.

She hated with a vindictive hatred the little pretty, fair-haired favourite, the proud, well-born Madeleine. This latter, in her mad fits, had claimed to have attended the "Sabbath," and to have been crowned Queen there. She said she had been adored by the others, and had been loved,—by the Prince himself. . . . Prince! what Prince? Louis Gauffridi, Prince of the Magicians.

Louise, whom such an avowal stung like a whip, was too much enraged to doubt its truth. Maddened, she believed the other's mad words, that she might thereby work her ruin. Her demon was backed up by the other demons in all these jealous hearts. With one voice they all chimed in, declaring that Gauffridi was indeed the King of the Wizards. Then it was noised abroad everywhere a great capture had been made, nothing less than a Priest-King of the Magicians, the Prince of Magic in all lands.

Such was the fatal diadem of fire and iron these she-devils forced on his brow.

All men lost their heads, even Romillion. Whether from hatred of Gauffridi, or fear of the Inquisition, he withdrew the matter from the Bishop's hands, and carried his two devil-possessed nuns, Louise and Madeleine, to the Convent of La Sainte-Baume, the Prior of which was Father Michaëlis, a Dominican and Pope's Inquisitor in the papal territory of Avignon, claiming to exercise the same office also for the whole of Provence. The primary question was only one of exorcising the evil spirits; but as the two women were bound to accuse Gauffridi, the latter was on the high-road to fall under the disciplinary powers of the Inquisition.

Michaëlis was to preach the Advent sermons at Aix before the Parlement there assembled. He at once saw how well these dramatic occurrences would serve to bring him into prominence, and seized the opportunity offered with all the eagerness our modern pleaders at Assizes display when a sensational murder comes their way or a curious case of crim. con.

The correct thing in affairs of this sort was to carry on the drama throughout Advent, Christmas-time, and Lent, and only come to the burning in Holy Week, on the eve of the great festival of Easter Day. Michaëlis reserved his chief efforts for the final Act, entrusting the bulk of the work to a protégé of his, a Dominican from Flanders, one Doctor Dompt, a Louvain man, who was already practised in exorcism, and well posted in these follies.

Besides, the very best thing the Fleming could do was to do nothing at all. In Louise he had a redoubtable helper, three times as zealous as the Inquisition, endowed with a fierce untiring energy and a burning eloquence, wild indeed and sometimes grotesque, but always terror-striking, a veritable brand of hell.

The matter resolved itself into a duel between the two devils, between Louise and Madeleine, fought out in public.

Simple folk who came there on pilgrimage to the Holy Balm

—a worthy goldsmith, for instance, and a draper, both natives of Troyes in Champagne—were ravished to see Louise's demon belabour the other demons so cruelly and cudgel the Magicians. They positively wept for joy, and wended homewards giving thanks to God.

A terrible sight, for all that (terrible even as depicted in the heavy, colourless, official report as drawn up by the Flemish Doctor), to watch the unequal contest,—to see the stalwart Louise, both an older and a stronger woman than her adversary, a true Provençal, as hard as the stones of her own desert of the Cran, day by day pelt and pummel and demolish her shrinking victim, so young and childish-looking, but already so sore a sufferer, love-sick and shame-sick, writhing in the pains of epilepsy. . . .

The Fleming's volume, together with the additional matter supplied by Michaëlis, in all some four hundred pages, is a brief abstract of the invectives, insults, and menaces which the woman vomited unceasingly for five long months, as well as of her sermons, for she would preach on any and every subject,— the sacraments, the coming appearance of Antichrist, the frailty of women, etc., etc. This over, in the name of her devils she would take to raving again, twice every day renewing her torture of poor Madeleine, without ever taking breath, without for one instant checking the awful torrent of her words, till the other, utterly confounded, "one foot in hell," to use her own words, fell into convulsions, knocking the floor with her faltering knees, and fainting body, and drooping head.

Louise is three parts a mad woman, it cannot be denied; no amount of knavery could have enabled her to keep the lists so long. Nevertheless her bitter jealousy teaches her, wherever she can find a chance to stab her victim's heart and wound her feelings, a dreadful lucidity is expressing herself.

All ordinary laws are clean upset. This impious, devil-ridden creature communicates as often and as freely as she will. She rates and rebukes personages of the highest dignity. The venerable Catherine de France, Lady President of the Ursulines, comes to see the wonder, questions her and instantly convicts her of downright misstatement and silly misconception. Thereupon the woman turns insolent and ends the matter by retorting, in the name of her devil, "Well! is not the Devil the Father of Lies?"

A friar, a man of sense, who is present, takes her at the word, and retorts, "Then you are lying!" and turning to the exorcists, "Why do you not stop this woman's mouth?" he gives them an account of a certain Martha, a woman at Paris who had falsely pretended to diabolic possession. For answer, they make her communicate in his presence. The Devil taking Communion, the Devil receiving God's body in the Sacrament! . . . The poor man is staggered, and humbles himself before the Inquisition. The sight is too much for him, and he dares not say another word.

One of Louise's favourite devices is to terrorise her audience, crying out suddenly, "I can see Magicians there, . . . there!" setting each individual trembling for his skin.

Triumphant at La Sainte-Baume, she extends her efforts to Marseilles. Her Flemish exorcist, now reduced to the extraordinary office of secretary and confidant of Satan, writes to her dictation five letters:

To the Capuchins of Marseilles, urging them to call upon Gauffridi to repent and be converted; to the same Capuchins, directing them to arrest Gauffridi, bind him hand and foot with a stole, and hold him prisoner in a certain house she designates; letters to the moderates, to Catherine de France, to the Doctrinaire Fathers, who themselves were for declaring against her. Eventually, reckless and regardless of consequences, she insults her own Lady Superior. "You told me," she says, "when I left you, to be humble and obedient . . . Well! I give you back your own advice!"

Verrine, Louise's devil, demon of the air and the wind, was for ever whispering in her ears mad words of folly and senseless pride, that wounded friends and enemies alike, and even the Inquisition. One day she deliberately made fun of Michaëlis, who she said was kicking his heels at Aix preaching in the desert, while all the world was thronging to La Sainte-Baume to hear her. "Preach away, Michaëlis! your words are true enough, but fall on deaf ears,—while Louise, who has never studied Theology, has comprehended the *summum bonum* and attained perfection!"

She was filled with savage self-satisfaction,—above all at her victory over Madeleine, whose spirit she had broken. One phrase had contributed more to this result than a hundred sermons, the cruel, brutal words, "You will be burned!" (December 17th). From that day the poor girl lost all heart, and said whatever the other wished,—became, in fact, her abject and submissive slave. She grovelled to everybody, asked pardon of her mother, of her Superior Romillion, of the audience, of Louise herself. If we are to believe what the latter says, the trembling girl drew her aside and besought her to take pity on her, not to be too harsh upon her.

The other, as gentle as a rock, as merciful as a reef of the sea, felt that she was hers, to do what she would with her. So she seized her victim, enveloped and strangled her, robbing her of the few sparks of vitality still left her,—a second enchantment, the reverse of Gauffridi's, a *possession* by fear and horror. The poor fainting creature stepped on beneath the rods and whips, and day by day they urged her further along the agonising road of repeated accusations, repeated attempts on the life of the man she still loved.

Had Madeleine shown a firm front, Gauffridi would undoubtedly have escaped; for everybody was set against Louise.

Michaëlis, even at Aix, the effect of whose sermons she had quite eclipsed and whose dignity she had treated so lightly, would sooner have quashed the proceedings altogether than leave the prestige with this woman.

Marseilles was ready to defend Gauffridi, terrified as its citizens were to see the Inquisition of Avignon pushing its advances so far as actually to seize a native of their town inside their own walls.

The Bishop in particular, and the Chapter, were for defending a priest of their own diocese. Their contention was that the whole affair meant nothing more than a piece of jealousy between rival confessors, another example of the well-known animus of the monks against the secular priests.

The Doctrinaire Fathers for their part would fain have hushed up the whole matter, being bitterly grieved at the scandal. Not a few of their number were so deeply chagrined they came near leaving all and quitting their House altogether.

The ladies were indignant, especially Madame Libertat, the lady of the Chief of the Royalists, who had surrendered Marseilles to the King. All bewailed Gauffridi's fate, and declared none but the Foul Fiend could attack so pure a lamb of God.

The Capuchins, whom Louise so peremptorily ordered to arrest him, were (like all the Orders connected with St. Francis) enemies of the Dominicans. They were jealous of the prominence given the latter by the events which had occurred amongst them. Moreover, their wandering life, which brought the Capuchin Fathers into such frequent contact with women, often involved them in questions of morals. They had an instinctive dislike to people's looking so closely into the private lives of ecclesiastics. They took sides for Gauffridi. Persons possessed of the Devil were not such rare phenomena it was impossible to get hold of one, and they soon found what they required. Their new protégée's devil, under Franciscan influence, said precisely the opposite of what St. Dominic's devil had announced. He said, and they wrote it down in his name, "That Gauffridi was in no sense a Magician, and could not be arrested."

This was quite unexpected at La Sainte-Baume. Louise was nonplussed, and could only say, that apparently the Capuchins had not made their devil swear to speak the truth,—a poor retort, which, nevertheless, was backed up by the trembling Madeleine.

This latter, like a whipped hound, trembling in dread of a repetition of the thrashing, was capable of anything, even of biting and tearing. Indeed, it was by her instrumentality that Louise in this emergency bit savagely and cruelly.

All she said herself was that the Bishop was, unknowingly, hurting God's cause, exclaiming likewise "against the Sorcerers of Marseilles," without mentioning any names. But the cruel and fatal words she put into *Madeleine's* mouth. A woman who had two years before lost her child was denounced by the latter as having strangled it. The accused, fearing torture, fled or kept herself in hiding. Her husband and father arrived in tears at La Sainte-Baume, no doubt hoping to move the Inquisitors. But Madeleine dared not withdraw what she had once said, and only repeated the odious charge.

Who was safe? From the moment the Devil was elected avenger of God's anger, and they started writing down under his dictation the names of those in danger of the flames of ecclesiastical punishment, each man shuddered at every hour at the horrid nightmare of the blazing stake.

Marseilles, confronted with so presumptuous an invasion of its privileges by the Papal Inquisition, should by right have looked for aid from the Parlement of Aix. Unfortunately the Marseillais were only too well aware of their own unpopularity at Aix. The latter city, a small place dominated by officialdom and full of magistrates and nobles, has always looked with jealous eyes on the wealth and magnificence of Marseilles, the Queen of the South. As a matter of fact, it was the adversary of the Marseillais, the Papal Inquisitor, who in order to anticipate Gauffridi's appeal to the Parlement, was the first to have recourse to its assistance. It was an intensely bigoted body, the bigwigs of which were chiefly nobles enriched in the preceding century at the time of the massacre of the Vaudois. Moreover, as lay judges, they were delighted to see an Inquisitor of the

Pope create a precedent of the sort, and admit that where a priest was concerned and a question of alleged Sorcery involved, the Inquisition could only proceed so far as the preliminary examination. It was as good as a formal resignation on the part of the Inquisitors of all their ancient privileges. Another point which pleasantly flattered the vanity of the men of Aix, as it had done in the case of those of Bordeaux, was this, that laymen though they were, they had been set up by the Church herself as censors and reformers of ecclesiastical morals.

In this business, where everything seemed bound to be extraordinary and miraculous, not the least miraculous feature was to see so savage a demon grow suddenly complimentary towards the Parlement, and turn politic and diplomatic. Louise enchanted the King's friends by a panegyric of the late King, Henry IV. who (who would have thought it possible?) was canonised by the Devil. One fine morning, *à propos* of nothing, she broke out into eulogiums "of that pious and sainted monarch who had but now risen to the skies."

An alliance of this sort between two such old enemies as the Parlement and the Inquisition, the latter henceforth assured of the assistance of the secular arm, of soldiery and executioner, a special commission despatched by the Parlement to La Sainte-Baume to examine the victims of diabolical possession, to hear their depositions and accusations, and draw up lists, was indeed a terrifying eventuality. Louise made no more ado, but denounced the Capuchins, Gauffridi's champions, in so many words, and declared "they would be punished temporally" in their persons and in their flesh.

The unhappy Fathers were quite broken-spirited, and their Devil had not another word to say. They went to the Bishop to tell him they could not really very well refuse to produce Gauffridi at La Sainte-Baume and make a formal act of submission; but this done, that the Bishop and Chapter might reclaim him and bring him once more under the protection of the episcopal jurisdiction.

Another effect, moreover, had no doubt been calculated upon, namely that the sight of the man they had loved so deeply would shake the equanimity of the two women, that the redoubtable Louise herself would be deeply moved by the promptings of her heart. As a matter of fact her sensibility *was* awakened at the approach of her guilty lover, and the Fury would seem to have shown a moment's weakness. I know of nothing more ardent than her supplication to God to save the man she has herself been driving to his death, "Great God, I offer you all the sacrifices ever offered since the beginning of the world, and that shall be offered to the end of time . . . all for Louis! . . . I offer you all the tears of the Saints and all the ecstasies of the angels . . . all for Louis! I would there were more souls yet, that the oblation might be more complete . . . all, all for Louis! Pater de cœlis Deus, miserere Ludovici! Fili redemptor mundi Deus, miserere Ludovici!" (O God the Father of Heaven, have mercy upon Louis! O God the Son, Redeemer of the world, have mercy upon Louis!)

Vain compassion!—and sinister, to boot! . . . What she would fain have had, was that the accused *should not harden his heart,* but plead guilty,—in which case he was certain to be burned under the existing jurisprudence of the country.

Louise herself was at the end of her forces, incapable of further effort. The Inquisitor Michaëlis, humiliated at owing his success solely to her, and exasperated with his Flemish exorcist, who had allowed himself to fall so completely under her ascendency and let all the world see into the secret springs of the drama, Michaëlis was now coming finally to crush Louise, to rescue Madeleine and, if he could, set her in the other's place in the popular imagination. The attempt was not ill conceived, and implies a certain comprehension of the appropriate *mise en scène.* Winter and the Advent season had been occupied by the awful Sibyl, the wild Bacchante. In the gentler weather of a Provençal springtide, in Lent, would have figured a more touch-

ing personality, a soft, feminine demon incarnate in a sick girl
and speaking from trembling lips. The child coming as she did
of a distinguished family, the nobility took an interest in her
case and the Parlement of Provence

Far from listening to his Flemish colleague, Louise's man,
Michaëlis, when the former tried to enter the privy council of
the Parlement, slammed the door in his face. A Capuchin,
another fresh arrival, cried out at the first word Louise uttered
in his presence, "Silence, accursed Devil!"

Meantime Gauffridi had arrived at La Sainte-Baume, where
he cut a very poor figure. A man of sense and ability, but weak
and sinful, he foresaw but too plainly the inevitable termination
of a popular tragedy of the sort, and in the cruel catastrophe
beheld himself abandoned, betrayed by the child he loved. He
gave himself up to despair, and when confronted with Louise,
stood before her as if she were his judge, one of those old ecclesiastical judges, cruel and subtle in his inexorable logic. She put
doctrinal questions to him, to all of which he answered *yes,*
granting her even the most disputed points,—for instance "that
the Devil may be believed in a Court of Justice on his word and
oath."

This lasted only a week—from the 1st to the 8th of January;
then the clergy of Marseilles claimed him. His friends, the
Capuchins, stated they had visited his lodging, and found nothing there connected with Magic. Four Canons of Marseilles
arrived armed with authority to take him, and carried him
home again.

Gauffridi was brought very low; but neither did his adversaries occupy a particularly proud position. Even the two Inquisitors, Michaëlis and the Fleming, were scandalously in
disagreement. The partiality of the latter for Louise and of the
former for Madeleine went beyond mere words and was em-
bodied in action. All this chaos of accusations, sermons, revelations, which the Devil had dictated by the mouth of Louise, the
Fleming, who had written it down, maintained was in its integ-

rity, and without exception God's own words, and feared any interference with it. He avowed much distrust of his chief Michaëlis, dreading lest, in the interests of Madeleine, he should falsify these papers in such a way as to ruin Louise. He defended them with all his might, shut himself up in his room and stood a regular siege. Michaëlis, who had the members of the Parlement on his side, could only get hold of the manuscript by using the King's name and breaking in the door.

Louise, who was afraid of nothing, was for setting up the Pope against the King. The Fleming laid complaint against his chief Michaëlis before the Papal Legate at Avignon. But the prudent Papal Court shrunk back terrified before the scandal of seeing one inquisitor levelling accusations against another. The Fleming found no support, and had nothing else to do but to submit. Michaëlis, to make him hold his tongue, gave him back the papers.

Those of Michaëlis which form a second portfolio, sufficiently dull and uninteresting and not to be compared for an instant with the other, are full of Madeleine and nothing else. They play music to her by way of calming her agitation. They note with the utmost care whether she eats or refuses her food. They fuss round her, in fact to excess, often in not over-edifying particulars. They ask her strange questions about the Magician, and about the localities of her person which might bear the Devil's mark. She was also actually examined. Though it would seem this had been done already at Aix by the physicians and surgeons of the Parlement (p. 70), Michaëlis, in his extreme zeal, examined her again minutely at La Sainte-Baume, and gives his observations in detail (p. 69). No matron was called in. The judges, lay and monkish, agreed for once, and having nothing to fear from each other's surveillance, mutually consented, it would seem, to wink at this neglect of the proper formalities.

But they had a stern judge in Louise, who, with her characteristic outspokenness, branded these indecencies with fiery words:

"They that were swallowed up by the Deluge had not done so wickedly as these men! . . . Nothing to equal the enormity was ever related of Sodom and Gomorrah! . . ."

She said further, "Madeleine is delivered over to impurity!" And indeed this was the saddest feature of all. The poor mad creature, blinded by her love of life, her joy at not being burned after all, or perhaps with some confused feeling that it was she now who could influence her judges, sang and danced at times with a shameful, indecent, alluring freedom of mien and gesture. The old Doctrinaire priest, Romillion, blushed for his Ursuline protégée. Shocked at seeing the judges admire her long hair, he said it must be cut off, and this stumbling-block removed.

She was gentle and submissive in her more composed hours, and they would have made another Louise of her if it had been possible. But her devils were vain and amorous; not eloquent and fierce like her rival's. When they should have been preaching they spoke only silly trivialities. So Michaëlis was forced to play the piece by himself. As Inquisitor-in-Chief, feeling bound to far outdo his subordinate, the Fleming, he declared he had already drawn out of the child's body an army of six thousand six hundred and sixty devils, only a hundred now remaining. The better to convince the public, he made her bring up the charm or spell she had swallowed, so he said, and extracted it from her mouth in the form of a glutinous, sticky substance. Who could hold out against this? The audience was left dumbfounded and convinced.

Madeleine was now on the high-road to save her life. The only obstacle lay in her own impudence; she kept continually saying injudicious things likely to rouse her judges' jealousy and exhaust their patience. She confessed that every object reminded her of Gauffridi, that he was constantly before her eyes. She did not try to hide her erotic dreams. "Last night," she would say, "I was at the 'Sabbath,' and the Magicians were adoring my statue, which was gilt all over. In its honour each of them made an offering of their blood, which they got by cutting their hands with lancets. *He*, he was there, on his knees, a rope round his neck, beseeching me to come back to him and not to betray him. . . . But I held back. . . . Then he said, 'Is there any here ready to die for her?' 'Yes, I am,' cried a young man, and the Magician immolated him."

Another time she saw him praying her just for one of her beautiful golden hairs. "And when I refused he said, 'Well, give me half a hair at any rate.' "

Meantime she assured them she was always firm in her resistance. But lo! one day, the door happening to stand open, the virtuous convert is away at top speed to rejoin Gauffridi once more.

She was recaptured,—at least her body was. But her soul?— Michaëlis was puzzled how to recapture it. By a happy inspiration, he thought of her magic ring. This he took from her, cut it in pieces, ground it to powder and burned it. Moreover, suspecting that her obstinacy, unaccountable in so gentle a creature, was fostered by invisible Sorcerers who slipped unperceived into the room, he stationed a man-at-arms there, a stalwart fellow armed with a sword, who lashed out in every direction and hacked the invisible tempters into bits.

But the best medicine towards Madeleine's conversion was the death of Gauffridi. On February 5th, the Inquisitor visited Aix to preach the Lenten sermons, saw the judges and stirred them up to action. The Parlement, readily adopting his suggestions, sent to Marseilles to arrest the rash offender, who seeing himself so well supported by the Bishop, the Chapter, the Capuchins and everybody, had never supposed they would venture on so bold a step.

Madeleine from one quarter, Gauffridi from another, arrived at Aix. Such was her excitement they were forced to bind her; her state of agitation was terrible, and anything might happen. A very bold experiment with a girl in her morbid condition was tried, to give her one of those frights that throw a woman into convulsions, that are sometimes fatal. A Vicar-General of the Archbishop's mentioned that there was in the Archiepiscopal Palace a dark, narrow charnel-house,—what in Spain they call a *pudridéro*, such as we see at the Escorial. In former days a quantity of old bones of dead men whose names were forgotten had been thrown there to rot. Into this sepulchral vault they brought the trembling girl, and exorcised the demon within her by putting these cold dead bones in contact with her cheeks. She did not die of horror, but from that time she was absolutely at their disposal; they had got what they wanted, the death of conscience, the extermination of all that was left of moral sense and free will.

She became a pliant instrument, ready to do whatever was desired, with a flattering alacrity seeking to guess what would be agreeable to her masters. They showed her Huguenots, and she cursed them. They confronted her with Gauffridi, and she told him by heart the counts of accusation against him more glibly than the King's officers could have done. Nor did this in any way prevent her snarling and snapping like a wild beast when she was taken to church and set to stir up the populace against Gauffridi by making her devil blaspheme in the name of the Magician. Beelzebub would exclaim by her mouth, "I forswear God, in the name of Gauffridi, I forswear God," and so on. Then, at the instant of the elevation of the host, "On me be the blood of the Just One, on me,—in the name of Gauffridi!"

A grim partnership, whereby this twofold devil damned the one out of the mouth of the other; for whatever he said through Madeleine, was surely imputed to Gauffridi. So that this crowd was eager and anxious to see the stake make a speedy end of the blasphemer, whose impiety, dumb though he remained, yet spoke loudly and hatefully by Madeleine's voice.

The exorcists asked her a cruel question, one they could have answered far better themselves than she could: "How is it, Beelzebub, you speak so ill of your bosom friend?" Her answer was in these appalling terms: "If there are traitors among men, why not among demons? When I feel myself with Gauffridi, I am his to do whatsoever he bids me. But when you force me, I betray him and make a mock of him."

However, she could not keep up this vein of horrid mockery. The demon of terror and servility seemed to have entered into every fibre of her soul, but there was room left for despair. She could no longer take the least nourishment; and these good folks who for five months had been racking her with exorcisms and who pretended they had relieved her of six or seven thousand devils, are obliged to admit she had no wish left but to die, and eagerly sought any means of suicide. Her courage failed, that was all. Once she pricked herself with a lancet, but had not determination enough to push it home. Another time, she grasped a knife, and when this was taken from her, tried to strangle herself. She drove needles into her flesh, ending by a mad attempt to force a long pin through one ear into her head.

What befell Gauffridi? The Inquisitor, who is so full of details about the two women, has next to nothing to tell us about him, passing lightly over so risky a subject. What little information he does give is strange enough. He relates how his eyes were bandaged while they searched with needles all over his body to find the insensible spot that meant the Devil's mark. On the bandage being removed, he learned with wonder and horror that in no less than three different places the needle had been driven home without his knowing it; so that he was manifestly marked triply with the sign of Hell. And the Inquisitor adds, "If we were at Avignon, the man would be burned to-morrow."

He saw his case was desperate and offered no defence. His only idea now was that some enemies of the Dominicans might perhaps save his life, and he expressed a wish to confess to the Oratorians. But this newly founded Order, which might fairly be called the *media via* of Catholicism, was too cold and too prudent to take such an affair in hand, to say nothing of its having already gone so far and reached such a desperate pass. Next he turned again for succour to the Begging Order, and making confession to the Capuchins, admitted all, and more than all the truth, hoping to buy his life at the price of infamy. In Spain, he would undoubtedly have been *relaxed,*—barring a period of penance in some monastery. But the French Parlements were more severe, and made a point, besides, of proving the superior integrity of the lay jurisdiction. The Capuchins, not over-firm themselves on the question of morals, were not of the sort to draw down the lightning on their own heads. They made much of Gauffridi, kept him safe and offered him consolation day and night,—but solely to the end that he might be induced to confess himself a Magician, and so, the practice of magic arts remaining the main count of accusation, a decent veil might be drawn over the crime of seduction by a confessor, an incident so compromising for the clergy.

Thus eventually his own friends, the Capuchins, by persistency, by gentle treatment and soft words, drew from him the fatal admission, which, so they said, was the salvation of his soul,—but which very certainly meant giving his body to the stake.

The man being settled and done with, they made an end with the two girls, who, however, were not to be burned. The finale was a broad farce. Before a great assembly of the clergy and Parlement Madeleine was brought forward; then addressing her, they formally called upon her devil, Beelzebub, to quit the field, or else give satisfactory reasons for his contumacy. He had no reply to make, but departed ignominiously.

Then Louise was produced, with her devil Verrine. But before driving out a spirit so friendly to the Church, the monks regaled the gentlemen of the Parlement, who were novices in these matters, with an exhibition of the *savoir-faire* possessed by the devil in question, making him go through an extraordinary pantomime. "How do the Seraphim and Cherubim and Thrones do before God?" "Difficult! difficult!" Louise answered; "they have no bodies." However, on the order being repeated, she did her best to obey, imitating the flight of the first, the divine ecstasy of the others, and finally the adoration of all, bending low before her judges, and prostrating herself head bowed to the earth. All saw the far-famed Louise, so proud and so indomitable, humiliated, kissing the floor, and with arms outstretched lying her length on the cold stones.

An extraordinary exhibition, foolish and indecent to the last degree, by which she was made to expiate her redoubtable success with the populace! Even now she partially won over the Assembly again by an adroit stab she administered to Gauffridi who was present in chains. "At the present moment," she was asked, "where is Beelzebub, the devil expelled from Madeleine?" "I see him plainly, there at Gauffridi's ear," was her cruel answer.

Enough surely of these horrors and abominations? Why inquire what the unhappy man said under torture? For he was subjected to the question, both ordinary and extraordinary. The revelations he must have made would no doubt throw considerable light on the dark and mysterious history of nunneries. The Parlement greedily collected all such particulars, as weapons that might prove useful, but they kept them to themselves "under seal of the Court."

The Inquisitor Michaëlis, much blamed by public opinion for so much animosity that was hardly distinguishable from petty jealousy, was recalled by his Order, which was sitting in Assembly at Paris, and did not see Gauffridi's execution. The latter was burned alive at Aix four days later (April 30th, 1611).

The reputation of the Dominicans, which had suffered in this affair, was not much mended by another case of *diabolic possession* which they got up at Beauvais (November of the same year) in such a way as to give themselves all the honours of war, and a report of which they printed at Paris. As one chief objection against Louise's devil had been that he could not talk Latin, this new victim of the Fiend, Denise Lacaille, could gabble a few words of that language. They made a great ado, frequently showed the woman in procession, and even took her

from Beauvais to Notre-Dame de Liesse. But there was no enthusiasm; this Picard pilgrimage had none of the dramatic
effects, the terrors of La Sainte-Baume. The Lacaille woman,
for all her Latin, did not possess the burning eloquence of her
Provençal predecessor, and had neither her fiery spirit nor her
savage energy. The only result of the whole thing was to give
the Huguenots something to laugh at.

What became of the two rivals, Madeleine and Louise? The
first, or rather her shadow, was kept within the papal territory,
for fear of her being induced to talk about the dismal and disrep-
utable affair. She only appeared in public to be stared at as an
edifying example of penitence, and was employed generally
along with a number of poor women in cutting wood to be sold
for charitable purposes. Her family were ashamed of her and
had cast her off and deserted her.

As for Louise, she had declared during the trial, "I shall win
no glory from it all. . . . The trial ended, I shall die!" But she
was wrong; she did not die, but went on killing instead. The
murderous devil that was in her raged more savagely than ever.
She began deliberately to denounce by name, Christian name
and surname, all whom she imagined mixed up with Magic and
Sorcery,—among others a poor young girl, by name Honorée,
"blind of both eyes," who was burned alive.

"Let us pray God," says the good Father Michaëlis, in conclusion, "that all may redound to His glory and the glory of His
Church!"

THE NUNS of LOUDUN

URBAIN GRANDIER

1633, 1634

In the *Mémoires d'État* composed by the renowned Father
Joseph, known to us only in fragments, having doubtless been
prudently suppressed as too instructive, the worthy Father explained how in the year 1633 he had had the good fortune to discover a heresy, an enormously widespread heresy, affecting a
countless multitude of confessors and directors of consciences.

The Capuchins, an admirably organised legion of defenders
of the Church, good watch-dogs of the holy flock, had scented
out and unearthed, not in the deserts, but in mid-France, in the
centre, at Chartres, in Picardy and everywhere, a formidable
quarry, the *alumbrados* of Spain (*illuminati* or Quietists), who
too fiercely persecuted in that country, had taken refuge in
France, and who among women, and above all in the nunneries,
were instilling the soft poison ticketed later on with the name of
Molinos.

The wonder is the thing had not been discovered sooner. It
could not very well be hidden, being so widely disseminated;
the Capuchins swore that in Picardy alone (a land where the
women are weak and the blood more fiery than in the South itself) this mania of mystic love had sixty thousand professors.
Was the whole body of clergy involved then? all the confessors,
all the directors? It must no doubt be understood that the official directors of consciences were supplemented by a great
number of laymen burning with the same zeal for the salvation

189

of female souls. One of this class, who was conspicuous at a later date no less for talent than for bold originality, was the author of the *Délices Spirituelles* (Spiritual Joys), Desmarets de Saint-Sorlin.

It is impossible to realise or understand the enormous power exercised by the Confessor over nuns, a hundred-fold more absolute at this time than in any previous age, unless the new conditions of the period are taken into account.

The reforms decided upon at the Council of Trent with regard to the closer seclusion of the inmates of Religious Houses, which had been largely ignored under Henri IV., when nuns entertained their fashionable friends, gave balls and danced at them, etc., these reforms began to be seriously enforced under Louis XIII. Cardinal de la Rochefoucauld, or rather the Jesuits who acted through him, insisted upon a high degree of external propriety. Need we say all entry into convents was prohibited for the male sex? One man, and one man only, went there every day, penetrating not only into the house, but wherever he wished, into each cell,—this comes out clearly in several cases, especially in the evidence given by David at Louviers. This reformation, this close seclusion, shut the door in the face of the world at large and excluded all inconvenient rivals, giving the right of familiar intercourse with Religious Women and the exclusive opportunity of influencing their minds to the Father Confessor.

What was likely to follow? This may be problematical, a matter of speculation, to dreamers; but practical men, and doctors, know better. As early as the sixteenth century the physician Wyer makes it clear enough to us by very plain examples. In his Book IV. he cites numerous cases of nuns having gone mad with love; while in Book III. he mentions a well-reputed Spanish priest, who having gone by chance when at Rome into a convent of nuns, left it a maniac, declaring that as brides of Christ, they were his, those of the priest, Christ's Vicar.

He had Masses said praying that God might grant him the grace to wed soon with the convent in question.[1]

If a mere passing visit could produce such an effect, we can understand what must have been the state of mind of the regular Director of nunneries of women, when he was alone with them, in the seclusion of the cloister, could spend all day with them, and receive at any hour the perilous confidences of their languors and weaknesses.

Nor are temptations of the senses the only factor to be reckoned with in these cases. We must likewise take account of the ennui and the irresistible craving to vary the conditions of existence, to escape from a monotonous life by the indulgence of some caprice or some fancy. Then what an age of new discoveries, of novelties of all sorts, it was! Travel, the Indies, discoveries of new worlds! Printing! last but not least, Romances! . . . When everything is on the move out of doors, every mind on the stretch, how suppose it possible to endure the crushing uniformity of monastic life, the long, weary services, unrelieved by anything more exciting than a dull sermon intoned through the nose?

Even laymen, in the midst of so many distractions, demand insistently of their confessors the pleasing variety of an occasional escapade, absolution for a certain degree of inconsistency of life.

The priest is hurried along by the current, and constrained to concede point after point. A vast, various, and learned literature develops out of Casuistry, or the art of making everything permissible,—a rapidly progressive literature moreover, in which yesterday's leniency would seem stern severity to-day.

Casuistry was for the laity, Mysticism for the cloister.

The complete suppression of individuality and the death of free will, this is the great principle of Mysticism. Desmarets gives us very clearly the true moral purport of it all. The pious

---
[1] Wyer, bk. iii. ch. 7.

devotee, he says, sacrificed in and for himself and annihilated, exists henceforth only in God. *Henceforth he can do no wrong.* His higher part is so divinely perfect, he has no consciousness left of what the other part is doing.[2]

One would have supposed that the zealous Father Joseph, after uttering so loud a cry of alarm against these corruptors of morals, would not have stopped there, that a full and searching inquiry would have been held, that this countless host, that in one province alone numbered sixty thousand Doctors of the Church, would be made known and minutely scrutinised. But no! they simply disappear, and no news is to be heard of them. Some, it is said, were cast in prison; but no trial was held, nothing done to break the deep silence. To all appearance, Richelieu had no mind to fathom the matter. For all his tenderness for the Capuchins, he was not so blinded by partiality as to follow their lead in a matter which would have put into their hands the duty of making inquiry into the conduct of all the confessors in the country.

As a rule, the monk both envied and hated the secular clergy. He was absolute master of the women of Spain; but was less appreciated by their French sisters on account of the dirtiness of his person; they preferred to call in the priest, or the Jesuit Father, an amphibious director, so to speak, half monk, half

---

[2] A very old doctrine, which reappears frequently in the Middle Ages. In the seventeenth century it is common in the French and Spanish cloisters, nowhere more clearly and naïvely expressed than in the lessons of a Normandy angel to a nun, reported in the papers relating to the Louviers affair (see following chapter). The angel teaches the nun in the first place "contempt for the body and indifference to the flesh. So much did Jesus despise the flesh that He exposed it naked to flagellation and open to the eyes of all men. . . ." He teaches her "complete abandonment of soul and will, holy, blessed, purely passive obedience; for example, the Blessed Virgin, who feared not Gabriel, but obeyed, and conceived. . . . Herein she exposed herself to no risk. For a spirit can cause no impurity. Quite the contrary, he purifies." At Louviers this noble doctrine was in the ascendant as early as 1623, and was taught systematically by a confessor of ripe age and well-supported authority, Father David by name. The gist of his teaching was "to kill sin by sin, the better to return to a state of innocence. This is what our first parents did." Esprit de Bosroger (Capuchin), *La Piété affligée* (Piety Afflicted), 1645; pp. 167, 171, 173, 174, 181, 189, 190, 196.

man of the world. If once Richelieu let loose the pack on Capuchins, Recollets, Carmelites, Dominicans, and the rest, no one would be safe among the clergy either. What director, what priest, however well meaning, had not on occasion used—yea, and abused—the pleasant jargon of the Quietists when dealing with his penitents?

Richelieu took good care not to worry the clergy at a time when he was already preparing for the General Diet at which he asked for a contribution for the war. One prosecution was allowed the monks, and only one, against a curé,—but a curé accused of Magic, which made it competent to confuse issues (as in the Gauffridi affair) to such good purpose that no single confessor, no single director, recognised the case as being like his own, and each could say in perfect security, "I have nothing to do with it."

Thanks to these judicious precautions, a certain degree of obscurity really envelopes the case of Urbain Grandier.[3] The historian of the affair, the Capuchin Tranquille, proves conclusively and satisfactorily he was a Sorcerer, and more than a Sorcerer, a Devil, and he is entitled in the documents of the trial (as they might have said of the goddess Ashtoreth) *Grandier of the Dominations!*

Ménage, on the contrary, taking a diametrically opposite view, is almost ready to rank him in the list of great men falsely accused of Magic, among the martyrs of liberty of conscience.

To see somewhat more clearly into the affair, we must not

---

[3] The work entitled *L'Histoire des diables de Loudun* (History of the Devils of Loudun), by the Protestant Aubin, is a serious and painstaking book, and its statements are confirmed by the Official Reports even of Laubardemont. On the contrary, Tranquille's book is a grotesque production. The *Procédure* is in the Bibliothèque Nationale at Paris. M. Figuier has given a lengthy and excellent account of the whole matter (*Histoire du merveilleux,*—History of the Miraculous). I am, as the sequel will show, against the judges, but by no means in favour of the condemned. It is absurd to make a martyr of him, out of dislike for Richelieu. The fact is he was a fool, a fop, and libertine, who deserved, not the stake, but imprisonment for life.

isolate Grandier, but let him occupy his proper place in the great diabolic Trilogy of those days, of which he and his doings formed only the Second Act; we must seek enlightenment on his case from the First Act, played out in Provence, as we have seen, in the dreadful business of La Sainte-Baume that ruined Gauffridi, and further enlightenment again from the Third Act, the affair of Louviers, which was a copy of Loudun (in the same way as Loudun had copied La Sainte-Baume), and which in its turn produced a Gauffridi and an Urbain Grandier.

The three affairs are one and identical. In all of them the libertine Priest, in all the jealous Monk and the maniac Nun by whose mouth they make the Devil speak,—and all end in the same way, by the death of the Priest at the stake.

One difference throws a strong light on these matters, and lets us have a clearer view than we can ever obtain in the fetid darkness of the Spanish and Italian monasteries,—the fact that while the nuns of these lands of Southern sloth were astonishingly passive and readily submitted to the life of the seraglio and worse things still,[4] their French sisters were of a very different temper. Their personality was vigorous, ardent, exacting; very devils (in no figurative sense) at once of jealousy and hate, they were equally indiscreet, loquacious, and spiteful. Their revelations were very precise, so extremely so towards the end as to arouse universal shame and disgust, the result being that in the course of thirty years three several scandals, forced into prominence by sheer horror and indignation, eventually died out drearily and ignominiously amid the groans of sick repulsion.

It was hardly at Loudun, in mid-Poitou, among the Huguenots and exposed to their scrutiny and jeers, in the very town where they held their great National Synods, that we should have expected a great scandal for the Catholics to have occurred. But it was just in these old Protestant towns that the latter were accustomed to live like conquerors in a subdued country, allowing themselves a very wide liberty of action, not unnaturally

---

[4] See Del Rio, Llorente, Ricci, etc.

supposing that people so often massacred and only recently defeated, would enter no protests. The Catholic inhabitants,—magistrates, priests, monks, a few nobles and a handful of artisans,—lived apart from the rest of the population quite like a colony of conquering aliens. This colony was further subdivided, as might be guessed, by the opposition existing between priests and monks.

The monks, a haughty and numerous band, as missionaries among a heretic population took the wall of the Protestant inhabitants, and acted as confessors to the Catholic ladies of the town. Such was the state of things when one day there arrived from Bordeaux a young curé, a pupil of the Jesuits, a cultivated and agreeable man, writing well and speaking better. He made a sensation in the pulpit, and soon afterwards in society as well. He was a native of Mantes and a born dialectician, but by education a *Meridional,* with the well-oiled tongue of Bordeaux and all the boasting, light-hearted effrontery of a Gascon. In a very short time he had contrived to set the whole of the little town by the ears, having the women on his side, the men against him,—all or very nearly all. He waxed superb, insolent, and insupportable, lost to all sense of proper reverence. He rained torrents of sarcasm at the Carmelites, and held forth publicly in the pulpit against the monks in general. The crowds were suffocating when he preached. Dignified and richly dressed, he paraded the streets of Loudun like a Father of the Church, while by night in a quieter way he would be lurking down back alleys or slipping in by back doors.

The women were at his beck and call. The wife of the "Avocat du Roi" was not insensible to his graces, and far more so the daughter of the "Procureur Royal," who had a child by him. Nor was this enough; this triumphant squire of dames, pushing his advantage farther and farther, began to assail the denizens of the nunneries.

There were to be found everywhere at that period Sisters of

the Ursuline Order, nuns vowed to the education of the young, lady missionaries in a Protestant land, expert at flattering and winning over the mothers and drawing the little girls under their influence. The Ursulines of Loudun formed a small convent of the daughters of poor but noble houses. The convent itself was ill supplied with this world's goods; the community having been endowed, at its first foundation, with little more than the house itself, a former Huguenot college. The Lady Superior, a person of good family and very well connected, burned with zeal to raise the status of her convent, to increase its numbers, to enrich and make it famous. She would very possibly have chosen Grandier, the man of the hour, for Confessor and Director, if she had not already had in these capacities a priest who possessed influence in the district for quite other reasons, being nearly related to the two principal magistrates. The Canon Mignon, such was his name, had no little influence over the Lady Superior. Both he and she learned in confession (the Ladies Superior of Convents used to confess the inmates) the hateful truth that the younger nuns dreamed of nothing else but this Grandier who was so much talked about.

Thus the Confessor whose authority was menaced, the husband whose honour was attacked, the father whose feelings were outraged, all these united their jealousy and indignation at the wrong done to family life, and swore a great oath to be Grandier's undoing. To attain this object, they had only to give him rope enough, as the saying is, and he would hang himself. Nor was it long before a scandal exploded that made noise enough to shake the town down pretty nearly.

The nuns, in the old Huguenot mansion they were settled in, did not feel altogether at their ease. Their boarders, children of the townsfolk, the younger Sisters possibly helping them, had found it a diverting amusement to terrify their companions by playing at ghosts, phantoms, and apparitions. Discipline was not over-strict among this miscellaneous collection of little girls, the spoilt children of rich parents. At night they would be scampering up and down the corridors, till they frightened both themselves and each other. Some were really ill with the effects, if not in body, at any rate in mind. But the object of all these terrors and illusions, complicated by the town talk they heard only too much of during the day, the ghost of these agitated nights was always Grandier. Several declared they had seen him, felt him of nights at their side, venturesome and victorious, and that they only awoke to full consciousness when it was too late. Was it all a case of self-deception,—or some trick of the novices? Was it really Grandier, who had bribed the portress or boldly climbed the convent walls? The matter has never been cleared up.

However, from that moment the three champions of family honour felt they had their man in their power. First of all they got from among the number of their humbler protégées two worthy souls to make declaration they could endure no longer to have as curé a debauchee, a sorcerer, a demon, a freethinker, who at church "bent one knee only and not two," a man who laughed at rules and regulations, and granted dispensations contrary to the Bishop's prerogatives. This last cleverly imagined charge set the Bishop of Poitiers against him, otherwise the natural defender of the priest, while giving up the latter to the malevolence of the monks.

The whole case was got up with consummate ability, it must be confessed. While having him accused by a couple of poor parishioners, it was found a further help to get him cudgelled by a nobleman. In this age of duelling the man who took a cudgelling inevitably lost ground with the public and was humiliated in the eyes of the fair sex; and Grandier fully realised the severity of the blow his prestige had received. Loving notoriety as he did, he went straight to the King himself, and throwing himself on his knees, claimed satisfaction for the insult to his cloth. The King was a pious king, and would probably have granted what was asked, had there not been people about him who told his Majesty it was a question of intrigue and the reprisals of injured husbands.

Brought before the Ecclesiastical Tribunal of Poitiers, Grandier was condemned to penance and to be banished from Loudun, in other words, degraded and dishonoured as a priest. However, the Civil Tribunal reopened the case, and found him innocent. He had, moreover, on his side the superior ecclesiastical authority to which Poitiers was subordinate, viz. the Archbishop of Bordeaux, Sourdis. This warlike prelate, an admiral and a gallant sailor quite as much as a priest, or more so, merely shrugged his shoulders at the tales of these peccadilloes. He acquitted the curé, but at the same time gave him the very judicious advice to go and live anywhere else rather than at Loudun.

This was just what the proud priest had no sort of mind to do. He was for savouring his triumph on the scene of battle and marching past before the ladies. He re-entered Loudun in broad daylight,—drums beating and flags flying; he carried a laurel brand as he walked, and all the fairest eyes of the city looked at his progress from the windows.

Not satisfied with this silly triumph, he now began to threaten and hint at compensation. His enemies, thus driven to bay and now in peril themselves, remembered the Gauffridi affair, in which the Devil, the Father of Lies, had been duly and honourably rehabilitated and accepted in court as a good truth-telling witness, worthy of credit and belief on the part both of the Church and the King's servants. In their desperate strait, they invoked a devil; and he came prompt to command, putting in his first appearance in the Ursuline convent.

The thing was risky, of course, but then, how many were interested in its success! The Lady Superior very soon found her convent, poor and obscure till now, attracting the eyes of the Court, the provinces, the whole world of France. The monks saw in it the triumph of their cause over their rivals the priests;

and an opportunity for reviving those fights with the Devil so popular in the preceding century, very often (as at Soissons) held before the church doors, and in which the populace with mingled terror and exultation beheld God's victory over his diabolic adversary, the admission "that God is in the elements" dragged reluctantly from the Devil, and the Huguenots convinced and brought to confusion out of the Demon's own mouth.

In this tragi-comedy the exorcist represented Almighty God, or if not quite that, at any rate the Archangel treading down the Dragon. He would step down from the platform, exhausted and dripping with sweat, but triumphant, to be borne shoulder high by the crowd and receive the blessings of the women who wept for joy to see such things.

This was why something of Sorcery must always be an ingredient in legal cases of this sort; the Devil supplied the only really interesting *motif*. Of course he could not always be shown leaving the accused's body in the form of a black toad,—as at Bordeaux in 1610; but at any rate the *mise en scène* was grand and imposing enough. The grim loneliness of poor Madeleine, the honours of La Sainte-Baume, in the Provence business, were no insignificant factors of success. Loudun had for its part the noisy rout and delirious frenzy of a whole army of exorcists distributed among several different churches. Last but not least, Louviers, as we shall see presently, by way of reviving interest in these rather out-of-date proceedings, inaugurated a series of midnight episodes, where, by the flickering torchlight, the devils, disguised as nuns, dug pits and extracted from them the magic talismans that had been there secreted.

The Loudun affair began with the Lady Superior and a lay Sister in attendance upon her,—who fell into convulsions and indulged in long diabolic rigmaroles. Other nuns copied them, —especially one bold spirit who recreated the rôle formerly played by Sister Louise at Marseilles, representing the same devil, Leviathan, the head demon of all cunning and calumny.

The little town is shaken to its foundations. The monks of all colours take possession of the nuns, divide them between them, proceed to exorcise them by threes and fours. They partition the churches between them, the Capuchins alone possessing themselves of two. These are crowded to excess, the whole female population flocking thither, and among the frightened, excitable congregation thus formed, more than one woman is heard screaming she also feels devils working within her. Six young women of Loudun are *possessed;* while the mere recital of these dreadful doings produces a like effect on two more at Chinon.

Everywhere it formed the absorbing subject of conversation, —at Paris, at Court. The Queen of France, a Spaniard by birth and a woman of ardent imagination and enthusiastic piety, sends her own Almoner; more important still, Lord Montagu, the old papal partisan and her Majesty's faithful servant, who saw everything and believed everything, reported everything to the Pope. The miracle was proved and confirmed; with his own eyes he had seen the wounds on a nun's body, the stigmata impressed by the Devil on the hands of the Lady Superior.

What had the King of France to say to it all? All his devotion was turned in the direction of the Devil, to Hell, to religious fear; and it is said Richelieu was delighted to keep it concentrated there. I doubt this myself; the devils were essentially Spanish and of the Spanish faction,—if they had talked politics at all, it would have been against Richelieu. It may be this was what he dreaded; at any rate he paid them the compliment of sending his niece to display a proper interest in the matter.

The Court was ready to believe; but it was not so on the spot, at Loudon. The local devils, wretched plagiarists of the demons of Marseilles, merely repeated by rote in the morning what had been taught them overnight from the well-known Manual of Michaëlis. They would never have known what to say, had not secret exorcisms, carefully rehearsed every evening for next day's comedy, taught them the proper graces of deportment and style for an effective appearance in public.

A firm and determined magistrate, the *Bailli* of the town, detected the fraud and came in person to expose its perpetrators, threatening and denouncing them. The Archbishop of Bordeaux tacitly coincided, when Grandier appealed to him. He sent an order to regulate the exorcists' zeal at any rate and put an end to their arbitrary proceedings; more than this his surgeon, who visited the young women, declared them not to be possessed at all. According to him they were not mad, not even touched with insanity,—but undoubted impostors and arrant shams.

Thus the century continues the great duel of Doctor against Devil, of Science and Enlightenment against the spirit of Falsehood and Obscurantism. We saw its commencement with Agrippa and Wyer; and now another physician, a man called Duncan, gallantly continued the same struggle at Loudun, and fearlessly printed the statement that the whole affair was only deserving of ridicule.

The Devil, reputed so stubborn, showed the white feather and uttered not another word. But the angry passions of both sides were too much excited for things to stop here. The tide flowed so strong in Grandier's favour that those attacked now became the attacking party. A kinsman of the accusers, an apothecary, was brought to book by a rich and well-born lady of the town, whom he had stated to be the curé's mistress, and was condemned, as a common slanderer, to make proper reparation.

The Lady Superior felt herself on the verge of ruin. It could easily have been proved, what an eye-witness saw later on, that her so-called stigmata were merely painted on, the colouring being freshened up every day. But she was related to a member of the King's Council, Laubardemont, and he saved her. At the moment he was entrusted with a commission to clear the ground at Loudun; and he now got himself nominated to bring Grandier to trial. The Cardinal was given to understand that the accused priest was the curé and friend of the *Cordonnière de Loudun,* one of the numerous agents of Marie de Médicis; that he had constituted himself secretary to his parishioner and had under her name composed a scandalous and unworthy pamphlet.

For the matter of that, Richelieu would gladly have shown himself magnanimous and treated the matter with contempt, but it was hardly possible for him to have done so. The Capuchins and Father Joseph speculated on this; for Richelieu would have given him a fine hold over him with the King, if he had shown a want of proper zeal. A certain M. Quillet, who had kept a careful eye on things, went to see Richelieu and warned him. But the Cardinal was afraid to listen to him, and appeared so ill-disposed towards his would-be benefactor that the latter judged it prudent to take refuge in Italy.

Laubardemont arrives on December 6th, 1663, with unlimited discretionary powers,—and his arrival marks the commencement of a reign of terror. He is the King's direct representative, wielding the whole weight of the Government of France,—a grim, ponderous sledge-hammer, to crush a fly.

The magistrates felt the affront; and the *Lieutenant Civil* notified Grandier of his intention to arrest him on the morrow. The latter paid no heed, and was duly arrested, instantly hurried out of the place without legal formalities of any sort, and thrown into the dungeons of Angers. Subsequently he was brought back again and confined (of all places in the world) in the house and bedchamber of one of his personal enemies, who had the windows walled up in an attempt to suffocate him. The detestable examination carried out on the suspected Sorcerer's person by driving in needles to discover the Devil's mark, was conducted by the very hands of his accusers themselves, who thus exacted a preliminary vengeance on him, a foretaste of more deadly penalties to follow.

He is dragged to churches to confront the mad women, to whom Laubardemont's arrival has restored the power of speech. There he finds a band of furious Bacchanals whom the condemned apothecary was busy intoxicating with his potions, throwing them into such paroxysms of rage that on one occasion Grandier came near perishing under their nails.

Unable to vie with the eloquence of the Devil-possessed Louise of Marseilles, they made up for the want of it by impudent cynicism. A vile sight truly!—young girls, taking advantage of the devils supposed to be prompting them to let loose the floodgates of their sensual delirium for the public delectation! For it was this and nothing else that attracted such crowds; they came to hear from women's mouths things that no modest female lips ever dare to utter.

And the absurdity of these scenes increased *pari passu* with the odiousness. The scraps of Latin that were whispered in their ears they pronounced all wrong. The public said scornfully that the devils had not passed their Fourth Standard. The Capuchins, not in the least disconcerted, replied that if the demons were weak in Latin, they spoke Troquois to perfection and very fine Double Dutch.

This ignoble farce, when seen from a distance of sixty leagues, from Saint-Germain or the Louvre, appeared something miraculous, terrifying, and appalling. The French Court wondered and shuddered; while Richelieu (no doubt to win popularity) condescended to a cowardly proceeding, having both exorcists and nuns paid for what they did.

So signal a favour encouraged the cabal, which now lost all sense of decorum and moderation. Words of senseless folly were succeeded by shameful acts. The exorcists, under pretext of the fatigued condition of the nuns, sent them on pleasure excursions outside the town, sometimes themselves accompanying them. The result was one of the number became enceinte, or at any rate seemed to be so. At the end of the fifth or sixth month this appearance vanished completely, and the demon that was in her confessed the trick he had played, in order to bring discredit on the poor nun by an illusory pregnancy. It is the learned historian of Louviers who supplies us with this fragment of the history of Loudun.[5]

It is credibly affirmed that Father Joseph arrived incognito, but seeing the case was hopeless, quietly withdrew again. The Jesuits also came, performed sundry exorcisms without much success, noted which way the wind of public opinion blew, and likewise beat a retreat.

But the monks, the Capuchins above all, were so deeply involved that only one course was left them, to save their own skins by inspiring terror in their neighbours. They laid cunning snares to catch the stout-hearted *Bailli* and his lady, whom they would fain have ruined and so stifled any retributive measures on the part of justice. Lastly, they urged the Commission to press the case against Grandier to a conclusion. Things were at a standstill, even their allies the nuns failing them at this crisis. After their fearful orgy of carnal frenzy and their shameless cries for human blood, two or three of them had swooned away, and filled with a sick disgust at their own vileness, became a horror and a loathing to themselves. In spite of the awful fate they must expect if they spoke out, in spite of the certainty of ending in a dungeon,[6] they openly declared within the church walls that they were lost souls, that they had played into the Devil's hands, that Grandier was an innocent man.

They ruined themselves, but did nothing to stop the course of events; and a general protest addressed by the town to the King was equally unavailing. Grandier was condemned to be burned (August 18th, 1634). So savage was his enemies' temper

---

[5] Esprit de Bossuet, p. 135.

[6] Such was still the custom. See Mabillon.

that before he went to the stake, they insisted on a second application of the needle to every part of his body in search of the Devil's mark. One of the judges would actually have liked his nails to be torn off, but the surgeon refused.

His persecutors dreaded the final scene and the victim's last words from the scaffold. Having found among his papers a written argument against the celibacy of the clergy, the same men who had pronounced him a Sorcerer, now thought him a freethinker. They remembered the bold words the martyrs of freedom of thought had hurled at their judges' heads, recalling the last, tremendous words of Giordano Bruno [7] and Vanini's dying defiance. So they arranged a compromise with Grandier. He was told that, if he kept a judicious silence, he should be spared the flames and should be strangled before the pile was kindled. The weak priest, a man of the flesh, yielded yet another and a last concession to the feeble flesh, and promised not to speak. He never opened his lips either on the road to his death or on the scaffold itself. Then when they saw him securely tied to the stake, everything ready and the embers so arranged as to wrap him swiftly in flame and smoke, a monk, his own confessor, without waiting for the executioner, set light to the faggots. The deluded victim had only time to exclaim, "Ah, you have cheated me!" before the rolling smoke rose round him and through the furnace of his torment only his shrieks were audible.

Richelieu in his *Memoirs* passes lightly over the affair, being evidently ashamed of the whole matter. He leaves it to be understood that he acted according to the reports supplied him, following the voice of public opinion in what he did. But there can be no doubt that by subsidising the exorcists, by giving the rein to the Capuchins' violence and ensuring their triumph throughout the country, he had directly encouraged knavery and imposture. Gauffridi, whose rôle had been recreated by Grandier, is

---

[7] These words, which he addressed to his judges after hearing his sentence pronounced, were: "This sentence, delivered in the name of a God of mercy, is perhaps more a cause of fear to you than to me." He was burned at the stake at Rome, February 17th, 1600.

soon to appear once more under still fouler circumstances in the affair of Louviers.

This very year of 1634 the devils, driven out of Poitou, appear in Normandy, copying and recopying the old absurdities of La Sainte-Baume, devoid equally of originality, fresh initiative, and creative imagination. The wild, fierce Leviathan of Provence, as travestied at Loudun, has lost his southern *verve*, and can only conclude the affair by making nuns and virgins speak volubly the vile language of the Cities of the Plain. Alas! presently, at Louviers, he will lose even this much of his old audacity; we shall find him succumbing to the heaviness of the northern atmosphere and growing a poor, mean-spirited creature of tricks and subterfuges.

THE NUNS of LOUVIERS
and SATANIC POSSESSION

MADELEINE BAVENT
1640-1647

Had not Richelieu refused to order the inquiry demanded by Father Joseph against the thirty thousand *illuminati* among the Father Confessors, we should doubtless have had some strange revelations as to the internal life of the convents and the morals of the nuns inhabiting them. Failing this, the history of events at Louviers, more instructive than anything told us about Aix or Loudun, proves that confessors, although possessing in *Illuminism* a new instrument of corruption, by no means neglected the old tricks of Sorcery, diabolic apparitions, angelic visitations, and the like.[1]

Of three successive Directors of the Convent of Loudun,

---

[1] It was only too easy to deceive women who wished to be cajoled. Celibacy was now more difficult than in the Middle Ages, the monastic fastings and bleedings being largely discontinued. Many died of a life so cruelly inactive and so liable to nervous over-excitation. The unhappy women took little pains to hide the martyrdom they suffered, but spoke of it to the other Sisters, to their Confessor, to the Virgin herself,—a circumstance deserving our sympathy and pity far more than our ridicule. We read in a report of an Italian Disciplinary Commission such an avowal on the part of a nun, who said naïvely to the Madonna, "of your gracious favour, Holy Virgin, grant me some one I may sin with" (in Lasteyrie, *Confession*, p. 205). It formed a genuine embarrassment for the Director, who, no matter what his age, was in real peril. The story of a certain Russian convent is well known,—how a man who had penetrated within its doors did not come out alive. In the French Houses the Director went inside, indeed it was his duty to do so, every day. The general belief among Religious Women was that a holy man

within thirty years, the first, David, is one of the *illuminati*, a *Molinist* (before Molinos); the second, Picart, *has dealings with the Devil* and uses magic arts; the third, Boullé, acts under the guise of an angel.

The great authority on the whole affair is a book entitled, *Histoire de Magdelaine Bavent, Religieuse de Louviers, avec son interrogatoir*, etc. (History of Madeleine Bavent, a Nun of Louviers, together with her Examination, etc.), 4to: Rouen, 1652.[2] The date of this work accounts for the perfect freedom with which it is written. During the "Fronde," a stout-hearted priest, an Oratorian, having found the nun in question in the prisons of Rouen, conceived the bold idea of writing down at her dictation the history of her life.

Madeleine was born at Rouen in 1607, and was left an orphan at nine years old. At twelve she was bound apprentice to a tradeswoman of the city, a worker in linen. The Confessor of the establishment, a Franciscan, was absolute master of the house, the linen-worker, who was chiefly employed in making nuns' robes, depending wholly on the Church's patronage. The monk made the apprentice girls, who were drugged probably with belladonna and other Wizards' potions, believe he was taking them to the "Sabbath" and marrying them to the great

---

can only sanctify, and a pure being purify. The people called them in mockery "the Sanctified" (Lestoile). This was a matter of very serious conviction in convents (see the Capuchin Esprit de Bosroger, ch. xi. p. 156).

[2] I do not know a more important, a more terrible book, or one better deserving to be reprinted (*Bibliothèque Z, ancien 1016*). It is the most striking of all such histories. Another work, *La Piété affligée* (Piety Afflicted), by the Capuchin Esprit de Bosroger, is a book that must live for ever in the annals of human folly and dulness. I have extracted from this, in the preceding chapter, some surprising statements which might well have involved its being burned by the common hangman; but I have carefully refrained from reproducing the amorous liberties which it makes the Archangel Gabriel take with the Virgin, his dove-like kisses, and so on. The two admirable pamphlets of the stout-hearted Surgeon Yvelin are to be found in the Bibliothèque de Sainte-Geneviève. The *Examen* and the *Apologie* are bound up with other documents in a volume inappropriately labelled *Éloges de Richelieu* (Letter x. 550). A duplicate of the *Apologie* occurs also in the volume numbered Z 899 in the same collection.

devil Dagon. He had his will of three of them, and Madeleine, at fourteen, made the fourth.

She was filled with ardent piety, especially towards St. Francis. A Franciscan convent had just been founded at Louviers by a lady of Rouen, widow of the *King's Procureur* Hennequin, hanged for malversation. The lady hoped by this good work to do something for the salvation of her husband's soul, and with this view consulted a holy man, an aged priest by name Father David, who superintended the new foundation. Outside the gates of the town, buried in the woods surrounding Louviers, the convent, a poor place gloomily situated, and established under such tragic circumstances, seemed a fit place for the austere life. David himself was known by a strange, violent book he had composed against the abuses that disgraced the Religious Houses, the *Fouet des Paillards* (A Whip for Wantons), as it was called.[3] Nevertheless, this stern moralist had some very curious notions as to what constituted purity. He was an *Adamite,* preaching the nudity Adam practised in his innocence. Obedient to his teaching, the Sisters of the convent at Louviers, by way of subjugating and humiliating the novices and breaking them in to discipline, required (no doubt in summer-time) these young Eves to resume the condition of our first mother. They made them take exercise in this state in certain private gardens, and even appear so in chapel. Madeleine, who had succeeded at sixteen in being received as a novice, was too proud (too pure-minded perhaps so far) to submit to this strange way of living. She incurred the displeasure of the authorities and was scolded for having endeavoured, at Communion, to hide her bosom with the altar-cloth.

She was equally reluctant to unveil her soul, and would not confess to the Lady Superior,—a usual practice in convents and one that the Abbesses found greatly to their liking. She preferred to entrust the care of her soul to the old priest, David, who separated her from the other Sisters,—while he

---

[3] See Floquet, *Parl. de Normandie,* vol. v. p. 63%.

returned the compliment by entrusting his body to her when he was ill. He did not hide from her his private, inner doctrine, the conventual theory of *Illuminism*: "The body cannot contaminate the soul; we must, by means of sin, which makes us humble and cures our pride, kill sin," etc. The nuns, saturated with these doctrines, and unobtrusively putting them in practice among themselves, appalled Madeleine with their abominable doings. She withdrew and kept apart from the rest, living in the outer purlieus of the convent, having secured the post of *tourière*.[4]

She was eighteen when David died. His advanced age can scarcely have allowed him to go very far with Madeleine but the curé Picart, his successor, pursued her with ardent importunity. At confession he spoke of nothing but love, and made her Sacristaness, that he might be able to be with her alone in the convent chapel. She did not like him; but the Sisters forbade her any other confessor, for fear of her divulging their little mysteries. This put her completely in Picart's hands. He assailed her when she was ill, when she was almost on her deathbed; moreover, he assailed her through her fears, leading her to believe that David had handed on to him certain diabolical talismans. Last of all, he assailed her through her feelings of compassion, shamming sick himself and beseeching her to visit him in his room. From that moment he was her master, and it would seem, confused her wits with magic potions. She dreamed of the Witches' Sabbath, fancied herself carried off thither in his company, where she was at once altar and victim. And it is only too true she was so in sad reality!

But Picart was not satisfied with the barren pleasures of the "Sabbath," but, defying scandalous tongues, boldly got her with child.

The nuns, whose turpitude he knew, were afraid of him.

---

[4] *I.e.*, the nun who attends to the turning-box of a convent, by means of which communication is kept up with the outside world.

Besides which they were bound to him by their worldly interests; it was his credit, his energy, the alms and gifts he attracted
from all quarters, which had enriched their convent. He was
even now building them a great church. The affair of Loudun has
sufficiently shown what were the ambitions and mutual rivalries
of these Houses and the jealous eagerness they displayed to out-
vie one another. Picart, in virtue of the good will of rich patrons,
found himself promoted to the rôle of benefactor and sacred
founder of the convent. "Dear heart," he declared to Madeleine,
" 'tis I am building this magnificent church. After my death
you will see wonders. . . . Will you not do as I wish?"

He was a great lord, and carried things with a high hand. He
paid down a dowry for her, and from a mere lay Sister raised
her to the position of a full-blown Sister, so that, being no longer
in charge of the turning-box, and living within the convent
itself, she might conveniently be delivered or contrive abortion,
as the case might be. Provided with certain drugs, and possessed of certain secrets, convents could dispense with the
necessity of calling in medical aid. Madeleine declares (*Examination*, p. 13) she bore several children. What became of these
infants she does not say.

Picart, already an oldish man, dreaded Madeleine's fickle-
ness, fearing she might form a new connexion with some other
confessor, to whom she could pour out her remorse. He adopted
a hateful means of attaching her irrevocably to himself. He
made her swear an oath pledging herself *to die when he should
die, and be with him where he should go.* The poor, faint-
hearted creature endured agonies of terror. Would he drag her
with him into the tomb? would he set her in Hell alongside of
himself? She fully believed herself a lost soul. She became his
chattel, his familiar spirit bound to do his will, and he used
her and abused her for every vile purpose. He prostituted her
in a fourfold orgy, carried out with his vicar Boullé and another
woman. He made use of her to win over the other nuns by a

magic talisman. The sacred wafer, dipped in Madeleine's blood and buried in the convent garden, was a sure way of agitating their senses and eluding their wits.

It was the very same year that Urbain Grandier was burned, and all France was talking of nothing else but the devils of Loudun. The Penitentiary of Evreux, who had been one of the actors in that drama, brought back appalling accounts of what had occurred to Normandy. Madeleine felt herself *possessed*, assailed, battered, by devils; a cat with fiery eyes pursued her with amorous advances. Little by little other Sisters caught the contagion, and began to experience strange, supernatural stirrings. Madeleine had asked help of a Capuchin, and later on of the Bishop of Evreux. The Lady Superior, who could not but be aware of the fact, was rather glad than otherwise, seeing the glory and riches a similar affair had brought to the Convent of Loudun. But for six years the Bishop was deaf to all such appeals, being no doubt afraid of Richelieu, who was trying at the time to initiate a reform of the Religious Houses.

His wish was to put an end to all these scandals. Only at his death and that of Louis XIII., in the general confusion that followed, under the Queen and Mazarin, did the priests really take up their dealings with the supernatural again, and resume their struggle with the Devil. Picart was dead, and interference looked less hazardous now in an affair in which that dangerous man might have involved many others in his own guilt. To fight the visions of Madeleine, another visionary of the same sort was sought for, and soon found. A certain Anne of the Nativity was introduced into the convent, a woman of sanguine and hysterical temperament, on occasion shown, a savage and half a madwoman, actually insane enough to believe her own lies. It was a stand-up fight, regularly arranged like a bout between two bulldogs; and the pair fell to sacrificing each other with outrageous calumnies. Anne declared she saw the Devil standing stark naked by Madeleine's side. Madeleine swore that she had seen Anne at the Witches' Sabbath, along with the Lady Superior, the Mother Delegate, and the Mother of the Novices. Not that there was a single novel feature; it was all a *réchauffé* of the two famous cases at Aix and Loudun. Both had the printed reports of those trials, and followed them slavishly, without a trace of discrimination or originality.

The accuser Anne and her devil Leviathan had the countenance of the Penitentiary of Evreux, one of the chief actors in the Loudun affair. By his advice the Bishop of Evreux orders the exhumation of Picart's body, so that his corpse being removed from the neighbourhood of the convent may remove the devils along with it. Madeleine, condemned without a hearing, is to be degraded, and examined to discover on her body the satanic sign-manual. Her veil and robe are torn off her wretched body, which is left to be the butt of an unworthy curiosity, ready to pry into her very vitals to find excuse to send her to the stake. The Sisters would entrust to no hands but their own this cruel search, in itself a terrible punishment. These virgin nuns, in the guise of matrons, verified her condition, whether pregnant or no, then shaved her in every part of her person, and pricking with their needles, driving them deep in the quivering flesh, sought if there was anywhere a spot insensible to pain, as the devil's mark is bound to be. But every stab hurt; failing the crowning triumph of proving her a Witch, at any rate they had the satisfaction of gloating over her tears and cries of agony.

But Anne was not satisfied yet; on the testimony of her devil, the Bishop condemned Madeleine, whom the examination vindicated from the suspicions entertained, to be immured in an *in pace* for life. Her removal, it was alleged, would calm the other nuns. But it was not so. The Devil raged only the more furiously; and a score of the Sisters were soon screaming, prophesying, and struggling.

The sight attracted the curious in crowds from Rouen, and even from Paris. A young surgeon of the latter city, Yvelin by name, had already been a spectator of the farce perpetrated at

Loudun, and now came to watch the one at Louviers. He was accompanied by a magistrate, a very clear-headed man and an Assistant Counsellor at Rouen. They devoted a steady and persevering attention to the matter, establishing themselves in the town and studying the phenomena systematically for seventeen days.

From the very first day they detected the imposture. A conversation they had had with the Penitentiary on entering the town was repeated to them (as a special revelation) by the devil in possession of Anne of the Nativity. On every occasion they accompanied the crowd to the convent garden. The scene and its accessories were extremely striking; the shades of night, the torches, the trembling and smoky lights, all produced effects which had been lacking at Loudun. The mode of procedure, however, was of the simplest; one of the *possessed* would declare, "You will find a talisman at such and such a spot in the garden." A hole was dug at the place indicated, and the charm duly discovered. Unfortunately, Yvelin's friend, the sceptical magistrate, refused to quit the side of the principal performer, the nun Anne. On the very edge of an excavation they were going to open up, he grasps her hand, and opening the fingers, finds the talisman (a little black thread) concealed there, which she was on the point of throwing into the hole.

Exorcists, Penitentiary, priests, and Capuchins, who were all present, were covered with confusion. The intrepid Yvelin, on his own authority, commenced an inquiry and saw to the bottom of the whole thing. Among fifty-two nuns there were, he declared, six *under possession,* diabolic or otherwise, who would seem to have deserved a taste of discipline. Seventeen others, *under a spell,* were merely victims, a troop of young women affected by the morbid excitement characteristic of cloister life. He details the symptoms with precision; the girls are otherwise normal, but hysterical, suffering from extreme disturbances and derangements of the womb, to all intents and purposes lunatic and deranged. Nervous contagion had destroyed their wits, and the very first thing to do is to isolate them from each other.

Next he scrutinises with a Voltairean keenness the various signs by which the priests recognise the supernatural character of the possession under which they labour. *They prophesy;* granted, but things that never happen. *They translate* tongues; granted, but without understanding the original (for instance, *ex parte Virginis* is made to mean "the departure of the Virgin"). *They know Greek* before the populace of Louviers, but cannot speak a word of it before the doctors at Paris. *They make extraordinary leaps and perform feats of strength,*—the easiest in the world, climbing a great tree-trunk a child of three could negotiate. In one word, the only thing they do really terrible and *unnatural* is to say filthy abominations no man would ever soil his lips with.

The surgeon was really doing a great service to humanity by tearing away the mask from them. For the business was being pressed, and more victims would soon have been added. Besides the talismans, papers were discovered which were attributed to David or Picart, and in which such and such individuals were declared Sorcerers and marked down for death. Everybody trembled, and the terror of ecclesiastical pains and penalties gained ground from day to day.

The evil days of Cardinal Mazarin were now come, and the first essays in ruling of the weak Anne of Austria. Order and good government were things of the past. "There was only one phrase left in the whole French language, *La Reine est si bonne* (the Queen is so good-natured)." This good nature it was gave the clergy their chance to gain the upper hand; lay authority being interred with Richelieu, bishops, priests, and monks were going to govern instead. But the impious audacity of the magistrate and Yvelin was like to compromise this agreeable hope. Voices of lamentation and protest reached the good Queen,— not the voices of the victims, but those of the scamps and impostors caught red-handed in their trickeries. The Court must go into mourning for the dire outrages done to the sacred cause of Religion!

This was a blow Yvelin was far from expecting, believing his favour at Court to be firmly based, as for ten years he had enjoyed the title of Surgeon to the Queen. Before his return from Louviers to Paris, his adversaries won from the weakness of Anne of Austria the appointment of other experts, of their own choosing, an old dotard in his second childhood, a Diafoirus of Rouen and his nephew, two clients of the clergy. These did not fail to find that the affair of Louviers was supernatural, above and beyond all human skill.

Any other man but Yvelin would have been discouraged. The Rouen experts, who were physicians, treated as altogether an inferior this mere barber-surgeon, this quack; while the Court gave him no support. He only stiffened his back and wrote a pamphlet, which will live. In it he accepts the great duel between Science and the Clergy, and declares (as Wyer had done in the sixteenth century) "that in such-like matters the proper judge is not the Priest, but the man of Science." After much difficulty he found a printer to risk putting it in type, but no one willing to sell it. Accordingly the heroic young fellow set himself in broad daylight to the task of distributing the little book. He posted himself at the most frequented spot in Paris, on the Pont Neuf, and standing at the feet of Henri IV., presented his brochure to the passers-by. There they could read the official report of the scandalous deceit,—the magistrate seizing in the very hand of the female devils the unanswerable evidence of their own infamy.

To return to the unhappy Madeleine. Her enemy, the Penitentiary of Evreux, the same who had ordered her to be pricked —personally marking the place for the needles!—now carried her off as his prey, and deposited her in the depths of the episcopal *in pace* at that town. Beneath a subterranean gallery was a cellar at a lower level still, beneath the cellar a dungeon where the prisoner lay rotting in damp and darkness. Her unfeeling companions, making sure she must soon perish in the dreadful place, had not common kindness enough to provide her with a little linen to dress her ulcer with. She suffered both from pain and from her filthy condition, lying as she did in her own excrements. The perpetual darkness was disturbed by a dreadful scampering of hungry rats, the object of much terror in prisons, as they will sometimes gnaw off the helpless prisoners' noses and ears.

But the horror even of these fearful surroundings did not equal that inspired by her tyrant, the Penitentiary. Every day he would come into the cellar overhead, to speak down the orifice of the *in pace,* threatening, ordering, confessing her in her own despite, making her say this and that against other people. Presently she left off eating entirely. He was afraid she was going to die, and took her out of the *in pace* for a brief while, lodging her in the cellar above. Then, furious at Yvelin's brochure, he threw her once more into the foul sewer down below.

This glimpse of light, this gleam of hope, kindled and so soon extinguished, all added to her despair. The ulcer had now closed, and her strength was somewhat recruited. She was seized with a heartfelt, wild desire for death. She swallowed spiders,—she merely vomited, without further bad effects. She pounded glass and gulped it down,—but in vain. Putting her hand on an old blunt knife, she tried hard to cut her throat,—but could not succeed. Next, choosing a softer place, her belly, she forced the iron into her inwards. For four whole hours she worked, and writhed and bled. But nothing answered her hopes; even this wound soon closed. To crown her woes, the life that she hated so, grew stronger within her. Her heart was dead indeed,—but what of that?

She became a woman once more, and alas! desirable still, a temptation for her gaolers, brutal fellows of the Bishop's household, who, in spite of the horrors of the place, the unhealthy and unclean condition of the wretched creature, would come to take their pleasure of her, deeming any outrage permissible on a Witch. An angel came to her succour, so she declared. She defended herself both from men and rats, but not from her own evil passions. A prison degrades the character. She began to dream about the Devil, to call upon him to visit her, to implore the renewal of the shameful, agonising delights he used to wring her heart with in the old days at Louviers. But he would come back no more; the power of dreams was done in her, her senses depraved indeed, but dulled and dead. Only the more eagerly did she recur to the thought of suicide. One of the gaolers had given her a poison to destroy the rats that infested her cell. She was on the point of swallowing it, when an angel stayed her hand (was it an angel or a demon?), reserving her for an existence of crime.

Now fallen into the most abject condition, to indescribable depths of cowardice and servility, she signed interminable lists of crimes she had never committed. Was she worth the trouble of burning? Many renounced the idea, and the implacable Penitentiary was the only one who still thought seriously of adopting such a course. He offered money to a Wizard of Evreux they had under lock and key if he would give such evidence as to ensure Madeleine's death.

But henceforth she could be utilised in quite a different way, as a false witness, an instrument of lying and slandering. Every time it was desired to ruin a man she was haled to Louviers, to Evreux,—the accursed phantom of a dead woman who went on living only to be the death of others. In this fashion she was brought along to kill with the venom of her tongue a poor man by name Duval. The Penitentiary dictated, and she said her lesson obediently after him; he told her by what sign she should recognise Duval, whom she had never seen. She duly identified him, and affirmed she had seen him at the Witches' Sabbath,— and he was burned on her testimony!

She confesses to this atrocity, and shudders to think she must

answer for it before God. After a while she fell into such contempt they did not so much as deign to watch her. The doors
stood wide open; sometimes she had the keys in her own possession. Where, indeed, should she have fled, now she was
grown a mere object of horror to all mankind? From henceforth
the universe rejected the odious creature and spued her out;
her only world was her dungeon.

Under the anarchy of Mazarin and his "good-natured" mistress, the Parlements were the sole and only authority left.
That of Rouen, till then the most favourable of them all towards
the clergy, yet waxed indignant at the insolence of their present
proceedings, the way they were domineering and burning. By a
mere decree of the Bishop's, Picart had been exhumed and his
body cast into the common sewer. Now it was the vicar Boullé's
turn, and they were trying him. The Parlement hearkened to
the appeal of Picart's family, and condemned the Bishop of
Evreux to return the body at his own cost to the tomb at
Louviers. It summoned Boullé to appear before it, discharged
his case, and on the same occasion finally removed the unhappy
Madeleine Bavent from Evreux, and took her also to Rouen.

There was much reason to fear the Parlement might call up
both the surgeon Yvelin and the magistrate who had detected
the nuns, *flagrante delicto,* in their imposture. Appeal was instantly made to Paris; and Mazarin threw the ægis of his protection over his fellow-rascals. The whole affair was to be laid
before the King's Council, an easy-going tribunal, which had
neither eyes nor ears, and whose first care was invariably to
bury, to hush up, to make a cloud of darkness, in any question
of law and justice.

Simultaneously, soft-spoken priests, in the dungeons of
Rouen, comforted Madeleine, received her confession, and for
penance ordered her to ask pardon of her persecutors, the Sisters
of Louviers. Henceforward, come what might, Madeleine, thus
tongue-tied, could not be brought up to bear witness against
them. This was a distinct triumph for the clergy,—a triumph

which the Capuchin, Esprit de Bosroger, one of the charlatan exorcists, has celebrated in his *Piété affligée,* a grotesque monument of human folly, in which, quite unknowingly, he incriminates the very people he believes himself to be defending. We have seen a little above (in a note) the noble words of the Capuchin in a passage where he gives as lessons of the angels a series of shameful maxims that would have utterly shocked Molinos.

The *Fronde* was, as I have said before, a revolt in favour of integrity of living. Fools have seen in it only the formal and ludicrous side, but the real basis was a solemn and serious moral reaction. In August, 1647, at the first breath of free criticism, the Parlement took action, and cut the knot. It decreed: *imprimis,* that the Sodom of Louviers should be destroyed, the young women dispersed and sent home to their families; *secundo,* that henceforward the Bishops of the Province should send four times a year Confessors Extraordinary to all nunneries to make sure that these filthy abuses were not being repeated.

Still a sop was needed for the clergy. They were given the bones of Picart to burn, and the living body of Boullé, who, after making a proper expression of contrition in the cathedral, was drawn on a hurdle to the Fish-market, and there delivered to the flames,—August 21st, 1647. Madeleine, or rather her dead carcass, remained in the prisons of Rouen.

SATAN TRIUMPHANT
in the SEVENTEENTH CENTURY

THE *Fronde* was essentially Voltairean. The Voltairean spirit, as old as France really, though long kept in abeyance, breaks out in Politics, and very soon afterwards in Religion. The King, with all his greatness, tries in vain to impose a solemn and serious attitude on his subjects. The undercurrent of mocking laughter is always audible.

Does it all mean nothing more then but laughter and derision? Far from that; it is the beginning of the reign of Reason. Kepler, Galileo, Descartes, and Newton triumphantly established the dogma of reason, of faith in the *unchangeableness of the Laws of Nature.* The Miraculous dares no more show its face on the stage, or if it does, it is promptly hissed off.

To put it better still, the fantastic miracles of casual caprice have had their day, and the great, universal, the standing Miracle of Nature appears instead, the more divine from the very fact of its definite subjection to law and order.

It marks the final victory of a general Revolt. So much may be seen in the bold forms assumed by these earliest protests, in the irony of Galileo, in the absolute scepticism from which Descartes starts to build up his system. The Middle Ages would have said, "It is the Spirit of the Wily One, the Foul Fiend."

No mere negative victory, however, but positive and firmly based.

The Spirit of Nature and the Sciences of Nature, those proscribed outlaws of an earlier day,—there is no resisting their restoration to power. It is Reality and hard fact chasing away the empty shadows of mediæval darkness.

Foolishly men had said, "Great Pan is dead." Then presently, seeing he was alive still, they had made him into a god of evil; and in the gloom and chaos of those days the mistake was possible enough. But lo! he is alive now, and with a life in harmony and sweet accord with the sublime and immutable laws that guide the stars of heaven, and no less surely govern the deep mystery of human life.

Two things may be predicated of this epoch, apparently, yet not really, contradictory: the spirit of Satan has prevailed, but Witchcraft is doomed.

Magic of every kind, whether diabolic or divine, is sick unto death. Sorcerers and Theologians, both are equally impotent. They are reduced to the condition of empirics, vainly imploring of some supernatural accident or the caprice of a Gracious Providence, those marvels that Science asks only from Nature, from Reason.

The Jansenists, with all their ardent zeal, obtain in a whole century but one insignificant, rather ludicrous, miracle. More unfortunate still, the Jesuits, rich and powerful as they are, cannot, at any price, get even one, but must rest content with the visions of a hysterical girl, Sister Marie Alacoque, a being of a quite abnormally sanguine idiosyncrasy. In face of such a show of impotence, Magic and Sorcery may well take heart of grace for their own failures.

Observe how in this decay of faith in the Supernatural, infidelity of one kind ensues upon infidelity of the other. The two were bound together in the thoughts and fears of the Middle Ages. They continued closely bound together in ridicule and contempt. When Molière made fun of the Devil and his "boiling cauldrons," the Clergy were sorely disturbed: they felt instinctively that faith in Paradise was being depreciated to a corresponding degree.

A purely lay Government, that of the great Colbert (who for a long period was king in all but name) takes no pains to conceal its contempt for these outworn questions. It purges the gaols of the Sorcerers the Parlement of Rouen still went on accumulating within their walls; eventually *forbids the Courts to take cognisance of charges of Witchcraft at all* (1672). The said Parlement protests, and protests with great plainness of speaking, that a repudiation of Sorcery implies risk to a great many other things as well. Who throws doubt on the nether mysteries, shakes belief in many a soul in the mysteries of heaven.

The Witches' Sabbath disappears; and why? The reason is, it is *everywhere* henceforth; it is a part of men's ordinary habits; its practices are those of everyday life.

It was said of the "Sabbath," "No woman ever returned from it in child." The Devil and the Witch-wife were reproached with being sworn foes of generation, of hating life and loving death and annihilation. And lo! it is precisely in the sanctimonious seventeenth century, when Witchcraft is a-dying,[1] that love of barrenness and fear of giving birth form the most general of diseases.

If Satan is a reading man, he has good cause to laugh when he peruses the Casuists, his successors and continuators. Yet a difference there is between them. Satan in dread days of old was careful for the hungry, and pitiful for the poor. But these others have pity only for the rich man. Crœsus with his vices and luxury and life at Kings' Courts, is needy, grievously poor, a beggar. He comes in Confession, humble, yet menacing, to

---

[1] I do not regard La Voisin as a Sorceress, nor as a true Witches' Sabbath the travesty she performed to amuse *blasé* noblemen of high rank, Luxembourg and Vendôme, her pupil, and the like. Reprobate priests, allies of La Voisin's, would say the Black Mass secretly for their benefit, undoubtedly with even more obscene details than it had ever included in old days when celebrated before a multitude. In some wretched female victim, a living altar, Nature was pilloried. A woman given up to vile mockery! what an abomination! . . . a sport far less of men than of her sister women's cruelty,—of a Bouillon, brazen, abandoned creature, or of the dark Olympe, deep-dyed in crime and learned in poisons (1681).

extract from the learned Father a licence to sin, within the bounds of conscience. Some day will be written (if anyone has the courage to write it) the surprising history of the cowardly expedients of the Casuist eager not to lose his penitent and the disgraceful subterfuges he is ready to resort to. From Navarro to Eseobar, a strange bargaining goes on at the expense of the wife, and some points are still left open to dispute. But this is not enough; the Casuist is fairly beaten, and gives up everything. From Zoccoli to Liguori (1670–1770), the defence of Nature is abandoned altogether.

The Devil had, as everyone knows, when attending the Witches' Sabbath, two faces, one above, gloomy and terrible, the other behind, ludicrous and grotesque. Nowadays, having no more use for it, he will of his generosity give the latter to the Casuist.

What must vastly divert Satan is the fact that his most faithful followers are to be found in those days among respectable folks, in serious households, ruled and governed by the Church.[2] The woman of the world, who raises the fortunes of her house by means of the great resource of the period, profitable adultery, laughs at prudence and boldly follows the promptings of nature. The pious family follows merely its Jesuit Confessor. To preserve and concentrate the family fortune, to leave a rich heir, the crooked ways of the new spirituality are entered upon. In shadow and secret, the proudest wife, at her *prie-Dieu,* ignores her self-respect, forgets her true nature, and

---

[2] Voluntary sterility is continually on the increase in the seventeenth century, especially among the more carefully regulated families, subjected to the strictest discipline of the Confessional. Take even the Jansenists. Follow the history of the Arnaulds, and see the steady ratio of decrease among them,—to begin with, twenty children, fifteen children; then five! and eventually not one. Can it be this energetic race (their blood mingled moreover with the gallant Colberts) finishes in enervation? Not so. The fact is it has little by little limited its output, so to speak, in order to make a rich eldest son, a great Lord and King's Minister. The end is gained, and the race dies of its ambitious carefulness, undoubtedly duly planned and purposed.

follows the precept of Molinos: "We are set here below to suffer! One thing only, a pious indifference, at long last, softens and lulls our pain,—and wins us respite. What is this respite? It is not Death. We feel to some extent what goes on beside us; without joining in it, or responding to its stimulus, we yet hear an echo of its movement, vague and gentle. 'Tis a sort of happy accident of Grace, which soothes and thrills us, never more so than in those abasements where free will is all eclipsed."

What refinement, what depth is here. . . . Poor Satan! how are you outdone! Bow down, and admire, and own the sons of your own engendering.

The doctors, who are in an even more true sense his lawful sons, who sprung from the popular empiricism known as Witchcraft, these his chosen heirs, to whom he left his noblest patrimony, are far too ready to forget the fact. They are basely ungrateful to the Witches who paved their way for them.

They do more. On this fallen monarch, their father and the author of their being, they inflict some sore lashes. . . . *Tu quoque, file mi!* (You too, my son!) . . . They supply the mockers with some cruel weapons to use against him.

Already the physicians of the sixteenth century derided the Spirit, which in all ages, from Sibyls to Witches, tormented women and harassed them with windy troubles. They maintained this is neither Devil nor God, but even as the Middle Ages said, "the Prince of the Air." Satan, it would seem from them, is simply a form of disease!

Satanic *possession,* they declared, was simply a result of the close, sedentary life, dull and yet harassing and exasperating, of the cloister. The 6,500 devils that dwelt in Gauffridi's Madeleine, the legions of demons that fought and struggled in the bodies of the tormented nuns of Loudun and of Louviers,— these doctors call them physical disturbances and nothing more. "If Æolus makes the earth shake," Yvelin asks, "why not a

girl's body?" The surgeon who attended La Cadière (the subject
of our next chapter) says drily, "Nothing else in the world but a
choking of the womb."

What a strange come-down! The terror of the Middle Ages
put to rout by the simplest of remedies, exorcisms *à la Molière,*
in fact, flying helter-skelter, to be seen no more!

Nay! this is assuming too much. The question is not so
simple as all that. Satan has other aspects besides, of which the
doctors see neither the highest nor the lowest,—neither his
grand revolt in Science, or those extraordinary combinations of
pious intrigue and stark impurity he contrives towards 1700,
uniting in one conglomerate Priapus and Tartuffe.

Historians suppose themselves to know the eighteenth century, and yet they have never observed one of its most essential
characteristics.

The more its surface, its higher levels, were civilised, illumi-
nated, saturated with light, the more hermetically sealed and
closed was the vast underlying region of the ecclesiastical world,
of the convent, of credulous womanfolk, morbidly ready to
believe anything and everything. In anticipation of Cagliostro,
Mesmer and the magnetisers who will come with the later
years of the century, not a few priests make a profit out of the
Sorcery of a departed age. All their talk is of bewitchments, the
dread of which they spread broadcast, and undertake to drive
out devils by means of various indecent exorcisms. Many play
the wizard, well assured the risk is small and burnings henceforth an impossibility. They know themselves sufficiently safe-
guarded by the civilisation of the times, the toleration preached
by their enemies the Philosophers, and the light indifferentism
of the scoffers, who think the last word has been said, when they
have raised a laugh. But it is just this laughing attitude which
enables such-like dark schemers to go on their way unafraid.
The new spirit is that of the Regent, sceptical and good-
naturedly tolerant. It is conspicuous in the *Lettres Persanes,*

and saturates through and through that all-powerful journalist who fills the century, Voltaire. Once let human blood flow, and his whole heart revolts; at all else he laughs. Little by little the guiding principle of the world at large apparently comes to be, "Punish nothing, and make fun of everything."

The spirit of toleration is such as to suffer Cardinal Tencin to live openly as his own sister's husband; such as to ensure the ruling spirits of the convents in peaceful, undisturbed possession of the nuns in their charge, so completely so indeed that cases of pregnancy amongst the latter were regularly announced, and births formally and legally declared.[3] The same spirit of tolerance excuses Father Apollinaire, caught in a vile and shameful act of exorcism,[4] while Cauvrigny, the *gallant* Jesuit, idol of the provincial nunneries, expiates his intrigues merely by a recall to Paris, in other words by a summons to higher preferment.

Similar was the punishment accorded the notorious Jesuit, Father Girard; he deserved hanging, but was loaded with honours instead, and died in the odour of sanctity. Indeed this is one of the most curious occurrences of the century, marking exactly the characteristic methods of the period, the rough-and-ready combination of the most contradictory modes of procedure. The perilous suavities of the *Song of Songs* formed, as usual, the preface, followed up by Marie Alacoque and her ecstasies, by the wedlock of Bleeding Hearts, seasoned with

---

[3] For instance, the most noble Chapter of the Canons of Pignan, who had the honour to be represented in the "Estates" of Provence, were equally proud of their recognised right to possess the nuns of that country. There were sixteen canons; and the Provost's offices received in a single year from the nuns sixteen declarations of pregnancy (*Histoire manuscrite de Besse,* by M. Renoux). This publicity had at any rate this advantage, that the especial crime of Religious Houses, to wit infanticide, was bound to be less common. The nuns, quietly submitting to what they held to be a necessary accident of their profession, at the cost of a trifle of shame, were humane and good mothers. At any rate they did not kill their children. The nuns of Pignan put theirs out to nurse with the peasants, who were ready to adopt them, make what use they could of them and bring them up with their own family. Thus it comes that not a few farmer folk thereabouts are known down to the present day as descendants of the ecclesiastical nobility of Provence.

[4] Garinet, p. 344.

the morbid, unctuous phrases of Molinos. Girard supplemented all this with the diabolic element and the terrors of bewitchment. He was the Devil, and the Exorcist to boot. The dreadful conclusion of the whole affair was that the unhappy woman he so barbarously immolated, far from obtaining justice, was harried to her death. Eventually she disappeared, probably imprisoned under a *lettre de cachet,* and cast for the rest of her days into a living tomb.

22

FATHER GIRARD
and CHARLOTTE CADIÈRE

THE Jesuits were much to be pitied. So favourably regarded at Versailles, "masters of all they surveyed" at Court, they had not the smallest prestige in the eyes of Heaven, not the most insignificant miracle to show. The Jansenists enjoyed an abundance at any rate of moving legends. Unnumbered crowds of sick folk, of the afflicted, the lame, the paralytic, found at the tomb of the Deacon Pâris a moment's healing and relief. The unhappy French people, bowed down under an appalling succession of scourges,—the Grand Monarque, in the first place, then the Regency and Law's wondrous system, which between them reduced such multitudes to beggary,—this unhappy people came to implore salvation of a poor man of righteousness, virtuous if weak-witted, a saint in spite of his many ridiculous attributes. And when all is said and done, why jeer? His life is indeed far more touching than ludicrous. No need for wonder if these good folks were moved to awe and veneration at their benefactor's tomb, and straight forgot their ills. True the cure was hardly ever permanent; still, what matter? The miracle had actually occurred, the miracle of genuine devotion, and loving faith, and heartfelt gratitude. Later on, an alloy of charlatanry was infused in it all; but at that time (in 1728) these extraordinary scenes of popular enthusiasm were still perfectly sincere.

The Jesuits would have given their ears to own the smallest of these miracles which they refused to credit. For more than half a century they had been at work decking with fables and pretty tales their legend of the Sacred Heart, the story of Marie Alacoque. For five-and-twenty or thirty years they had been striving to persuade the world that their ally, James II., not content with curing the King's evil (in his quality as King of France, which he never was), amused himself after his death in making the dumb to speak, the halt to run, the squint-eyed to see straight. Unfortunately, after cure, their outlook was more oblique than ever; and as for the dumb, it was discovered, alas! that the individual who played this part was a known and proved impostor, a woman who had been caught red-handed in cheatery. Her habit was to travel the countryside, and at every chapelry renowned for the holiness of its patron saint, to be miraculously healed and receive the alms of the edified worshippers,—going through the same performance at each successive shrine.

For miracle-working, give us the South for choice,—a land abounding in superstitious women, quickly stirred to nervous excitement, good subjects for somnambulism, miraculous manifestations, the holy stigmata, and the like.

The Jesuits had at Marseilles a Bishop of their own kidney, Belzunce, a man of good heart and courage, famous ever since the date of the Great Plague, but credulous and extremely narrow-minded, under shelter of whose authority much might be attempted that would otherwise have been over-risky. As his right-hand man they had established a certain Jesuit from Franche-Comté, a man of keen intelligence and no little ability, who for all his austerity of external demeanour was yet an agreeable preacher in the florid, somewhat worldly style ladies admire. A true Jesuit, competent to win success in either of two ways, whether by feminine intrigue or by the most straight-laced piety, Father Girard had otherwise neither youth nor good looks to recommend him. He was a man of forty-seven, tall, dry-as-dust, tired-looking; he was rather deaf, had a squalid look about him, and was for ever spitting (pp. 50, 69, 254).[1] He had been a teacher up to the age of thirty-seven, and still retained some of the tastes he had learned among schoolboys. For the last ten years—since the Great Plague, that is to say—he had been a confessor in nunneries. He had been highly successful, and had acquired a large measure of ascendency over his penitents by imposing on them the very regimen that seemed *primâ facie* most diametrically opposed to the temperament of these Provençal nuns, viz. the doctrine and discipline of mystic self-annihilation, passive obedience, and the absolute and utter abnegation of self. The fearful incidents of the Plague had broken their spirit, enervated their heart, and affected them with a sort of morbid languor. The Carmelites of Marseilles, under the direction of Girard, carried this species of mysticism to great lengths,—at their head a certain Sister Rémusat, who was reputed a veritable saint.

The Jesuits, in spite of all this success, or perhaps just because of it, removed Girard from Marseilles. They were anxious to employ him in the task of raising the status of their House at Toulon, which sorely needed it. Colbert's magnificent Foundation, *The Seminary of Naval Almoners*, had been entrusted to the Jesuits to gradually wean the young priests attached to it from the mischievous ascendency of the Lazarist Fathers, to whose spiritual superintendence they were in almost every instance subject. But the two Jesuits appointed were far from competent for the task. One was a fool, the other one (Father Sabatier) a man of a singularly violent temper, notwithstanding his years. He had all the blunt insolence of the old type of naval martinet, and scorned any sort of moderation. He was blamed by people at Toulon, not for keeping a mistress or even going with a married woman, but with doing so openly, insolently,

---

[1] Dealing with a matter which has been the subject of so much controversy, I shall quote freely,—especially from a folio volume entitled, *Procédure du P. Girard et de la Cadière*, Aix, 1733. To avoid a multiplicity of footnotes, I merely give in my text the page of the book in question.

and outrageously, in such sort as to drive the injured husband to despair. His chief wish was that the latter should before all things realise his shame and feel all the pangs of marital jealousy. Eventually things were pushed so far that the poor man died of chagrin.[2]

However, the rivals of the Jesuits afforded even greater cause for scandal. The Observantine Fathers, who acted as spiritual directors to the nuns of Saint Claire of Ollionles, lived in open concubinage with their penitents; nay! they were not satisfied with this iniquity, but even failed to respect the little girls who were pupils at the nunnery. The Father Superintendent, one Aubany, had violated one, a child of thirteen, afterwards flying to Marseilles to escape the vengeance of her relatives.

Girard, now nominated director of the *Seminary* of Toulon, was destined, by his apparent austerity of character and his very real dexterity of management, soon to regain ascendency for the Jesuits over a body of monks so deeply compromised and of parish priests of small education and of a very common stamp.

In this land where men are rough and hasty, often harsh in speech and rugged in appearance, women appreciate highly the gentle gravity of men of the North, liking and admiring them for speaking the aristocratic, the official language, French.[3]

Girard on his arrival at Toulon must have known the ground thoroughly well already. He already possessed a devoted ally there, a certain Madame Guiol, daughter of a cabinet-maker in a small way of business; she was in the habit of paying occasional visits to Marseilles, where she had a daughter in a Carmelite convent. This woman put herself absolutely at his disposal, as much as and more than he wished; she was well on in years (forty-seven), extremely hot-spirited, utterly corrupt

---

[2] Bibliothèque de la ville de Toulon, *Pièces et Chansons manuscrites,* 1 vol. folio,—an extremely curious collection.

[3] That is the tongue of Northern and Central France, descended from the old Langue d'Oïl, as contrasted with the Langue d'Oc, still spoken in the South. The latter is often called a *patois,* but it is really a distinct language.

and unscrupulous, ready to serve him in any capacity, whatever he did or whatever he was, be he saint or sinner.

Besides her daughter in the Carmelite convent at Marseilles, she had another who was a lay sister with the Ursulines of Toulon. The Ursulines, a society of teaching nuns, constituted in all localities a nucleus of social intercourse; their parlour, which was frequented by their pupils' mothers, formed a halfway house between the cloister and the world outside. Here by the Sisters' complacence, no doubt, Father Girard came in contact with the ladies of the town, amongst the rest with a lady of forty, and unmarried, a certain Mlle. Gravier, daughter of a former Contractor of Government Works in the Royal Arsenal. This lady had a friend and familiar, a sort of shadow accompanying her wherever she went, Mlle. Reboul, her cousin, daughter of a ship's captain, who was her heir and who, though of pretty near the same age (thirty-five), quite expected to succeed to her property. Round these two grew up by degrees a little coterie of Father Girard's female admirers, who chose him as their Confessor. Young girls were sometimes admitted, for instance, Mlle. Cadière, a tradesman's daughter, Mlle. Laugier, a sempstress, Mlle. Batarelle, daughter of a waterman of the port. Books of devotion were perused, and occasionally little suppers indulged in. But nothing interested them so strongly as a series of letters in which were recounted the miracles and ecstasies of Sister Rémusat, who was still living at the time. (She died in February, 1730.) What a crown of glory for good Father Girard, who had led her so near to Heaven! The letters were read and admired with tears and exclamations of delighted wonder. If not literally ecstatic as yet, these women were surely not far from the confines of ecstasy. And indeed, Mlle. Reboul, in order to gratify her kinswoman, was already in the habit occasionally of producing strange phenomena in herself by the familiar device of quietly holding her breath and pinching her nose with her fingers.[4]

---

[4] See the *Trial;* also Swift, *Mechanical Operations of the Spirit.*

Of this band of women, old and young, the most serious-minded was undoubtedly Mlle. Catherine Cadière, a delicate, invalidish young girl of seventeen, entirely devoted to piety and works of charity, and showing a sad, thin face, which seemed to declare that young as she was she had felt more deeply than any the great misfortunes of the time, the calamities of Provence and her native Toulon. This is easily accounted for. She was born during the terrible famine of 1709, while just at the epoch when a girl is growing into a woman, she witnessed the appalling scenes of the Great Plague. These two sinister events, quite beyond the range of ordinary experience, seemed to have left a permanent mark on her personality.

This melancholy blossom was a pure product of Toulon, of the Toulon of that date. To understand its genesis, it is indispensable to recall what this town is now, and was then.

Toulon is a thoroughfare, a place of embarkation, the gateway of a vast harbour and a gigantic naval arsenal. This is what first strikes a traveller's eye and prevents him seeing Toulon itself. Still there is a town there, a city of venerable antiquity. It contains two distinct populations, officials and functionaries from other parts, and the genuine Toulonnais, the latter not over well-disposed towards the former, envious of the government employé and not unfrequently disgusted at the arrogance of naval men,—all this concentrated within the gloomy streets of a place still shut in and half strangled by the narrow girdle of its fortifications. The most striking feature of the little black-browed town is its situation midway between two great oceans of brilliancy, the wondrous mirror of the roadstead and the majestic amphitheatre of its bare mountains of a dazzling grey that well-nigh blinds your eyes at midday. All the more gloomy seem the streets. Except such as run directly to the harbour and derive some light from its expanse, these are in deep shadow all day long. Grimy alleyways of small hucksters' shops, poorly set out, and the goods all but invisible to anyone coming from the glare of daylight,—such is the general aspect. The centre of the town is a labyrinth of intricate lanes, hiding a number of churches and old monastic buildings, now turned into barracks. Turbulent brooks, heavy and foul with household refuse, rush fiercely down the middle of the narrow ways. The air is stagnant, and you are surprised, in so dry a climate, to find so much damp everywhere. In front of the new theatre an alley known as the *Rue de l'Hôpital* connects the Rue Royale, itself a narrow thoroughfare, with the still narrower Rue des Canonniers (St. Sebastian), seeming at the first glance to be a *cul-de-sac*. Still the sun does cast one look into it at high noon, but finds the spot so dismal he instantly passes overhead and restores the lane to the shadowy dimness proper to it.

Among its black-browed houses the smallest was that inhabited by the Sieur Cadière, huckster and second-hand dealer. The only entrance was through the shop, and there was one room on each floor. The Cadières were honest, pious folks, and Madame Cadière a very mirror of perfection. Nor were these good people in absolute poverty; not only was the little house their own property, but like most of the *bourgeois* of Toulon city, they possessed a *bastide*. This generally includes a building of sorts and a small rocky messuage producing a trifle of wine. In the great days of the French navy, under Colbert and his son, the prodigious activity of the port was highly profitable to the town. The wealth of France poured thither in a constant stream. All the great lords who passed that way were accompanied by their household and domestic servants, a wasteful crew that left many fine pickings behind. But all this came to an abrupt conclusion, and an activity artificially fostered came to a dead stop. There was not money enough even to pay the Arsenal artificers' wages, while the ships of war under repair were left indefinitely on the stocks, and the hulls eventually sold for what they would fetch.[5] Toulon suffered severely under the effects of all this. During the siege of 1707 the place seemed only half alive. But how much worse the dreadful year of 1709, the '93 of Louis

---

[5] See an excellent MS. dissertation by M. Brun.

XIV., when all calamities, a cruel winter, plague and famine, were concentrated simultaneously on the ruin of fair France! The trees of Provence themselves were not spared. Intercommunication ceased entirely, and the roads swarmed with starving mendicants! Toulon shuddered, ringed round with robbers who intercepted all traffic.

To cap all, Madame Cadière found herself pregnant in this terrible year. She had three boys already. Of these the eldest remained at home to help his father in the shop. The second was a pupil at the Preachers' College, being intended for a Dominican monk, or Jacobin, as the name was. The third was studying for the priesthood at the Jesuit Seminary. Husband and wife both desired a girl, while the latter prayed God she might turn out a saint. She spent her nine months in constant prayer, fasting or else eating nothing but rye bread. Eventually she bore a daughter, Catherine, who was an extremely delicate and, like her brothers, a rather unhealthy child. No doubt the damp, ill-ventilated house, as well as the insufficient diet of a saving and more than abstemious mother, had something to say to this. Her brothers suffered from glandular swellings, which sometimes broke out into open sores, and little Catherine had the same in her childish days. Without being exactly ill, she showed the invalidish prettiness common with sickly children. She grew tall without growing strong. At an age when other girls feel their strength and activity overflowing, and experience all the exhilaration of youth, she was already declaring, "I have not long to live."

She had the small-pox, which left her somewhat marked. We do not know if she was pretty, but it is very certain she was dainty and charming, possessing all the engaging contrasts of young Provençal maidens and their twofold nature. At once vivacious and dreamy, gay and melancholy, a well-conducted, pious child, with harmless interludes of frivolity. At intervals between the long church services, if she was taken to visit the *bastide* with other girls of her own age, she raised no difficulties about doing as they did, singing, dancing, or touching the tambourine. But such days were rare. More often her great pleasure was to climb to the very top of the house (p. 24), to get nearer the sky and catch a glimpse of daylight, perhaps to see a little bit of sea, or a pointed summit of the great waste of surrounding mountains. These were solemn then as now, but at that date somewhat less forbidding in aspect, less bare and denuded of trees, sparsely clothed in the refreshing green of arbute trees and larches.

This dead city, at the time of the Plague, numbered 26,000 inhabitants, an enormous mass of humanity to be crowded into so minute a space. Besides, from this space must be subtracted the ground occupied by a ring of great monasteries and convents built up against the town walls, Minims, Oratorians, Jesuits, Capuchins, Recollets, Ursuline Sisters, Visitandines, Bernardines, Refuge, Good Shepherd, and right in the centre of the town the enormous House of the Dominicans. Add in the parish churches, presbyteries, episcopal palace, etc., and it will be evident the clergy filled all the room, while the people had next to nothing.

Easy to see how fiercely the disease, concentrated in so small a focus, must have burned. Moreover, its own good nature was fatal to the town, which magnanimously took in refugees from the stricken city of Marseilles. These were just as likely to bring the Plague with them as certain bales of wool which were held responsible for the introduction of the contagion. The notables were panic-stricken and on the point of flight; they were for scattering over the country, when the chief of the Consuls, M. d'Antrechaus, a brave-hearted hero, stopped them, sternly asking, "And the people, gentlemen, what is to become of them, if, in this poverty-stricken town, the rich desert the place and take their purses with them?" [6] He succeeded in staying the panic and forced everybody to remain. The horrors of Mar-

---

[6] See M. d'Antrechaus' book, and the excellent little pamphlet by M. Gustave Lambert.

seilles were attributed to the free communication permitted between the inhabitants; so D'Antrechaus tried an exactly opposite system, viz. to isolate the citizens, to shut each household up in its own domicile. At the same time two enormous hospitals were established, one in the roadstead, one on the mountainside. Whoever did not go to one or the other of these was bound to remain within doors under penalty of death. D'Antrechaus for seven long months kept his stupendous wager, performing the seemingly impossible task of keeping and feeding in their own houses a population of 26,000 souls. For all this time Toulon was a sepulchre, nothing stirring all day long after the morning distribution of bread and the removal of the dead that followed it. The doctors most of them perished, and all the magistrates except D'Antrechaus. The gravediggers died to a man, and were replaced by deserters under sentence of death. These wretches displayed a savage haste and brutality; the bodies of the dead were thrown from the fourth story, head downwards, into the carts. A mother had just lost her daughter, a little girl. Horrified at the thought of seeing the poor little corpse treated in this violent fashion, she gave the men money to carry it decently downstairs. On the way the child came to itself and opened its eyes. She was taken upstairs again, and recovering completely, actually became the grandmother of the learned M. Brun, already referred to as the author of the admirable History of the Port of Toulon.

The poor little Cadière girl was then precisely the same age as this rescued victim of the Plague, viz. twelve, an age abounding with so many perils for her sex. The universal closing of the churches, the suppression of all Feasts and Holy Days (Christmas above all, so merry a time at Toulon), all this was for the child the end of the world. She seems never to have really recovered the shock, and the same is true of the town. It never lost its deserted look; all was ruin and mourning, a city of widows and orphans and crowds of desperate men. In the midst of all, a grand, a gloomy spectre, D'Antrechaus, who had witnessed the death of all he cared for, sons, brothers, and fellow-magistrates, and who had nobly ruined himself,—so much so that he had to live at his neighbours' tables, the poor disputing among themselves the honour of feeding him.

The child informed her mother she would never wear the fine clothes she had again, and they were sold. All she cared for now was to tend the sick, and she was for ever enticing her mother to the Hospital situated at the bottom of their street. A neighbour, a little girl of fourteen, Laugier by name, had lost her father, and was living in great poverty with her widowed mother. Catherine went to see her constantly, taking her her food and clothes and everything she could. She asked her parents to pay the expenses of apprenticing Laugier to a sempstress, and such was her ascendency over their minds they did not refuse this heavy outlay. Her piety, her loving little heart, made her all-powerful. Her charity was a passion; she not only gave money, but affection as well. She would fain have made Laugier as perfect a character as herself, and took delight in having her near her, and often sharing her bed with her. Both had been received among the *Daughters of St. Theresa,* a tertiary order which the Carmelites had organised. Mlle. Cadière was the shining light of the affiliation, and at thirteen seemed a fully trained Carmelite Sister. She had borrowed from a Visitandine certain books of mysticism which she devoured eagerly. The girl Laugier, at fifteen, offered a marked contrast, showing no predilection for anything but eating, and looking pretty. She *was* this, and for this reason had been made sacristaness of the Chapel of St. Theresa,—an appointment which gave great opportunities for familiarities with the priests. So much so that when her behaviour earned her a well-deserved threat of expulsion from the congregation, a higher authority, a Vicar-General, was so indignant as to declare that, if this were done, he would lay an interdict on the chapel (pp. 36, 37).

Both the girls shared the temperament of their native Provence, one of excessive nervous excitability, and from very early years had been subject to what were locally styled *vapours of the womb*. But the effects were quite different in each,—to the last degree carnal in Laugier, a greedy, indolent, violent-tempered creature, purely cerebral in the case of the pure, gentle-minded Catherine, who as the result of her ill-health or her vivid imagination absorbing her whole nature, had no conception of sex whatever. "At twenty, she was like a child of seven." All her thoughts turned to prayer and almsgiving, and she refused to entertain the idea of marriage. The mere word set her weeping, as if she had been asked to desert God.

Someone had lent her the Life of her Patron Saint, St. Catherine of Genoa, and she had bought a copy of the *Château de l'Ame* (Fortress of the Soul) of St. Theresa. Few Confessors cared to follow her in this excursion into mysticism, and those who talked ineptly of these holy things offended her. She could find satisfaction neither in her mother's Confessor, a priest attached to the cathedral, nor in a Carmelite Father, nor yet in the old Jesuit Sabatier. At sixteen she had as her Director a priest of St. Louis, a man of high-strung piety. She spent whole days in church, till her mother, by this time a widow and who required her help, pious woman as he was herself, used to punish her when she came home at last. But it was no fault of hers; she forgot everything in her ecstatic trances. The girls of her own age looked upon her as so saintly a being that sometimes at Mass they believed they saw the Holy Wafer, drawn by the attraction of her love and longing exercised, fly to her and enter in between her lips of its own accord.

Her two younger brothers entertained widely divergent sentiments towards Girard. The elder of the two, the one at the Preachers' College, felt for the Jesuit the antipathy characteristic of the Dominican Order. The other, who was studying for the priesthood with the Jesuits, regarded Girard as a saint and a great man, and had made him his peculiar hero. Catherine loved her youngest brother, who was a weakling in health like herself. His never-ending praises of Girard were bound to take

effect. One day she encountered him in the street, and seeing him
so grave and serious and yet so kind and benignant-looking, an
inner voice cried within her, *Ecce homo* (behold the man, pre-
destined to direct your conscience). The following Saturday
she went to confess to him; "and he told me, 'Mademoiselle,
I have been expecting you.'" She was filled with wonder and
emotion, never dreaming her brother might have warned him,
but thinking the mysterious voice had spoken to him as well,
and that both shared this celestial boon of heavenly admoni-
tions (pp. 81, 383).

Six summer months rolled by without Girard, who confessed
her every Saturday, having made any advances. The scandal
attaching to the old Jesuit Sabatier was sufficiently deterrent.
It would have been his more prudent course to be content with
the more obscure attachment, and stick to the Guiol woman,
a very mature charmer it is true, but a very devil incarnate for
ardour and enterprise.

It was Charlotte herself who, in all innocence, made the first
advances toward her Father Confessor. Her brother, the hot-
headed Jacobin, had thought good to lend to a lady of his
acquaintance, and circulate through the town, a satiric piece
entitled, *La Morale des Jésuites* (Morals of the Jesuits). The
latter soon got wind of it, and Sabatier swore he would write to
Court to demand a *lettre de cachet* to clap the obnoxious Jacobin
in prison. His sister is anxious and alarmed, and goes with tears
in her eyes to beg and implore Father Girard's intervention. On
her coming to him again after a short interval, he tells her,
"Courage, mademoiselle; your brother has nothing to fear; I
have arranged the matter." She was melted by his kindness, and
Girard was not slow to perceive his advantage. A man of such
influence, the King's friend, and God's favoured instrument, and
who had shown himself so good and kind! What more moving
for a young and generous heart? He took his courage in both
hands, and said (but still in his usual equivocal phraseology),
"Put yourself in my hands; give yourself up wholly and entirely

to me." Without a blush, in her angelic purity of mind, she promised "I will," understanding merely that she was to have him henceforth for sole and only director of her conscience.

What did he propose to do with the girl? Would he make her his mistress, or his tool for charlatanry? Doubtless Girard was drawn both ways, but I believe his inclination was to adopt the second alternative. He had a wide choice, and could find sensual gratification elsewhere without the same risk. Mlle. Cadière was protected by a God-fearing mother; she lived with her relations, a married brother and the two Churchmen, in a house of the most confined dimensions, the only means of entering which was through the elder brother's shop. She scarcely ever went abroad except to church. Great as was her simplicity, she divined by a sort of instinct anything that was impure and houses of a dangerous character. A band of women, penitents of the Jesuit Fathers, were fond of meeting at the top of a certain house, where they indulged in little gormandisings and foolishness of other sorts, shouting in their Provençal dialect, "Long live the Jesuiticals!" A neighbour, disturbed by the noise, came on the scene and surprised them lying flat on their bellies (p. 56), singing and eating fritters,—the expenses, it was said, being all defrayed from the alms-box. Mlle. Cadière was invited to join this coterie, but was disgusted by what she saw, and never came again.

She was only open to attack on the spiritual side, and Girard's designs seemed limited to getting the mastery of her soul. To win her subjection, to make her accept the doctrines of passive obedience he had taught at Marseilles, such apparently was all he wanted. He thought example would be more efficacious than precept, and instructed the woman Guiol, his familiar spirit and abject servant, to carry the young saint to that town, where Mlle. Cadière had a friend of her girlhood, a Carmelite nun, daughter of Madame Guiol. The astute schemer pretended, by way of inspiring her companion with confidence, that she too experienced ecstatic stirrings of spirit, and fed her with a string of ridiculous tales. She told her, for instance, how on one occasion finding a cask of wine turned sour in her cellar, she fell to her prayers, and instantly the wine grew good again. Another time she felt a crown of thorns wounding her brow, but to comfort her the angels had served up a good dinner, which she enjoyed along with Father Girard.

Charlotte secured her mother's permission to visit Marseilles with her good friend, the excellent Madame Guiol, Madame Cadière paying expenses. It was in the hottest month of that blazing climate, in August (1729), a season when the whole countryside is burnt up, and offers a landscape of bare rocks and gravel reflecting the fierce sunlight. The poor girl's brain, parched by the heat and weakened by the fatigues of travelling, received only too readily the sinister impressions of conventual mortification. The most striking type of this was afforded by the afore-mentioned Sister Rémusat, little better than a corpse already, and who actually died shortly afterwards. Charlotte was lost in admiration of such high perfections, while her artful companion plied her with the alluring suggestion of following in her steps and succeeding to her prestige.

During her temporary absence, Girard, left behind in the hot, stifling oven of Toulon, had lamentably deteriorated. He was constantly visiting the little Laugier girl, who also thought she had ecstasies, to *comfort* her,—which he did so effectually that all of a sudden she found herself enciente! When finally Mlle. Cadière came back to him all spirituality and mystic ecstasy, Girard, whose feelings were widely different, entirely carnal in fact and pleasure-seeking, "cast over her a breath of desire" (pp. 6, 383). She was kindled by it, but (it is evident) in her own peculiar fashion, in a spirit of purity, holiness, and generosity, anxious to spare him from a fall, devoting herself to save him to the point of being ready to die for him (September, 1729).

One of the privileges attaching to her sanctity was a gift of seeing to the bottom of men's hearts. It had several times been her lot to discover the secret life and private morality of her confessors, and warn them of their faults,—rebukes which some of them, astounded and disconcerted, had taken in a contrite spirit. One day during this summer, seeing Madame Guiol on her way home, she suddenly accosted her with the words, "Ah! bad woman, what have you been doing?" "And she was quite right," Guiol admitted subsequently herself. "I *had* just been doing a sinful act." What was this act? Probably the betrayal of Laugier to Father Girard's passion. We are strongly tempted to think so, seeing how ready she was next year to do the same with the girl Batarelle.

Laugier, who often shared Charlotte Cadière's bed, may very likely have made her the confidante of her happiness and described the holy man's love-making and fatherly caresses,— surely a harsh trial for the good child and a cause of much searching of heart. True she was thoroughly well acquainted with Girard's great axiom, That with holy men every act is holy. But on the other hand her innate sense of right and wrong and all her previous upbringing compelled her to believe that an inordinate complacency towards any created being was a mortal sin. This agonising perplexity between two contradictory doctrines was too much for the poor girl; she suffered fearful storms of doubt, and firmly believed herself *possessed* of the Devil.

Here again she showed the goodness of her heart. Without humiliating Girard, she told him she had the vision of a soul tormented by the lusts of the flesh and in peril of mortal sin, that she felt in her an imperative need to save this soul, to offer the Evil One victim for victim, to acquiesce in diabolic *possession* and sacrifice herself in lieu of the other. He raised no objection, but permitted her to be *possessed,* but for a year only (November, 1729).

She was aware, like everybody else in the place, of the scandalous intrigues of the old Jesuit, Father Sabatier, a reckless, insolent transgressor, without a trace of Girard's judicious prudence. She saw the contempt into which the Jesuits (whom she counted as the pillars of the Church) could not but fall. One day she said to Girard, "I have had a vision,—a storm-tost sea, a ship full of souls, beaten about by the tempest of unclean thoughts, and on the deck two Jesuit priests. I cried to the Redeemer, whom I saw in Heaven, 'Lord! save them, and drown me . . . I take all the shipwreck on myself.' And Almighty God granted my prayer."

Never once, during the course of her trial and when Girard, now her bitterest enemy, was seeking her death by every means, did she recur to these visions. Never did she condescend to expound these parables, whose meaning was so plain, her nobility of spirit shrinking from all speech of the kind. She had vowed herself, according to her own conviction, to certain damnation. Shall we say that, out of pride, deeming herself virtually dead and unaffected by carnal emotions, she defied the uncleanness the Demon was staining the man of God with. One fact is beyond doubt, she had no precise knowledge of sensual concerns, that in all this mystery she foresaw nothing but pain and demoniac tortures. Girard was cold and cruel, utterly unworthy of such devotion. Instead of being melted, he played on her credulity by means of an ignoble trick. He slipped into the box where she kept her papers one in which God informed her that for her sake He would in very deed save the ship. But the wily priest took care not to leave this ridiculous document there; by repeated study of it she might have discovered it was a forgery. The same angel that had brought the paper carried it off again next day.

With the same want of proper feeling Girard, seeing her agitated and unable to pray, gave her unconditional leave, without a thought of possible consequences, to communicate as often as she chose, every day, in different churches. The result was to make her worse; bursting with the Demon already, she was but setting the two enemies side by side within her distracted body, where they fought an evenly matched battle. She felt as if she must die under the horrid strain; she fell in a dead faint, remaining in this condition for several hours. By December she hardly left the house at all, being indeed pretty much confined to her bed.

Girard had only too good excuses for visiting her, and he observed considerable prudence, always getting her young brother to conduct him to her room, at any rate as far as the door. The sick-room was at the top of the house, and the girl's mother always remained discreetly in the shop downstairs. He could be alone with her as much as he pleased, and if he chose might turn the key in the lock. By this time she was very ill, and he treated her like a child, leaning forward a little over the head of the bed, taking her face between his hands and kissing her as a father might,—a caress which she invariably received with respect and affectionate gratitude.

Pure as she was, she was intensely sensitive. The slightest contact, which another girl would never have noticed, produced a condition of unconsciousness,—a mere touch near the bosom was enough. Girard observed the fact, and it suggested bad thoughts. He threw her at will into this sort of sleep, without her entertaining a thought of stopping him. Her confidence was complete; her only feeling was one of reluctance and something of shame to take such freedoms with so holy a man and waste so much of his precious time. His visits grew longer and longer, and the result to be foreseen soon followed. The poor girl, ill as she was, intoxicated Girard beyond all power or self-control. Once, on awaking, she found herself in a highly ridiculous and highly indecent posture; another time she caught him caressing her person.

She blushed, groaned, remonstrated. But he told her with the utmost effrontery, "I am your master, your God. . . . You are bound to endure all things in the name of obedience." Towards Christmas, in the festal season, he laid aside his last scruples. On waking she exclaimed, "Great God! how I have suffered!" "I am sure you have, poor child!" he answered in a tone of pity.

Henceforth she complained less, but was never able to account to herself for what she felt in her sleep.[7]

Girard understood better, but not without terror, what he had done. In January or February an only too significant sign warned him she was with child. To cap his difficulties, Laugier also found herself in the same condition. The religious meetings and picnics, so to speak, above mentioned, accompanied as they were by a somewhat indiscreet indulgence in the cheap but seductive wine of the country, had been followed primarily by a state of mental excitation naturally to be expected among so inflammable a race, by a condition of contagious ecstasy. With the more cunning and experienced it was all pretence; but with Laugier, a young girl of a sanguine and headstrong temperament, the ecstasy was real. She exhibited in her little room at home veritable excesses of delirium and swooning fits, particularly when Father Girard came to see her. Her pregnancy began a little after that of Charlotte Cadière, no doubt about the time of the Twelfth Night celebrations.[8]

The danger was imminent. The girls did not live in a desert; they were not buried in a convent, where everybody was concerned to hush the matter up, but in the glaring light of an inhabited quarter,—Laugier surrounded by inquisitive friends and neighbours of her own sex, Cadière in the bosom of her own family. Her brother, the Jacobin, began to look suspiciously on the lengthy visits her confessor paid her. One day he insisted on staying by her, when Girard arrived; but the latter put him out of the room, and his mother indignantly turned her son out of the house.

Things were ripening for an explosion. No doubt but the young man, so harshly treated, driven from home, bursting with resentment, would go to complain loudly to his masters, the Preaching Fathers. The latter, quick to seize so excellent an

[7] pp. 5, 12, etc.

[8] pp. 37, 113.

opportunity, would hasten to repeat the scandal, and set to work surreptitiously to rouse the town against the Jesuit. This latter took a sudden and extraordinary resolution, to retaliate by a bold stroke and save his skin by crime. The man of pleasure was turned into a man of sin.

He knew his victim intimately. He had seen on her person the traces left by the scrofulous sores she had suffered from as a child. These do not heal cleanly like an incised wound, the skin always remains reddened at the spot, exceptionally thin and tender. Such marks she had on her feet, and another in a sensitive, dangerous place, just under the breast. He conceived the devilish idea of reopening these wounds, and giving them out as stigmata, like those of St. Francis and other saints had received from Heaven, holy men who, aspiring to *imitation* of the Crucified and complete conformity with His blessed body, came to bear the mark of the nails and of the lance-thrust in the side. Were not the Jesuits in despair at having nothing to offer in opposition to the miracles of the Jansenists? Girard felt sure of delighted acceptation of so unexpected a miracle, and he could hardly fail to be supported by the members of his own order and their house at Toulon. One, the old Sabatier, was ready to believe anything; he had already been Charlotte's confessor, and the fact had redounded to his honour. Another, Father Grignet, was a pious fool, who would see whatever he was told to. If the Carmelite Fathers thought good to entertain any doubts, why, they should have a hint from such high quarters that they would deem it prudent to keep these to themselves. Even the Jacobin Cadière, hitherto his persistent and jealous enemy, would find it best to change his attitude, and credit a circumstance that would redound so much to the glory of his family and constitute him the brother of a saint.

"But surely," it will be objected, "the thing may be explained on natural grounds. Countless examples, perfectly well authenticated, are known of genuine stigmata." [9]

---

[9] See in particular A. Maury, *Magie*.

Probability points the other way. Directly she noticed what had occurred, she was vexed and ashamed, fearing Girard would be annoyed at this revival of her childish complaint. She hurried to consult a neighbour, a Madame Truc, who dabbled in medicine, and bought of her (pretending it was for her young brother) an ointment that cauterised the wounds.

What method did the cruel priest employ to make the wounds? Did he use his nails? did he resort to a small knife he always had with him? Or else did he draw the blood to the surface in the first instance, as he undoubtedly did afterwards, by vigorous sucking? The victim was unconscious, but not insensible to pain; there cannot be a doubt she felt the pangs in her sleep.

She would have deemed it a deadly sin not to tell Girard everything, and however much afraid of displeasing and disgusting her friend, she informed him of the facts. He looked, saw, and began the comedy he had resolved to play, reproaching her for wishing to get cured and so opposing the will of God. " 'Tis the celestial stigmata," he cried, and dropping on his knees, fell to kissing the wounds on the girl's feet. For her part, she crosses herself, bows to the earth, cannot credit the thing. Girard is only the more earnest and scolds her for her incredulity; then he makes her show him her side and is lost in admiration of the wound there. "I, too, am marked," he tells her, "but my stigmata are eternal."

Thus is she constrained to believe herself a living miracle. What helped her to acquiesce in so strange a marvel was the circumstance that Sister Rémusat had just died. She had seen her in glory, and her heart borne aloft by angels. Who was to be her successor on earth? Who was to inherit the sublime gifts that had been hers, the celestial privileges she had been so richly endowed with? Girard offered Charlotte Cadière this succession, and corrupted her by appealing to her pride.

Henceforth she was a changed woman. In a spirit of vainglory she sanctified all she experienced in the way of bodily derangements. Repulsions and shudderings natural to pregnancy, but the meaning of which she utterly failed to grasp, she put down to violent activities of the Spirit within her. The first day of Lent, being at table with her family, she suddenly beholds the Lord. "I would fain lead you to the Desert," he tells her; "to have you share in the ineffable ardours of the Forty Days, to have you share in my pain and agony. . . ." The vision left her trembling, afraid to think of the sufferings she must undergo. But she, and she only, can be sacrifice in herself for a whole world of sinners. She dreams of blood, sees nothing but blood, beholds Jesus as it were a sieve distilling blood. She spat blood herself, and lost still more in another way. But simultaneously her nature seemed transformed, and the more she suffered, the more she began to feel the pricks of love. On the twentieth day of Lent she sees her own name joined with Girard's. Then at last pride, stirred and stimulated under the new feeling that had come over her, pride teaches her comprehension of the *especial domination* Mary (Womanhood) has over God.

She knows *how much the angel is* inferior to the least and lowliest saint, whether male or female. She sees the palace of the Almighty's glory, and is joined in union with the Lamb of God! . . . To cap her illusion, she feels herself lifted from the ground, rises several feet in the air. She can scarce believe it, but a credible witness, Mlle. Gravier, assures her of the fact. All the neighbours come to marvel and adore, Girard bringing with him his colleague Grignet, who drops on his knees and weeps for joy.

Not venturing to see her every day at home, Girard would have her pay frequent visits to the Church of the Jesuit Fathers. Thither she would drag her feeble limbs at one o'clock, after the morning services were over, during the dinner hour. No one was in the building at that time, and Girard gave himself up, before the altar, in front of the cross, to transports which the abominable sacrilege only made more ardent. Did his victim feel no scruples? Can she really have been hoodwinked? Her conscience would seem, with all her exalted enthusiasm, which was still sincere and genuine enough, to have already grown somewhat dulled and darkened. Underlying the bleeding stigmata, the cruel favours of the celestial bridegroom, she began to find mysterious compensations. Her swoons were blissful periods, in which she declared she enjoyed agonies of ineffable delight and a mystic flood of grace, culminating "at last in perfect and complete consent" (p. 425).

At first she was surprised and agitated at these novel experiences, and spoke of them to Madame Guiol. But the latter only smiled, telling her she was a little fool to make so much of nothing, and adding cynically that she felt just the same things herself.

Thus did these faithless friends do their best to corrupt a young girl of great natural goodness, and whose belated senses only awoke at last under the odious, overmastering constraint of religious authority misapplied.

Two things stir our sympathy in her pious dreams. The first is the pure and holy ideal she formed in her own mind of a union of faithful hearts, firmly believing she saw the name of Girard and her own united together for all eternity in the Book of Life. Another touching feature is the way her kind heart, her pretty childish ways, show through all her aberrations. On Palm Sunday, seeing all assembled round the merry domestic board, she wept for three hours without stopping to think that "on the same day nobody invited Jesus to dinner."

Nearly all through Lent she was all but unable to eat, her stomach rejecting even the little food she did take. During the last fortnight of the time she fasted rigorously, and reached the last degree of weakness. Will it be believed that Girard, far from leaving the dying girl to breathe her last breath in peace, actually began to practise fresh violence upon her? He had prevented her wounds from closing; and now a new one made its appearance in her right side. Finally, on Good Friday, to crown the cruel farce, he made her wear a crown of iron wire, which, piercing her forehead, set drops of blood coursing down her face. It was all done with hardly an attempt at secrecy. First of all he cut off her long hair, which he carried away with him. The crown he had ordered of a certain Bitard, a tradesman of the port, who made bird-cages. She never showed herself to those who came to see her wearing this crown; only the effects were visible, the drops of blood staining her face red. The marks of these were imprinted on napkins, and the *Veronicas* thus manufactured were taken away by Girard to be presented no doubt to pious clients of his.

The girl's mother was involved in spite of herself in the imposture. Nevertheless she began to be afraid of Father Girard, becoming more and more convinced the man was capable of anything, while someone (very likely Madame Guiol), very much in his secrets, had told her that, if she said one word, her daughter would not have twenty-four hours to live.

As for Charlotte herself, she never spoke anything but the truth on this point. In the account she dictated of the events of this Lenten season she says expressly it was a crown with sharp points, which was pressed down on her head, and so caused the bleeding.

Nor did she make any concealment where the little crosses she was in the habit of giving her visitors came from. According to a pattern Girard supplied her with, she ordered these from one of her relatives, a carpenter in the Arsenal.

She lay, on Good Friday, for four-and-twenty hours in a swoon (which they called an ecstasy), given up to Girard's tender mercies, and various debilitating and dangerous practices on his part. Already he saw this saint and martyr, this miraculous and transfigured being, showing more and more evident marks of pregnancy. He desired, yet feared, the violent solution of the difficulty by means of abortion. This he tried to provoke by a daily administration of perilous potions and certain reddish-brown powders.

Her death would have been most satisfactory to him, and the best solution of his embarrassments. Failing this, he would like to have removed her from her mother's influence, and buried her in a convent. He was well acquainted with these establishments, and like Picart (*see above in the Louviers affair*), with what adroitness and discretion things of the sort are hushed up within their walls! He wanted to send her either to the Carthusian nunnery of Prémole, or to the house of St. Claire of Ollioules. He even broached the subject on Good Friday but she seemed so feeble they dared not let her leave her bed. Eventually, four days after Easter, Girard being present in her bedroom, she had a painful evacuation, and was suddenly relieved of a heavy lump of what appeared to be coagulated blood. Girard took up the vessel, went to the window, and carefully examined it. But the girl, who had no suspicions about what had occurred, called the serving-maid, and gave her the vessel to empty. "What foolish rashness!" Girard could not help exclaiming, and he was imprudent enough to repeat the same remark again afterwards (pp. 54, 388, etc.).

We do not possess equally precise details with regard to Laugier's miscarriage. She first noticed the fact of her pregnancy during this same Lent, having previously experienced strange convulsions and the beginnings of stigmata of a ludicrous sort, one being a small wound she had given herself with a pair of scissors when working at her trade as a seamstress, the other an open cutaneous sore in the side (p. 38). Suddenly her pious ecstasies turned into blasphemous despair. She spat on the crucifix; she cried out against Girard, screaming, "Where is he, that devilish father, who has brought me to this pass? . . . It was easy enough to abuse a poor girl of twenty-two! . . . Where is he? He should come here, and not leave me in the lurch like this." The women about her were themselves Girard's mistresses. They went in search of him, but he was afraid to face the angry transports of the girl he had betrayed.

The good dames, whose interest it was to minimise the scandal, could surely find some means of settling the matter quietly without his interfering.

Was Girard a wizard, as was alleged at a later stage? Really the hypothesis would seem almost credible when we see how easily the man, without being either young or handsome, had fascinated so many female hearts. But strangest of all was the fact that, after compromising himself so deeply, he could still defy public opinion. For the time being he seemed to have bewitched the whole town.

As a matter of fact, the Jesuits were recognised as being immensely powerful, so that no one cared to join issue with them. It was even deemed a trifle dangerous to speak ill of them in whispers. The main body of ecclesiastics consisted of comparatively insignificant monks belonging to Mendicant Orders, possessing neither influential connections nor high-placed protectors. Even the Carmelites, for all their jealousy and the chagrin they felt at losing Charlotte Cadière, even they said nothing. The girl's brother, the young Jacobin, moved by his mother's scared remonstrances, fell back on measures of politic circumspection, made friends with Girard, and eventually became his creature as completely as the other brother had done, —going so far even as to second him in carrying out an extraordinary manœuvre calculated to foster a belief that Girard was possessed of the gift of prophecy.

Any small opposition he had to fear was from the very individual he seemed to have the most completely subjugated. Charlotte, though still his obedient servant, yet began to exhibit some faint signs of an independence soon to assert itself. On April 30th, during a country expedition which Girard had politely organised for his lady friends, and to which, in company with Madame Guiol, he sent his band of young devotees, Charlotte Cadière fell into a state of profound reverie. Moved by the beauties of springtide, so especially delightful in these parts, she lifted up her heart to God, declaring with an accent of genuine piety, "You only, my Lord and Saviour! . . . I want no one but you only! . . . Your angels cannot content me." Then presently, one of her companions, and a very light-hearted young woman, having in Provençal fashion hung a little tambourine round her neck, Charlotte did as the rest did, romped, danced, threw a rug round her by way of girdle, played the strolling gipsy, and generally indulged in a hundred innocent frivolities.

She was strangely moved. In May she got her mother's leave to make a journey to La Sainte-Baume to visit the church of the Magdalene, the saint *par excellence* of penitent young women. Girard allowed her to go, but only under escort of two trusty emissaries to look after her, viz. Guiol and Reboul. On the road, however, though still falling occasionally into the old ecstasies, she was evidently grown weary of being the passive instrument of the fierce spirit (infernal or divine) which troubled her peace. The termination of her year of diabolical *possession* was now approaching; and, indeed, she appeared to have regained her emancipation already. Once outside the gloomy streets of her native Toulon, which cast so strong a spell over her spirit, and restored to the free air of the country, to the sights of Nature and the light of the sun, the captive recovered her own soul, made head against the alien soul indwelling in her, dared to be herself and exercise her own free will. This was far from edifying the two spies Girard had set over her, who immediately on returning from this brief expedition (from May 17th to 22nd) warned him of the alteration. This he was able to verify for himself; for she struggled now against the state of ecstasy, reluctant it would seem to obey any impulses but those of reason and common sense.

He had supposed her his, by his personal fascination, by his authority as a priest, last but not least by the fact of possession and carnal habit. Now he found his hold was gone; the tender soul, which after all had not so much been conquered as surreptitiously surprised, was reasserting its natural bent. This wounded him to the quick; his old trade of schoolmaster, the despotism he had wielded over children whom he could chastise at will, and subsequently over nuns not less at his mercy, had left deep in his heart a harsh, jealous love of domineering. He made up his mind to regain his power over Charlotte Cadière at any cost, and punish her first essay at revolt,—if revolt it can be called, this timid aspiration of a downtrodden soul to lift its head again.

On May 22nd, when, as her habit was, she confessed to him, he refused her absolution, saying she was so much to blame he must next day inflict a great, a very great penance on her.

What penance was it to be? Fasting? But she was already weak and exhausted. Long prayers, another usual form of penance, were not approved of by the Quietists; in fact, directors holding their tenets actually forbade them. There only remained corporal punishment, the discipline of the rod. This was very generally, indeed lavishly employed—in convents no less than in schools, being short, sharp, and easy of application. In rude and simple times the church itself was often the scene of such executions; and we see in the old *Fabliaux,* those naïve records of mediæval manners and customs, how the priest, after confessing husband and wife, would proceed without more ado on the spot, behind the confessional box, to lay the lash across their backs. Schoolboys, monks, nuns, all were chastised in the same homely fashion.[10]

---

[10] The Dauphin himself was whipped cruelly. The young Boufflers (a boy of fifteen) died of chagrin at having suffered the same indignity (Saint-Simon). The prioress of the Abbaye-aux-Bois, threatened by her superior *"with disciplinary chastisement,"* appealed to the King; for the credit of the convent she was relieved of the disgrace of a public whipping, but sent back to the superior for proper measures to be taken, and doubtless the punishment was duly inflicted on the quiet. By degrees it came to be recognised more and more how dangerous and immoral the practice was. Fear and shame led to degrading supplications and unworthy compromises. This had come out only too clearly in the famous trial which under the Emperor Joseph revealed the secret places of the Jesuit colleges, the report of which trial was reprinted later under Joseph II., and again in our own day.

Girard felt sure a girl like Charlotte Cadière, unused to humiliation, and modest in the highest degree (all she had undergone was in her sleep and unconsciously to herself), would suffer excessively from a shameful chastisement, which would infallibly break her spirit and destroy whatever spring was yet left her. She was bound perhaps to be even more deeply mortified than another would have been, to suffer (if the truth must be told) in her vanity as a woman. She had borne so much, fasted so rigorously!—and then her miscarriage had come as a climax. Her body, naturally delicate, seemed little better than a shadow. The more certain was she to dread letting any part of her poor emaciated, marred, and aching person be seen. Her legs were swollen, and she suffered from a little infirmity of the flesh that could not but humiliate her extremely.

We have not the heart to relate in detail what followed. It may be read in the three depositions she made, so naïve and so manifestly sincere. Not being under oath, she makes it a duty to declare even matters which it was for her own interest to conceal, even such as might be most cruelly abused to her own disadvantage.

First Deposition, made in reply to unexpected questioning before the Ecclesiastical Judge, who was sent to pay her a surprise visit; here we have throughout words springing naturally from a young and innocent heart, speaking as in face of God Himself.

Second Deposition, before the King, that is to say, before the magistrate representing him, the King's "Lieutenant Civil and Military" at Toulon.

Third and Last Deposition, before the High Court of the Parlement of Aix (pp. 5, 12, 384 of the "Trial" folio).

Observe that all three, in remarkably close agreement, are printed at Aix, under the eyes of her enemies, in a volume, the intention of which is (as I shall prove later on) to minimise Girard's criminality and draw the reader's mind to every circumstance unfavourable to Charlotte Cadière. And yet whoever issued it has found himself unable to help giving these depositions, which tell so crushingly against the man he favours.

With monstrous inconsistency, Girard first terrorised the unhappy child, then with a brusque change of front, shamefully and barbarously took foul advantage of her panic fear.[11]

There is no question here of love as an extenuating circumstance. Far from it; he did not love her, which adds to the horror of it all. We have seen the cruel drugs he administered, and shall presently see how he abandoned her in her need. He begrudged her her superiority to the other degraded women he had to do with; he hated her for having (how innocently!) tempted him and compromised his reputation. Above all, he could never forgive her for keeping her soul her own. His only wish was to break her spirit; yet he was filled with hope to hear her say, "I feel I shall not live long,"—a phrase she often made use of now. Scoundrel and libertine!—showering dishonouring kisses on her poor broken body, longing she were well dead all the while!

How did he account to her for these atrocious contrasts of caresses and cruelty? Did he represent them as trials of her patience and tests of obedience? Or did he appeal boldly to the real basis, the fundamental doctrine, of Molinos' teaching, "That it is by dint of sinning sin must be killed?" Did she believe it all? Did she not realise at all that these pretensions of justice, expiation, penitence, were nothing more nor less than a cloak for licentiousness?

After a while she preferred not to realise it, in the extraordinary crisis of moral deterioration she underwent after May 23rd, and in June, under the effects of the hot, enervating time of year. She owned him her master, partly from fear of him, partly out of a strange, slavish sort of love, persisting in the farce of receiving at his hands day by day light penances for her

---

[11] This is put in Greek in the book of Depositions, and falsified twice over, on p. 6 and again on p. 389, in order to extenuate Girard's guilt. The most exact version here is that of her deposition before the "Lieutenant-Criminal" of Toulon, pp. 12 *sqq.*

lapses. Girard treated her very cavalierly, not even taking the trouble to hide from her his relations with other women. He was for sending her to a convent. Meantime she was his plaything; and knowing this, she yet suffered him to have his will of her. Weaker and weaker, more and more debilitated by repeated shame and suffering, a prey to ever-increasing melancholy, she had little left to live for, and would often repeat the words (no ill tidings to Girard), "Ah! I feel, I feel I shall die before very long!"

23

CHARLOTTE CADIÈRE
at the CONVENT *of* OLLIOULES

THE abbess of the convent of Ollioules was young for an abbess, being only thirty-eight. She was a woman of wit, intelligence, and great vivacity. Impetuous in her likes and dislikes, and easily carried away by any impulse of heart or senses, she was conspicuously lacking, however, in the tact and moderation required for the government of such an establishment.

The religious house in question depended upon two sources of income. On the one hand, it had from Toulon two or three nuns belonging to consular families, who, bringing with them handsome dowries, did pretty much what they pleased, living in communion with the Observantine monks, who were confessors of the convent. On the other, these same monks, whose order had extensive ramifications at Marseilles and throughout the country, were able to get the nuns little girls as boarders and paying novices,—an ill-omened connection, fraught with peril for the children, as the Aubany affair showed clearly enough.

No serious confinement within bounds, and little discipline indoors. In the burning nights of summer in this African climate (more oppressive and exhausting than elsewhere in the stifling gorges of Ollioules) nuns and novices came and went with little to control their freedom. What occurred at Loudun in 1630 was repeated exactly at Ollioules in 1730. The majority of the sisters (twelve, or thereabouts, out of the fifteen the house numbered), a good deal neglected by the monks, who preferred the well-born ladies of society, were poor, languid, disappointed creatures, whose only consolations were gossip, childish games, and dubious familiarities amongst themselves, and between them and the novices.

The abbess was afraid Charlotte Cadière would see too much of all this, and raised difficulties about receiving her. Then suddenly changing her mind, she took just the opposite side, and in a charming letter, far more flattering than a little girl had any right to expect from such a great lady, she expressed the hope that she would give up Girard as her director. Not that she wished to transfer her allegiance to the Observantine Fathers, who were quite unworthy of such a trust; the bold and brilliant idea she had conceived was to make the girl her own, to be Charlotte's confessor herself.

The lady abbess was vain and ambitious, and hoped to appropriate the marvellous child for her own purposes. She thought she could easily gain an ascendency over her mind, being convinced of possessing greater powers to please than an old Jesuit Father, and would fain have exploited the girl saint for the profit of her house.

She paid her the signal honour of receiving her at the threshold of the outer door. She kissed her, and generally took possession of her; presently leading her to the fine chamber she occupied as lady abbess, she told her they would henceforth share it in common. She was enchanted with her modest bearing and rather sickly elegance, as well as with a certain mysterious, affecting touch of strangeness about her. Charlotte had suffered extremely during the short journey, and the abbess was for getting her to bed at once,—in her own bed. She told her she was so fond of her she wanted her to share it, that they should sleep together like sisters.

In view of the object she had in view, this was perhaps an injudicious step. It was going too far; to lodge the saint in her own apartments would have been quite enough. By yielding to this curious caprice of having the child sleep with her, she made her appear too much in the light of a little favourite. Such intimacy, very much practised among ladies of the world, was a thing forbid in convents, a thing to be done surreptitiously, and a bad example for a lady superior to set.

The abbess was astonished, however, to find her protégée hesitate. Doubtless modesty and humility were not the only factors in this reluctance. Still less would it have been due to any repugnance for the lady's person; relatively speaking, she was a younger woman than poor Charlotte Cadière, enjoying a vitality and health she would fain have communicated to her little sick friend. She pressed her tenderly to consent.

To make her forget Girard was her object, and she expected much from this close intimacy at all hours of the day and night. It was the especial foible of lady abbesses, their most cherished pretension, to confess their nuns,—as is permitted by St. Theresa. This was bound to come of itself, under the pleasant conditions arranged. The girl would surely make her confessors only trifling confidences, keping the innermost privacy of her heart for the one person of her predilection. Of evenings, at night, behind the bed-curtains, under the caresses of a companion eager to penetrate her soul, she would let slip many a secret,—both of her own and other people's.

She was unable just at first to shake herself free from such pressing importunities, and shared the lady abbess's bed. The latter deemed her hold secure now,—doubly secure, and on two different grounds; she was hers both as a saint and as a woman, —I should say as a girl, nervous, sensitive, and from very weakness, perhaps sensual. She had her legend composed, her words, every remark that escaped her, written down. Moreover, she carefully collected the most homely details of her physical existence, sending the report to Toulon. She would so gladly have made her an idol, her little doll and darling. On such slippery ground the downward road was no doubt easy and rapid, but the girl had scruples, and was in a way afraid. She roused herself to a great effort that might have been supposed beyond her exhausted strength. She asked humbly to quit this dove's nest, this downy bed, and pampered existence,—to share the ordinary life of the novices or of the boarders.

Great the surprise and mortification of the abbess, who deemed herself insulted. She was deeply offended at what she called her ingratitude, and never forgave her.

A warm welcome awaited her from the rest of the community. The mistress of the novices, Mme. de Lescot, a nun from Paris, equally clever and good-hearted, was a superior woman to the abbess. She seems to have realised what Charlotte was really, the victim of an unfortunate destiny, a young heart full of God's Holiness, but cruelly marred by abnormal accidents of fate, bound to bring her headlong to shame and some sinister end. Her only preoccupation was to watch over her, to guard her against her own imprudent impulses, to explain and excuse whatever seemed most inexcusable in her conduct.

Barring the two or three noble ladies who lived with the monks, and had small liking for the high abstractions of mysticism, all loved the girl and thought her a very angel from heaven. Their sensibility, which wanted an object, was concentrated on her, and her alone. They found her not only pious and supernaturally religious, but a good girl and a good sort, a charming and diverting companion. Ennui was a thing of the past; Charlotte both amused and edified them with her dreams,—truly, by this I mean sincerely, recounted and always overflowing with the purest tenderness. She would say, "I travel everywhere at night, even to America. I leave letters everywhere, to tell the people to be converted. To-night I shall come and find you, even though you were to lock yourself in your room. We will go together into the Sacred Heart."

Miraculous! One and all, at midnight, received, so they declared, the delicious visit. They firmly believed they felt Charlotte kiss their cheeks, and lead them away into the Heart of Jesus (pp. 81, 89, 93). They were very frightened and very happy. The most soft-hearted and credulous of them all was a nun from Marseilles, Sister Raimbaud by name, who enjoyed this felicity no less than fifteen times in three months, or, in other words, every six days pretty nearly.

All pure fancy—as is sufficiently proved by the fact that Cadière was with each and all of them at identically the same moment. Still the abbess was hurt, in the first instance because she was jealous at feeling herself the only one left out in the cold, in the second place being convinced that Charlotte, however buried she might be in her dreams and visions, would be only too certain eventually to hear from so many bosom friends about the scandals of the establishment. They were not hard to see. But as nothing could penetrate Charlotte Cadière's mind otherwise than by special illumination from on high, she believed herself to have discovered them by revelation. Her gentle heart was stirred to its depths, and she felt profound compassion for God, who was so vilely outraged. Once more she imagined herself bound to pay for the rest, to save the sinners from the chastisements they had deserved by exhausting in her own person whatever fiercest cruelty the fury of the devils might inflict.

This all burst upon her unexpectedly and overwhelmingly on June 25th, St. John's Day. In the evening she was with the sisters in the novices' room. Suddenly she fell back writhing and screaming, and presently became unconscious. On her waking, the novices crowded round her, waiting inquisitively to hear what she would say. But the mistress, Mme. Lescot, guessed of what sort this would be, and felt sure she would ruin herself. She carried her off straight to her own room, where she found her body to be scarified all over and her linen stained with blood.

How came Girard to fail her in the midst of these struggles, internal and external? This was a thing she could not understand. Surely did she need support; yet he never came, or if he did, only to the public parlour, at long intervals and for a hurried visit.

She writes to him on June 28th (by her brothers, for though

she could read, she scarcely knew how to write), summoning him in the most ardent and pressing terms. He answers her appeal by pleading for delay; he has to preach at Hyères, he has a sore throat, etc. Contrary to all expectation, it was the abbess herself who eventually got him to come. No doubt she was anxious about the discoveries Cadière had made as to the internal economy of the convent. Convinced she would speak of these to Girard, she wanted to anticipate her revelations. She wrote the Jesuit a letter of the most flattering and tender character (July 3rd; p. 327), begging him, when he came, to see her first, as she wished, unknown to everyone, to be his pupil, his disciple, as the humble-hearted Nicodemus was our Lord's. "I shall be able, quietly and unobtrusively," she writes, "to make great strides in virtue, under your guidance, by favour of *the blessed freedom my position gives me. Our new novice affords a pretext* that will serve to conceal and at the same time forward my purpose" (p. 327).

An extraordinary, a reckless step to take, that shows how ill-balanced was the lady abbess's mind. Having failed to supplant Girard with Charlotte, she was for trying to supplant Charlotte with Girard. Without preface or preparation she went straight to the point, as great ladies will, who are still well able to please, and whose overtures are certain to be instantly accepted, even going so far as to refer to the *freedom* she enjoyed!

This false step was determined by the belief that Girard had pretty well ceased to care for Charlotte by this time, as indeed was the case. But she might have guessed he had other difficulties on his hands at Toulon. He was disturbed and anxious about another affair, no longer involving a mere child, but a lady of ripe age, easy circumstances, and good position, the best-conducted of all his penitents, Mlle. Gravier to wit. Her forty years had been unavailing to protect her; Father Girard would tolerate no independent lamb in the fold. One fine morning she was astounded and deeply mortified to find herself pregnant, and gave vent to bitter recriminations (July; p. 395).

Girard, preoccupied by this fresh misadventure, looked coldly upon the very unexpected advances made by the abbess of Ollioules. He suspected her of laying a trap for him in conjunction with the Observantine Fathers, and resolved to be very cautious. He saw the abbess, already half regretting her imprudent letter, and then Charlotte afterwards, but only in the convent chapel, where he heard her confession.

The latter could not but be wounded by the slight, and no doubt his behaviour was very strange and to the last degree inconsistent. He would disturb her peace of mind with frivolous, flattering letters, and little playful, almost loverlike, threats and teasings (*Dépos. Lescot.* and p. 335),—then scornfully refuse to see her except in public.

In a note written the same evening she pays him out cleverly, telling him how at the moment he gave her absolution she had felt herself marvellously detached both from her own personality *and from every human creature.*

The very thing Girard most desired! The threads of his life were sorely entangled, and Charlotte was only a further embarrassment. Far from being annoyed at her letter, he was delighted at what she said, and made *detachment* the text of an urgent sermon. At the same time he insinuated how great was the need of prudence on his part. He had received, he told her, a letter in which he was seriously warned of the errors he had committed. However, as he was leaving on Thursday (the 6th) for Marseilles, he would pay her a flying visit (pp. 329, July 4th, 1730).

She waited for him, but no Girard appeared. Her agitation was intense; the flood rose to its height and became a raging, tempestuous sea. She confided in her bosom friend Raimbaud, who would not leave her, but slept the night with her (p. 73), against the rules, saving appearances by saying she had come to her room in the early morning. It was the night of July 6th, a night of concentrated, overpowering heat, in the narrow, shut-in furnace of Ollioules. At four or five, seeing her struggling in sharp agony, she "thought she had the colic, and went to the kitchen in search of fire." During her absence Charlotte had recourse to extreme measures, which could certainly not fail to bring Girard there without a moment's delay. Whether by reopening the wounds on her head with her nails, or in some way forcing the iron-pointed crown over her brow, she continued to drench her face with blood, which ran down in great gouts. The pain transfigured her whole appearance, and her eyes glittered strangely.

The scene lasted a good two hours. The nuns crowded in to see her in this extraordinary condition, and were lost in admiration. They were for bringing the Observantine Fathers, but Charlotte would not allow them.

The abbess, for her part, would have taken good care not to let Girard know, having no wish for him to see her in her present pathetic condition, which was too touching by far. However, the kind-hearted Mme. Lescot saw to this, and had the father duly informed. He came, but instead of going up to her chamber at once, like a true charlatan, he had an ecstasy of his own in the chapel, where he remained a whole hour prostrate on his knees before the Blessed Sacrament (p. 95). Going upstairs at last, he finds all the nuns assembled round Charlotte. He is told how for a moment she had looked just as if she were at Mass, moving her lips for all the world as if she were receiving the wafer. "Who should know it better than I?" was the impostor's ready answer. "An angel had given me notice. So I said Mass, and gave her communion from Toulon." The sisters were overwhelmed by the miracle, one of them actually being ill for two days afterwards. Then Girard, addressing Cadière with unseemly levity, "Ah! ha! little sweet-tooth," he cried, "so you are robbing me of half my share?"

The rest withdraw respectfully, and leave him face to face with his pale-eyed, bleeding, enfeebled victim,—and for these very reasons the more strongly moved. Any other man would have been touched; what more naïve, more striking avowal could she give of her dependence than this irresistible craving she had to see him? This avowal, expressed in her bleeding face and wounded brow, must surely stir his compassion. She was humiliating herself, but who could fail to pity her under the circumstances? She was constrained then for once to yield to Nature's impulses, this innocent being? In her short and unhappy life, then, the poor girl saint, so much a stranger to things of the senses, did know one hour of human weakness. What he had had of her without her consciousness could count for little or nothing. Now, with consent of soul and will, he was to have all.

Charlotte is very brief, as may be supposed, about all this. In her deposition she says shamefacedly she lost consciousness, and scarcely knew what happened. In a confession made to her friend, Madame Allemand (p. 178), without formulating any complaint, she makes clear all that occurred.

In return for this vivid outburst of devotion towards him, this charming impatience to see him, what did Girard do? Scolded her! The flame that would have caught another man and set him on fire, chilled Girard. His tyrannous heart would tolerate only women whose will was dead within them, unresisting playthings of his passions. And this girl, by the vigorous initiative she had taken, had forced him to come to her!—the scholar was leading the master. The irritable pedant treated the whole situation as he would have done a barring-out at school. His libertine severities, his selfish coldness, and the evident pleasure he felt in inflicting pain horrified the unhappy girl, and left her with no other feeling but remorse.

Another abomination! The very blood shed for him had no effect but to suggest the idea he might utilise it to his own advantage. In this interview, the last perhaps, he wished to bind over the poor creature at any rate to discretion, to make her think herself, though deserted by him, still under obligations towards him. He asked if he was to be less favoured than the nuns who had witnessed the miracle. She made her wounds bleed for him to see, and the water with which he washed off this blood was then drunk between him and her,[1] by which odious communion he believed himself to have bound her soul to his.

This took up two or three hours, and it was nearly midday. The abbess was scandalised, and thought good to come herself with the dinner and make them open the door. Girard drank tea; as it was a Friday, he pretended he was fasting, having taken in good provision no doubt at Toulon. Cadière asked for coffee. The lay Sister in charge of the kitchen was surprised on such a day (p. 86). But without this stimulant the girl would have fainted. It gave her a little strength, and she kept Girard still by her side. He remained with her (it is true, the door was not locked now) till four o'clock, wishing to efface the sinister impression left by his behaviour of the forenoon. By dint of a string of lies promising friendship and protection, he somewhat reassured the excitable creature, and restored her to calmness. She conducted him to the door on his leaving at last, and walking behind him, she took, like the child she really was, two or three little jumps of joy. He said drily, "Silly little madcap!" and that was all (p. 89).

She paid cruelly for her weakness. The same evening, at nine o'clock, she had a fearful vision, and they heard her screaming, "Oh, my God, begone! Leave me, leave me!" On the 8th, at the morning Mass, she did not stay for the communion (no doubt deeming herself unfit), but took refuge in her room. The scandal was great; but so great a favourite was she, that a nun who had run after her invented a merciful lie and swore she had seen Jesus communicating her with his own hand.

Mme. Lescot, with equal judgment and adroitness, wrote in the accredited legendary form, as mystic ejaculations, pious sighs, holy tears, any words they could drag from her torn and

---

[1] This was a custom of the *Reiters,* the northern soldiery, to make themselves blood-brothers by this sort of communion (see Michelet, *Origines du Droit*).

bleeding heart. A very rare occurrence—there was a conspiracy of kindness among women to shield a fellow-woman; and nothing could speak more highly in the poor girl's favour or be a surer testimonial to her powers of pleasing. In a month she was the spoiled child of all the Sisters. Whatever she did, they defended her: innocent *in any case,* they saw in her only a victim of the devil's wicked assaults. A worthy, stout-hearted woman of the people, daughter of the locksmith of Ollioules, and keeper of the turning-box at the convent, Matherone by name, after surprising certain indecent liberties on Girard's part, declared none the less, "It is nothing; she's a saint." Once when he was speaking of withdrawing her from the convent, the woman cried out, "Take away our Mademoiselle Cadière! . . . Why, I will have an iron door made, to stop her going out of the house." Her brothers, who came to see her every day, alarmed at the state of things they found and the advantage the abbess and her monks might turn them to, plucked up courage, and in an open letter, which they addressed to Girard in the name of Charlotte Cadière, recalled the revelation she had had on June 25th as to the way of life followed by the Observantine Fathers, telling him "it was high time to carry out God's purposes in this matter," —no doubt to demand an inquiry being held, to accuse the accusers.

The challenge was over-bold and altogether injudicious. Almost dying as she was, Charlotte Cadière was very far from any such ideas. Her friends thought perhaps the man who had caused the mischief might possibly allay it, and begged Girard to come and confess their protégée. The result was a terrible scene. In the confessional she gave vent to screams and lamentations, audible thirty yards away. The curious amongst the nuns enjoyed a fine opportunity of eavesdropping, which they did not fail to benefit by. Girard was in torment, and kept repeating, quite unavailingly, "Calm yourself, calm yourself, mademoiselle!" (p. 95).—All very well to give her absolution, but alas! she could not see her way to absolve herself. On the

12th she had so sharp a pain below the heart she thought her ribs would burst. On the 14th she seemed at death's door, and her mother was summoned. She received the *Viaticum*. The following day "she made a general apology, the most touching and expressive ever heard," which "dissolved us in tears" (pp. 330, 331). The 20th she fell into a sort of death agony that was unendurably pathetic. Then by a sudden and favourable change that saved her life, she enjoyed a very soothing vision. She saw the penitent Magdalene forgiven and transfigured in glory, holding the place in heaven which Lucifer had lost (p. 332).

Still Girard could not make sure of her discretion except by corrupting her yet further and stifling her remorse. Now and again he would come (to the convent parlour) and kiss her, then regardless of appearances. But more often still he would send his pious protégées to see her. Madame Guiol and others visited her, overwhelming her with caresses and embraces; when she confided her secret to them with tears of shame, they only smiled, and told her all this was only part of the divine liberties the elect enjoyed; that they had had their share too, and were in the same case with her. Indeed, they openly boasted of the delights of such an association amongst women. Nor did Father Girard disapprove of their mutual confidences and their thus sharing the most disgraceful secrets. So habituated was he to these abominations, and looked upon it all so much as a matter of course, that he actually spoke to Charlotte about Mlle. Gravier's pregnancy. He wanted her to have her invited to Ollioules, calmed her irritation, and persuaded her her condition might very well be an illusion of the Evil One that could be dissipated by proper means (p. 395).

All this disgusting information made no impression on Charlotte Cadière, though it could not but rouse her brothers' indignation, who knew how true it all was. The letters written by them in her name are exceedingly curious. Savage and furious in their inmost hearts, regarding Girard as a consummate scoundrel, yet obliged to make their sister speak with respect and tenderness, they yet write in such a way that here and there, to anyone reading between the lines, their rage is evident.

As for Girard's letters, these are laboured productions, manifestly composed in view of a possible trial to come. We will quote from the only one he never had an opportunity of falsifying, one dated July 22. It is bitter-sweet in tenor and gallant in tone, the letter of a reckless, hot-headed man. This is the gist of it:—

"The Bishop arrived this morning at Toulon, and intends to visit Cadière. . . . Arrangements will be made beforehand as to what can be done and said. If the Vicar-in-Chief and *Father Sabatier* come to see her and ask to see (her wounds), she will tell them she has been forbidden to act or speak.

"I am hungry to see you again and to *see everything*. You know I only ask *my rights*. It is long since I have *seen anything more than half* (he means at the grating of the parlour). I shall tire you out? Well, then! do not tire me out too"—and so on.

An extraordinary letter in every way. He is suspicious at one and the same time both of the Bishop and even of the Jesuit, his own colleague, old Father Sabatier. It is at bottom the letter of a guilty man in terror of discovery. He knows perfectly well she has in her possession his letter and papers, in a word stuff enough to ruin him outright.

The two young men answer in their sister's name by an animated letter, the only one that rings true. They answer line by line, without invective, but with a bitterness that is often ironic, and which displays a concentrated fire of indignation. In it their sister promises to obey her correspondent, *to say nothing either to the Bishop or the Jesuit.* She congratulates him on having "so much courage to exhort others to suffer." She throws his odious gallantry back in his face, but in equally odious words,—in this part a man's hand is manifest, it is the work of a couple of clumsy schoolboys.

The next day but one they went to tell him she wished to quit the convent instantly. He was terribly startled, thinking the papers were going to escape along with her. So profound was his terror it robbed him of his presence of mind, and he was weak enough to go weeping to the parlour at Ollioules, where he threw himself on his knees before her, and asked her if she would have the courage to leave him (p. 7). This touched the poor girl, who told him *no,* came forward and allowed him to embrace her. And all the time the Judas only wanted to deceive her and gain a few days' breathing space, time to get support from high quarters.

By the 29th all is changed. Charlotte is still at Ollioules, asking his pardon and promising submission (p. 339). It is very evident he has brought powerful influence to work, that by this date they have received threats,—perhaps from Aix, or later on from Paris. The bigwigs of the Jesuit Order have written, and Court protectors from Versailles.

What were the two brothers to do in this dilemma? Doubtless they consulted their chiefs, who probably warned them not to press Girard too hard on the ground of immorality as a *confessor;* this would have been to offend the whole of the clergy, whose dearest prerogative confession is. On the other hand, they were to isolate him from the clerical body, by insisting on the singularity of his tenets, and bring the *Quietist* in him into prominence. With this weapon alone they could do great execution. In 1698 a curé of a village near Dijon had been burned for *Quietism.* They conceived the idea of composing (apparently from their sister's dictation, who was really an entire stranger to the plan) a memoir, in which Girard's *Quietism,* exaggerated and sublimated, should be established, or as a matter of fact denounced. This consists in an account of the series of visions she had had during Lent. In these the name of Girard is already in the heavens; she sees it, united with her own name, in the Book of Life.

They dared not carry the memoir in question directly to the Bishop; but they got it stolen by their friend, his almoner, young Father Camerle. The Bishop read it, and other copies circulated in the town. On August 21st, Girard being at the palace, the prelate said to him, laughing, "Well! well! Father, so your name's in the Book of Life, is it?"

He was panic-stricken, and believed himself undone. He wrote to Charlotte in terms of bitter reproach, once more tearfully demanding his papers. Charlotte was greatly surprised, and swore the memoir had never been out of her brothers' hands. When she discovered this was untrue, her despair knew no bounds (p. 363). The most cruel pains of mind and body assailed her, and a moment came when she verily thought her flesh was melting. "I became more than half mad. I felt such a craving for pain! Twice I grasped the scourge, and so fiercely, I drew blood abundantly" (p. 362). In the midst of this wild frenzy, which shows equally the ill-balance of her brain and the infinite sensitiveness of her conscience, Guiol put the finishing touch to her agony by describing Girard to her as a man almost at death's door. Her pity rose to the highest pitch (p. 361).

She was sure now to let the papers go; though it was only too plain they were her only protection and defence, alone capable of proving her innocence and the nature of the wiles to which she had fallen a victim. To give them back was to run a serious risk of herself and her seducer changing places. It might be said, and there would then be nothing to disprove the lie, that it was she had led a holy man astray, and all the odium would be concentrated on her unhappy head.

But, if the only alternative lay between perishing herself or ruining Girard, she very much preferred the first. A demon (Guiol, no doubt) tempted her with this very bait, the extraordinary sublimity of such a sacrifice. She wrote to her saying God claimed of her a bloody sacrifice (p. 28). She was able to quote saints for her example, who, when accused, made no attempt at justification, but rather accused themselves and died as meek as lambs. This was the course Charlotte Cadière deliberately adopted. When charges were alleged against Girard in her presence, she invariably justified him, saying, "He speaks the truth; I told lies" (p. 32).

She might very well have returned merely Girard's own letters, but in the generosity of her heart she was ready to do whatever she was asked; so she gave him the drafts of her own into the bargain. He secured at the same time both these drafts in the handwriting of the Jacobin and the copies which the other brother made to send to him. After this he had nothing to fear. No sort of control was possible; he could excise, add, destroy, erase, falsify at his good pleasure. His task as a forger was perfectly easy, and he worked with a will. Out of eighty letters there remain sixteen, and even these appear to be elaborate compositions, manufactured after the event.

Girard held all the cards, and could laugh at his enemies, whose turn it now was to tremble. The Bishop, a man of the great world, knew his Versailles far too well, and what influence the Jesuits wielded there, not to treat them with consideration. He even thought it politic to say a gracious word to Father Girard to make up for his malicious remark about the Book of Life, and told him with an amiable smile he would like to act as sponsor to a child of any of his relatives at the font.

The bishops of Toulon had always been great lords. The episcopal register contains all the chief names of Provence, Baux, Glandèves, Nicolai, Forbin, Forbin d'Oppède, as well as famous Italian names like Fiesci, Trivuleio, La Rovere. From 1712 to 1737, under the Regency and Fleury, the Bishop of Toulon was a La Tour du Pin. He was a very rich man, holding *in commendam* the abbeys of Aniane and Saint Guilhem of the Desert in Languedoc. He was said to have behaved well during the Plague in 1721. Otherwise, he was an almost constant absentee, lived a purely worldly life, never saying Mass, and having the reputation of something more than gallantry.

He arrived at Toulon in July, and though Girard would gladly have dissuaded him from going to Ollioules and visiting

Charlotte Cadière, his curiosity was too strong to resist the temptation. He saw her at one of her good times, and was taken by her looks. He thought her a good, saintly little personage, and was so far convinced of the reality of her revelations from on high as, rather inconsiderately, to speak to her of his affairs, and interests, and future, consulting her much as he might have done a common fortune-teller.

Still he hesitated, in spite of her brothers' prayers, to remove her from Ollioules, and out of Girard's reach. Means, however, were found to fix his resolution. The report was spread at Toulon that Charlotte had shown a wish to fly to the desert, as her model St. Theresa had tried to do as a child of twelve. This notion, so it was said, was put in her head by Girard, in order to carry her off some fine morning, get her beyond the bounds of the diocese, whose chief glory she was,—in a word, to make a present of this treasure to some far-away religious house, where the Jesuits, having an exclusive monopoly, would exploit for their own benefit her miracles and her visions, and all the attractions she exercised as a young and popular saint. The Bishop was much aggrieved, and sent word to the abbess to deliver Mlle. Cadière to no one but her mother, who was shortly to remove her from the convent and take her to a *bastide* belonging to the family.

Not to offend Girard, they got Charlotte to write to him to the effect that, if the change of residence was inconvenient to him, he could procure a coadjutor, and so give her a second confessor. He understood the hint, and preferred to disarm jealousy by giving up Cadière altogether. He broke off relations (September 15th) by a very judiciously worded, humble, and piteous epistle, in which he endeavoured to leave her still his friend and well-wisher. "If I have committed faults against you," he writes, "still you must always remember I had every wish to help you. . . . I am and shall always be your devoted friend in the Sacred Heart of Jesus."

Nevertheless the Bishop was far from being reassured. He

thought the three Jesuits—Girard, Sabatier, and Grignet—were
for putting his suspicions to sleep, and then one fine day, with
an order from Paris, carrying off the girl with them. He took the
decisive step, September 17th, of sending his carriage (a light,
fashionable, unclerical conveyance called a *phaeton*), and having her driven to her mother's *bastide* in the near neighbourhood.

To calm her feelings and protect her person, and set her
generally in the right way, he sought a confessor for her, addressing himself in the first instance to a Carmelite who had
been her director before Girard. But the monk, who was an
old man, refused, and others in all probability followed his
example. The Bishop was obliged to take a stranger, a new arrival three months before from Franche-Comté, one Father Nich-
olas, Prior of the Barefooted Carmelites. He was a man of forty,
at once able and courageous, of a very determined, not to say
obstinate character. He showed himself well worthy of the
confidence reposed in him by declining the duty at first. It was
not so much the Jesuits he was afraid of as Charlotte Cadière
herself. He expected little good of her, considering the angel
was likely enough to be an angel of darkness, and fearing the
foul fiend, under the gentle guise of a young girl, would only
strike the fouler blows.

But the mere sight of her reassured him not a little; she
seemed innocent enough, and only too glad to have found a
man at last who was sure and trustworthy, and able to give her
firm support. She had suffered sorely from the continual state
of uncertainty Girard had always kept her in. From the first
day she talked more freely than she had done for a month past,
telling him about her life and sufferings, her pieties and visions.
Even the coming of night did not stop her—a hot night of
mid-September. All stood open in the chamber, the three doors
as well as the windows. She went on almost till dawn, by the
side of her sleeping brothers. Next day she began again, sitting in the vine-trellised summer-house, speaking in the most
edifying fashion of God and the sublimest mysteries of religion.

The Carmelite was astounded, asking himself if the devil could possibly praise God so eloquently.

Her innocence was self-evident. She seemed a good-hearted, docile girl, meek as a lamb and frolicsome as a puppy. She was eager to play bowls (a common amusement at the *bastides*), and he did not refuse to play too.

If a spirit dwelt in her, at any rate no one could say it was a "lying spirit." Watching her long and closely, none could doubt that her wounds really bled at times. Her new confessor, unlike Girard, carefully avoided any indecent investigations to verify the fact, contenting himself with what he saw of the stigmata on her feet. He was only too frequently witness of her ecstasies. A violent heat would suddenly take her at the heart and circulate all through her frame; then she would lose consciousness, fall into convulsions, and begin talking wildly.

The Carmelite understood perfectly that in Charlotte Cadière there were two distinct persons, the girl herself and the demon that possessed her. The first was right-thinking, and even exceptionally innocent of heart, ignorant of wrong, for all the wrong she had suffered, comprehending little of the very things that had troubled her so sorely. Previous to her confession, when she spoke of Girard's kisses, the Carmelite told her roughly, "Why, they are very deadly sins." "Oh, God!" she replied, weeping, "then I am undone, for he did many other worse things to me."

The Bishop often came to see her, the *bastide* making a convenient object for his walks. When he questioned her, she answered simply and unsuspiciously, and told him at any rate the beginning of what had occurred. The Bishop was very angry, deeply mortified and indignant, doubtless guessing what was left unsaid. He came within an ace of raising a terrible hue-and-cry against Girard. Without a thought of the dangers of provoking a struggle with the Jesuits, he entered completely into the Carmelite's ideas, admitting she was bewitched,—*ergo* that *Girard was a wizard*. He was for instantly inhibiting him formally, ruining and disgracing him. But Charlotte pleaded for the man who had so deeply wronged her, and refused to be avenged. Throwing herself on her knees before the Bishop, she conjured him to spare Girard, not to speak of such severe measures. With touching humility, she declared, "Enough that I am enlightened now, that I know how sinful I was" (p. 127). Her brother, the Jacobin, seconded her prayers, foreseeing all the perils involved in such a contest, and doubting if the Bishop had firmness enough to carry it through.

She was now much calmer. The burning heats of summer were over, and the gracious month of October come, when Nature at last showed a more kindly face. The Bishop reaped a lively gratification from the fact of her having been saved by his instrumentality. The poor girl, removed from the stifling conditions of Ollioules, freed from all contact with Girard, well guarded by her relatives and the good, brave-hearted monk, last but not least protected by the Bishop, who grudged no trouble and consistently gave her his countenance, she entirely recovered her serenity. Like the parched grass that revives under the October showers, she lifted up her drooping head and bloomed afresh.

For some seven weeks she appeared perfectly sensible and well behaved. So delighted was the Bishop, he would fain have had the Carmelite, with Cadière to second him, deal with the rest of Girard's penitents and bring them to a similar condition of sweet reasonableness. They were to come to the *bastide,* —one may guess how much against the grain and with how ill a grace. Nothing, in fact, could well be more unseemly than thus to confront women of the sort with the Bishop's protégée, a young girl barely recovered from a state of ecstatic deliriousness.

The situation was critical, verging indeed on the ludicrous. Two factions were brought face to face,—Girard's women on the one side, the Bishop's on the other. On the Bishop's part Madame Allemand and her daughter, partisans of Charlotte

Cadière's; on the opposite the rebels, the Guiol woman at their head. The Bishop opened negotiations with the latter to induce her to enter into relations with the Carmelite and bring her friends to confess to him. He sent his registrar to her, and later on a procurator, a former lover of Madame Guiol's. Meeting with no success, the Bishop played his last card, and summoned them all to the Palace. There they denied one and all the reality both of ecstasies and stigmata, of which they had previously boasted. One of the party, no doubt Guiol, with equal effrontery and malicious artfulness, astounded his lordship yet more by offering to show him there and then they had no mark whatever on any part of their bodies. They had supposed him giddy-headed enough to fall into the snare. He scored cleverly, however; he refused flatly, but expressed his thanks to the ladies who, at the expense of their modesty, would have made him Father Girard's imitator, setting all the town grinning at his adroitness.

The Bishop's proceedings turned out a dead failure. On the one hand, these insolent women merely laughed at him, while on the other, his supposed success with Mlle. Cadière ended in disappointment. No sooner back in gloomy Toulon and installed in the confined Ruelle de l'Hôpital, than she suffered a relapse. She was again on the very scene, with all its dangerous and sinister associations, that had witnessed the first commencement of her malady, in the actual battlefield where the two opposing factions were engaged. The Jesuits, with the Court of France, as all could see, at their back, had on their side the politicians, the diplomats, the *moderate men*. The Carmelite had only the Bishop, not supported even by his own colleagues, or by the curés. However, he had a weapon in reserve. On November 8th he extracted from Cadière a written authorisation to make public her confession, if circumstances required it.

This was a bold step that set Girard trembling by its very audacity. He was not a brave man, and he would have been undone if his cause had not been the Jesuits' too. He lay *perdu* in the recesses of their house. On the other hand, his colleague Sabatier, an old man of a sanguine, choleric temperament, went straight to the Palace and forced himself into the Bishop's presence, bearing in his gown, like Popilius, peace or war. He put his back, so to speak, to the wall, and gave the prelate to understand that an action at law with the Jesuits meant his professional ruin, that he would remain Bishop of Toulon to the end of his days, and never be Archbishop. More than that, with the freedom of speech allowable to an apostle so influential at Versailles, he told him plainly that if the business should prove a revelation of a Jesuit Father's morals, it would throw no less searching a light on those of a certain Bishop. A letter, obviously put together by Girard (p. 334), would seem to show that the Jesuits lay all ready in ambush to launch formidable countercharges against the prelate, declaring his life "not merely unworthy of the episcopal dignity, but *abominable.*"

The wily and perfidious Girard, the apoplectic Sabatier, bursting with rage and spite, would have seconded the calumny with might and main. Such men would not have failed to say all this ado was for a girl's sake, that if Girard had tended her when sick, the Bishop had enjoyed her favours when restored to health. What annoyance such a scandal must occasion in the well-ordered life of a great nobleman and gentleman of society! It would have been too ridiculous a piece of Quixotism to take up arms to avenge the virtue of a little crack-brained invalid girl, and for her sake to come to blows with all respectable men! Cardinal de Bonzi died of disappointed love at Toulouse, but, at any rate, it was for a fair and high-born lady, the Marquise de Ganges. Here his lordship ran the risk of ruining himself, of being overwhelmed by shame and ridicule for the daughter of an old-clothes-man in the Rue de l'Hôpital!

These menaces of Sabatier's produced the more effect, inasmuch as the Bishop was already, for other reasons, less eager in Charlotte's behalf. He was annoyed with her for falling ill again, and thus spoiling his success. She was putting him in the wrong by her inconsiderate relapse, and he could not help bearing her a grudge for not getting well.

He told himself Sabatier was quite right; it would be a piece of silly good-nature to compromise himself. The change was sudden and instantaneous, like conversion by the grace of heaven. He saw the light in a moment of time, like St. Paul on the road to Damascus, and straightway went over to the Jesuits.

Sabatier stuck to his guns. He put pens and paper before him, and made him write out and sign on the spot an interdiction directed against the Carmelite, his agent with Charlotte Cadière, and another for her brother, the Jacobin (Nov. 10, 1730).

TRIAL of CHARLOTTE CADIÈRE
1730, 1731

Wʜᴀᴛ this dreadful blow was for the Cadière family may be imagined. The sick girl's seizures became frequent and appalling, while, cruel aggravation, a regular epidemic of the same sort spread amongst her bosom friends. Her neighbour, Madame Allemand, who also was subject to ecstasies, but who had hitherto taken them as coming from God, was seized with sudden terror and thought hell was upon her. The good lady (she was now fifty) remembered that for certain she had often had unclean thoughts; she believed herself delivered up to the devil, saw nothing but devils about her, and though well looked after by her daughter, ran from her own house and asked asylum with the Cadières. The latter's house henceforth became uninhabitable, and business out of the question. The elder brother was furious, and gave vent to his rancour against Girard, crying repeatedly, "It will be a case of Gauffridi . . . the man shall be burned, he shall be burned too!" And the Jacobin added, "Sooner than put up with it, we would spend the family savings to the last penny."

In the night of the 17th–18th November, Charlotte yelled and choked till they thought she was going to die. The elder Cadière brother, the dealer, lost his head, and started shouting out of the window, screaming to the neighbours, "Help! help! the devil is strangling my sister!"—who came running up with next to nothing on. The doctors and surgeons diagnosed her state to be *a suffocation of the womb,* and ordered her to be cupped. Whilst the cupping-glasses were being fetched, they managed to open her clenched teeth and made her swallow a taste of brandy, which brought her round. Meantime the physicians of the soul were likewise coming on the scene one after the other, first an old priest, Mme. Cadière's confessor, soon followed by sundry curés of Toulon. The noise, the shouts, the arrival of the priests in full fig, the paraphernalia for exorcism, had quickly collected a crowd in the street. New arrivals kept asking what the matter was,—and were answered, "It is Charlotte Cadière, bewitched by Girard." The pity and indignation of the populace may be imagined.

The Jesuits were intensely dismayed, but anxious to throw off their panic. They were guilty of a very barbarous act; going away to the Palace, they demanded imperatively that legal steps should be taken against Cadière, and the attack delivered that very day. The result was, the poor girl, on the very bed where she lay, but now almost at death's door, directly after the awful crisis she had gone through, received without the smallest warning a visit from the police. . . .

Sabatier had refused to leave the Bishop before he had summoned his judge, his ordinary, the Vicar-General Larmedieu, and his apparitor (or episcopal procurator), Esprit Reybaud, and directed them to take instant proceedings.

The thing was impossible really, illegal in Canon Law. *A preliminary declaration as to the facts was required* before proceeding to interrogations. Another difficulty: the ecclesiastical judge had no power to order such a visit *except for a refusal of the sacrament*. The two Church legists were bound to point out these objections; but Sabatier would not hear a word. If things were to be delayed in this way by an adherence to cold, formal legality, his shot would miss fire, and no one would be tempted at all.

Larmedieu, or Larme-Dieu (what a touching name!) was a complacent judge, well disposed to the clergy. He was none of those hard-bitten magistrates who rush straight before them, like wild boars blind with fury, along the high-road of the law without seeing anybody or drawing any distinctions between individuals. He had shown great consideration in the affair of Father Aubany, superintendent of Ollioules. He had put the law in motion so slowly as to give Aubany time to make good his escape. Then, on learning he was at Marseilles, as if Marseilles had been miles away from France, an Ultima Thule, or the Terra Incognita of the old maps, he took no further steps. Here all was different; the same judge who had been so paralytic where Aubany was concerned had wings for Cadière,— and the wings of the lightning.

At nine o'clock in the morning the inhabitants of the alley were watching inquisitively the arrival of a very imposing procession, Messire Larmedieu at its head, followed by the prosecutor of the Episcopal Court, the pair of them respectfully escorted by two vicars of the parish, doctors in theology. They invaded the house, and summoned the sick girl before them. She was made to give an oath to tell the truth against herself, an oath to incriminate herself by revealing to justice what were really secrets of her own conscience and the confessional.

She need not have answered, no proper formalities having been observed. But she raised no difficulties, and swore as she was directed,—which was equivalent to throwing up her case and delivering herself into their hands. For, once bound by the oath, she told everything, even the shameful and ludicrous details it is so cruel for a young girl to have to confess.

Larmedieu's official report and his first interrogatory point to a fixed and settled plan between himself and the Jesuits. This was to display Girard as the dupe and victim of Charlotte Cadière's wiles. A man of fifty, a doctor of the Church, a schoolmaster, a director of religious women, who has remained so innocent and credulous through it all as to be trapped by a little girl, a mere child! The artful, abandoned creature deceived him, it would seem, about her visions, but did not succeed in alluring him to share her wild doings.

Furious at her failure, she revenged herself by imputing to

him every abomination the imagination of a Messalina could suggest to her.

Far from the interrogatory giving any confirmation of all this, the most touching feature is the victim's gentleness. Obviously her accusations were only dragged from her by means of the oath she had taken. She is gentle towards her enemies, even towards the treacherous Guiol, who (her brother says) betrayed her, did everything she could to corrupt her, and eventually ruined her by inducing her to give up the papers that would have been her safeguard.

The Cadières were appalled by their sister's simplicity. In her respect for her oath she had given herself away completely, made herself the butt for the contempt, ribaldry, and lampoons even of men who were ill-disposed to the Jesuits, and libertines and fools of every sort and description.

As the thing was done, they wished at any rate it should be accurately recorded, that the report drawn up by the priests might be verified by a more formal legal act. From accused, as she was made to appear, they constituted her accuser, taking the offensive themselves and engaging the King's magistrate, the "lieutenant, civil and military," Marteli Chantard, to come and take her deposition. In this document, at once lucid and brief, are distinctly established, first, the fact of *seduction;* further, the *expostulations* she had addressed to Girard with regard to his licentious caresses, expostulations he only laughed at; further, the advice he had given her to *let herself be possessed by the devil;* lastly, the *sucking* by means of which the impostor kept her wounds open.

The King's official, the lieutenant, ought to have dealt with the case in his own court. For the ecclesiastical judge having failed in his extreme haste to fulfil the proper formalities of ecclesiastical law, his action was really null and void. The lay magistrate, however, had not the courage of his opinions. He consented to assist at the clerical inquest, accepted Larmedieu as assessor, and actually sat to hear evidence in the Bishop's Court at the Palace. The latter's registrar, and not the royal "lieutenant's" registrar, wrote the report of the proceedings. Did he report impartially? This is open to legitimate doubt, when we see how this same clerical registrar systematically intimidated the witnesses, and went every evening to show their depositions to the Jesuits.[1]

The two joint vicars of Charlotte Cadière's parish, who were heard first, gave their evidence drily, showing no bias in her favour, but none against her, and none for the Jesuits (Nov. 24th). The latter now foresaw a complete fiasco, and losing all shame and at the risk of shocking public opinion, resolved on a bold and decisive stroke. They extracted an order from the Bishop to imprison Cadière herself and the principal witnesses she proposed to tender. These were the two Allemand ladies and Mlle. Batarelle, of whom the latter was confined in the Refuge, a convent prison, the other two in a house of correction, the Bon Pasteur (Good Shepherd), where madwomen were shut up and common street-walkers subjected to correction. Charlotte (Nov. 26th) was dragged from her bed and handed over to the Ursuline Sisters, penitents of Father Girard, who duly provided her with a bed of rotten straw.

Then, a reign of terror being thus established, they could hear witnesses. One was the woman Guiol, notorious for having selected the witnesses (Nov. 28th), two highly respectable, specially procured girls for Girard—an adroit, venomous tongue, chosen to inflict the first sting and start the open sore of calumny. The other was Laugier, the little sempstress Charlotte Cadière was supporting and the expenses of whose apprenticeship she had paid. With child by Girard, this Laugier had indulged in recriminations against her seducer; now she purged this fault by mocking at Charlotte and throwing dirt at her benefactress —but clumsily, like the abandoned creature she was, attributing

---

[1] Page 80 of the folio edition, vol. i., p. 33 of the 12mo.

bold, shameless speeches to her, quite inconsistent with her general behaviour. To these succeeded Mlle. Gravier and her cousin, Mlle. Reboul, and in fact the whole gang of the Girardines, as they were called at Toulon.

Nevertheless things could not be so cleverly arranged but that the truth peeped through here and there. The wife of a "procureur," in whose house the Girardines used to meet, said with brutal frankness there was no standing it, they turned the whole place upside down so; she described their noisy laughter, the feasts paid for out of the collections they levied for the poor, etc., etc. (p. 55).

Much anxiety was felt lest the nuns should side with Mlle. Cadière. The Bishop's registrar was sent to inform them (as if on the Bishop's authority) that any who spoke ill-advisedly would be punished. By way of putting still stronger pressure on them, they brought back from Marseilles their gallant Father Aubany, whose ascendency over them was well known. The matter of violating the little girl was arranged, and her relatives given to understand the law would do no more for them. The child's honour was estimated at eight hundred livres, and this sum paid on Aubany's behalf. This settled, he came back full of zeal, a Jesuit to the backbone, to his flock at Ollioules, —and the poor flock trembled not a little on the father's informing them that he was commissioned to warn them that, if they were not discreet, *they would be put to the question.*[2]

For all this, they failed to elicit what they wanted from the fifteen nuns. Barely two or three were for Girard, and all detailed facts, especially facts relating to July 7th, which directly incriminated the Jesuit.

His colleagues in despair adopted heroic measures in order to secure proper evidence being given. They established themselves on permanent guard in an intermediate hall leading to the court, where they stopped the witnesses, cajoling or threatening them, as the case might be, and if they were against Girard,

[2] *Trial,* 12mo., vol. ii., p. 198.

barring their entrance altogether and impudently putting them to the door again.[3]

The ecclesiastical judge and the King's "lieutenant" were simply cat's-paws in the hands of the Jesuits. This the whole town realised with horror, while in the course of December, January, and February the Cadière family formulated and circulated a complaint on the grounds of refusal of justice and subornation of witnesses. The Jesuits themselves felt the position was no longer tenable, and appealed for assistance *from higher quarters.* The best thing would apparently have been a simple decree of the Great council, citing the whole case before its own judges, and so hushing up everything,—as Mazarin did in the Louviers business. But the Chancellor was D'Aguesseau, and the Jesuits were not desirous the matter should be referred to Paris. They retained the case in Provence, and obtained a decision from the King (Jan. 16th, 1731) that the Parlement of Provence, in which they had many friends, should give the verdict on evidence to be called by two of its counsellors at Toulon.

As a matter of fact a layman, M. Faucon, and a clerical counsellor, M. de Charleval, presently arrived, and at once took up their lodging with the Jesuits (p. 407). These hot-headed delegates took so little pains to conceal their violent and cruel partiality that they launched against Charlotte Cadière a personal citation, such as was commonly served on the accused party, while Girard was politely requested to attend and left at liberty meantime; in fact, he went on saying Mass and confessing penitents just the same as before. But the complainant all the while was under lock and key, in her enemies' hands, lodged with Girard's devoted adherents and exposed to any and every species of cruelty.

The welcome accorded her by the good Ursuline Sisters had been for all the world the same as if they had been commissioned to do her to death. As a sleeping-room, they had

---

[3] *Ibid.,* 12mo., vol. i., p. 44.

assigned her the cell of an insane nun who befouled everything round her, and she lay on the madwoman's straw amid the horrid stench she occasioned. With the utmost difficulty her relatives managed next day to get a blanket and a mattress admitted. They gave her as gaoler and nurse a lay Sister, Girard's protégée and familiar spirit. She was daughter of the same Mme. Guiol who had been Charlotte's betrayer, a creature well worthy to belong to such a mother and quite capable of dark deeds, a peril to her prisoner's modesty and possibly even to her life. The latter was condemned to a penance of all others the most cruel for her, forced abstention from confession and communion. She began to fall ill again directly she ceased to communicate. Then her inveterate enemy, Sabatier the Jesuit, came to the cell, and essaying a new and extraordinary departure, tried to win her over, to *tempt her with the sacred wafer!* Truly an unseemly bargaining! Going, going, gone!— to receive communion, she must confess herself a slanderer, and so unworthy of the sacrament. She might even have done this, out of excessive humility. But in ruining herself she would have been ruining the Carmelite and her own brothers into the bargain.

Reduced to employ the artifices of the Pharisees, they glossed her words. What she spoke in a mystic sense was perversely taken as meant to apply to material reality. To avoid all these snares, she exhibited the last quality we should have expected from her, a remarkable degree of presence of mind (see in particular p. 391).

The most perfidious trick of all, contrived on purpose to alienate public sympathy and set the profane laughing at her, was to give her a lover. It was alleged she had proposed to a young scamp to elope with her and scour the wide world together.

The great nobleman of those days, who liked to have little lads as pages, were always ready to take into their service the prettiest of the peasants' children on their lands. This the Bishop had done with one of his farm-tenant's boys, whom he trained to polite arts. Later on, when his favourite grew up, he had him tonsured by way of giving him an air, and turned him into an abbé with the title of his lordship's almoner—all by the time he was twenty. Such was the young Abbé Camerle. Brought up with the servants and broken to all sorts of dirty work, he was like many another country lad, when the rust has been partly, but not entirely, rubbed off, a scampish young lout, both simple and subtle at one and the same time. He was quick to notice that the prelate, from the moment of his arrival at Toulon, took an interest in Charlotte Cadière, and was not well disposed towards Girard. He thought to please and amuse his patron by constituting himself at Ollioules the spy of the suspicious relations subsisting between the two. But the instant the Bishop changed front and showed he was afraid of the Jesuits, Camerle exhibited an equal zeal and activity on Girard's behalf and in helping him against Mlle. Cadière.

Like another Joseph, he declares that Mlle. Cadière (*à la* Potiphar's wife) had tempted him, endeavoured to shake his virtue. Supposing it had been the truth, supposing she had paid him the compliment of showing some weakness towards him, surely this would only have made it the more cowardly of him to punish her for it and take advantage of a thoughtless word. But a training like this, first as page, then as seminarist, produces neither honour nor love of women.

She made a ready and excellent defence, and covered her accuser with confusion. So victorious were her answers, that the two unworthy commissioners of the Parlement cut short the confrontations and cut down the numbers of her witnesses. Of sixty-eight originally called by her, they allowed only thirty-eight to appear (12mo., vol. i., p. 62). Observing neither the delays nor the formalities of justice, they hurried on to the final scene of confrontation. Yet with all this lustre, they gained nothing; again on February 25th and 26th she repeated without any variation her damaging depositions.

So furious were they that they regretted bitterly they had no executioner or torture "to make her sing out a bit." This was always *ultima ratio;* in every century the Parlements resorted to it. I have before me at the present moment an eloquent panegyric of torture,[4] written in 1780 by a learned member of Parlement, promoted to a seat on the Great Council, and dedicated to the King (Louis XVI.), and approved in most flattering terms by his Holiness Pius VI.

However, in default of torture which would have "made her sing out," they induced her to speak by better means still. On February 27th, early in the day, the lay Sister who acted as her gaoler, Mme. Guiol's daughter, brings her a glass of wine. The girl is astonished; she is not thirsty, she never drinks wine in the morning, and still less wine without water. The lay Sister, a rough, sturdy servant-girl, such as are kept in convents to master disorderly or mad members of the community, and punish the pupils, overrules the weak invalid's objections with threats and domineering insistence. She does not want to drink, yet drinks nevertheless. Moreover, she is forced to drink it all off, to the very dregs, which have a disagreeable, salty taste (pp. 243–7).

What was this unpleasant beverage? We have already seen, at the time of her miscarriage, how expert the former Director of Nuns was in the administration of drugs. In this case the strong wine would have been enough by itself, acting on a constitution weakened by sickness. It would have been quite sufficient to intoxicate her, to draw from her during the course of the same day some stammering words or other, which the Registrar would have twisted into a flat contradiction of her previous evidence. But a drug was added as well (perhaps the witches' herb, which clouds the mind for several days), in order to prolong this condition, so that they might obtain formal testimony from her that would render it impossible for her to retract her denial.

We have the deposition she made on February 27th, showing a sudden and complete change of front, being, in fact, a direct

---

[4] Muyart de Vouglans, at the end of his *Loix criminelles,* fol., 1780.

plea for Girard! Strangely enough, the Commissioners never notice so marked an alteration. The extraordinary and shameful spectacle of a young girl in a state of intoxication rouses no surprise or suspicion. She is made to declare Girard never laid hand upon her, that she herself felt neither pleasure nor pain, that all the sensations she experienced arose from an infirmity she labours under. Only the Carmelite, and her brothers, had persuaded her to recount as actual occurrences what was never anything better than a dream. Not satisfied with whitewashing Girard, she blackens her own friends, overwhelming them with monstrous charges and virtually putting the rope round their necks.

The surprising thing is the clearness and precision of the deposition, in which the hand of the practised Registrar is very evident. The astonishing circumstance is that having begun so well, they did not go on. Examination is held on one day only, the 27th. Nothing on the 28th; nothing from the 1st to the 6th of March.

Presumably on the 27th, under the influence of the wine, she was still able to speak and say something or other capable of being arranged consecutively. But by the 28th, the poison having exerted its full effects, she would seem to have been either in a stupor or in an unseemly state of delirium (like that common at the Witches' Sabbath), and it was out of the question to produce her in public. Besides, once her wits were thoroughly confounded, it was an easy matter to give her other potions, without her knowing or remembering anything about it.

At this stage it was, I make no doubt, during the six days between February 28th and March 5th or 6th, that an occurrence took place, so repugnant in itself and so sad for the unhappy child, that it is merely hinted in three lines, without either herself or her brothers finding the heart to speak of it more particularly (p. 249 of the fol. edition, lines 10–13). They would never have mentioned it at all, had not the brothers been accused and seen plainly their own lives were threatened.

Girard went to see Charlotte, and once again took impudent, immoral freedoms with her!

This took place, according to what the brother and sister say, *since the case began.* But from November 26th to February 26th Girard was in a state of prostration and humiliation, invariably beaten in the war of witnesses he was waging with Cadière. Still less did he dare to see her after March 10th, the date when she recovered her full wits and left the convent where he had kept her confined. He only saw her during those five days when he was still her master, and the unhappy girl, demoralised by the effects of the poison, was no longer herself.

Madame Guiol had formerly betrayed Charlotte, and her daughter could do the same again. Girard, who had by then won the game by the contradiction she had given to her own statements, had the heartlessness to come to her prison, see her in the condition he had brought her to, dull or despairing, abandoned by heaven and earth alike, and if any power of clear thinking was left her, given up to the horrid pain of having, by her deposition, been the murderess of her own kith and kin. The end was come, and her fate was sealed. But the other trial was only beginning, against her brothers and the stout-hearted Carmelite. Remorse may have urged her to try and move Girard and induce him to drop the prosecution directed against them, and above all not to put her to the question.

The prisoner's condition was deplorable, and called for leniency. Minor infirmities arising from a purely sedentary life caused her much suffering, while as a consequence of her convulsions, she suffered from a *prolapsus vulvœ,* which was very painful at times (p. 343). What proves Girard to have been no casual criminal, but a man of perverted sentiment and abandoned character, is that in all this he saw only a better and surer means of confirming his advantage. He argued that if he adopted these means, she would be so far humiliated in her own eyes she would never pluck up a spirit again, never recover courage to recant her recantation. He hated her by this time, and yet in jocose phrases of odious obscenity he spoke of this last infirmity, and seeing the poor creature defenceless, did her the outrageous indignity of touching it (p. 249). Her brother asserts the fact positively, though briefly and shamefacedly, without pursuing the subject further. Questioned on the matter herself, she answers in three letters, "Yes!"

Alas! her soul was not now her own, and she was long in regaining anything like composure. It was on March 6th she was to be brought up to confirm everything and finally and irretrievably undo her brothers; but when the time came she was choking, and unable to speak. The gentle-hearted Commissioners informed her the torture-chamber was next door, and explained to her the action of the wedges that would squeeze her bones, the rack and the iron spikes. Her body was so weak her courage failed her; and she endured to face her cruel master, who was in a position to laugh and triumph, having humiliated her in person, and still more deeply in conscience, making her the murderess of her own brothers!

No time was lost in profiting by her weakness. The Parlement of Aix was at once appealed to, and its approval obtained that the Carmelite and the two Cadière brothers should presently be charged, and be tried separately, so that after Charlotte should have been condemned and punished, their case might next be taken and pushed to a conclusion through thick and thin.

On March 10th she was conveyed from the Ursuline convent at Toulon to St. Claire of Ollioules. Girard was not sure of her, and contrived that she should be carried thither, like some redoubtable brigand of that ill-reputed road, between troopers of the Marshal's posse. He demanded that at St. Claire she should be kept a close prisoner under lock and key. The Sisters were touched to the point of tears to see their poor sick favourite arrive so, scarce able to drag herself along, and escorted by armed men. Everybody pitied her; and two gallant individuals, M. Aubin, Procureur, and M. Claret, Notary, were found ready to draw up for her formal statements by which she retracted her retractation—terrible documents, in which she details the threats of the Commissioners and of the Lady Superior of the Ursulines, particularly the fact of the drugged wine they forced her to drink (March 10th to 16th, 1751, pp. 243, 248).

Simultaneously, these intrepid friends of justice drew up and forwarded to Paris, addressed to the office of the Great Seal, what was known as an "appeal against abuse of procedure," exposing the irregular and faulty methods of the court and the wilful breaches of law and justice involved in the high-handed doings of (1) the official in charge and the King's "lieutenant," and (2) the special Commissioners. The Chancellor d'Aguesseau showed himself weak and flaccid to the last degree, upholding the odious proceedings hitherto and allowing the case to be referred to the Parlement of Aix, open to such strong suspicion since the disgrace its two members had just covered themselves with.

This settled, they laid hands again on the victim, and from Ollioules had her dragged to Aix, once more in charge of the Marshal's men. The custom then was to sleep midway at a half-way house, a roadside tavern. Arrived there, the Brigadier explained that by his orders he was to sleep in the young woman's bedroom. They had actually pretended to think it likely that the sick girl, who could barely walk, would make her escape and jump out of the window. A vile design truly,—to entrust her chastity to the self-restraint of the soldiery of the Dragonnades! What a triumph it would have been! What an excuse for ribaldry, if she had arrived at her destination *enceinte!* Luckily her mother had come up on her departure, had followed the cortège in spite of all remonstrances, and even the men-at-arms had not dared to drive her away with their butts. She stayed all night in the room, both of them keeping up and awake, and so protected her child's virtue (12mo. ed., vol. i., p. 52).

Her destination was the Ursuline convent at Aix, the Sisters of which were to guard her under orders from the King. But the Lady Superior pretended she had not yet received the order, and what followed shows only too plainly how ferocious women are when once stirred by passion, and how they lose all womanly qualities. She kept her four hours at the door, in the open street, a show for the passers-by (vol. x. of 12 mo. ed., p. 404). There was time enough to call together the *populace,* the Jesuit rabble, the *good working-people* of the Church to howl and hiss, and a crowd of children, if need be, to throw stones. It meant four long hours in the pillory. Meantime any impartial spectators there may have been present were asking whether the Ursuline Sisters had orders to let the girl be killed. What tender gaolers the good Sisters made for their sick prisoner may be imagined.

The soil had been excellently well prepared. An active combination of Jesuit magistrates and intriguing ladies had organised a complete system of intimidation. No advocate would ruin his future chances by defending so ill-reputed a client. No one was willing to put up with the mortifications her gaolers kept in readiness for anyone who should face their parlour every day to hold interview with Cadière. Under these circumstances the defence of the prisoner devolved upon the Syndic of the Aix Bas, M. Chandon. He did not decline the formidable task; but, in much perplexity, he would have preferred a compromise. This the Jesuits refused. Then he showed the stuff he was made of, that he was a man of unassailable honour and an admirable courage. A trained lawyer, he exposed the monstrous irregularity of the proceedings. This meant an irreconcilable quarrel with the Parlement, no less than with the Jesuits. He brought out clearly and distinctly the spiritual incest of the confessor, though he did not, from motives of decency, specify how far his licentious practices had gone. He refrained likewise from speaking of the Girardines, the pious disciples he had got with child, —a fact perfectly well known, but which no witness would have been willing to testify to. Eventually he brought the charge most likely to be practically effective under the circumstances against the criminal priest, attacking him *as a Sorcerer.* The advocate was greeted with a storm of mockery. He undertook to prove the existence of the Devil from a series of texts from Holy Writ, starting with the Gospels,—and his audience only laughed the louder.

The truth had been very adroitly distorted by making the honest Carmelite into a lover of Charlotte's, and the originator of a huge conspiracy of calumny directed against Girard and the Jesuit Fathers. Now the whole tribe of idle loungers and empty-headed worldlings, sneerers and philosophers alike, made fun of both sides equally, entirely impartial between Carmelites and Jesuits, but overjoyed to see the monks engaged in civil war among themselves. The *Voltaireans,* to anticipate by a few years the name they will presently be known by, the Voltaireans are actually biassed to some extent in favour of the Jesuits, polished men of the world, in preference to the old Mendicant Orders.

So it goes on, confusion growing ever worse confounded. It rains pasquinades, directed more especially against the victim. A love affair plainly, people say, and look at the whole thing in the light of an amusement. Not a student or a scholar but makes his rhymes on Girard and his pupil and revives the old Provençal skits on Madeleine (of the Gauffridi affair), her six thousand imps, the fear these show of the whip, and miracles of the lash which put to flight those infesting Charlotte Cadière (MS. in the Toulon Library).

As to this particular point Girard's friends found no difficulty in clearing his reputation. He had acted entirely within his rights as a director of consciences and in accordance with ordinary usage. The rod is the attribute of fatherhood, and he had acted for his penitent's good and "for the cure of her soul." It was the custom of the age to thrash demoniacs, thrash madmen, thrash other sufferers from disease. It was the accredited means of driving out the enemy, be this who or what it might, demon or sickness. It was the popular view too; a worthy working-man of Toulon, observing Cadière's unhappy condition, declared roundly the only cure for the poor patient was a good bull's pizzle.

Girard, with the powerful supporters he possessed, had really no need to justify himself. And as a matter of fact he takes mighty little trouble to do so. His defence is charming in its off-handedness. He does not condescend so much as to be self-consistent in his depositions; he contradicts his own witnesses. He appears to make a joke of the whole thing, and says, with the swaggering tone of a great lord of the Regency days, that if he *has* been shut up alone with her, as they state, "it only happened on nine occasions."

"And why else did he do it, the good Father," his friends would ask, "except for the purpose of observing, judging, gauging precisely what he was to make of it?" This is the bounden duty of a director in such circumstances. Read the life of the famous St. Catherine of Genoa. At night her confessor used to conceal himself and remain in her bedroom to witness the wonders she wrought, and catch her out miracle-working, so to speak, *flagrante delicto*.

"But the unfortunate thing in this case was that hell, that never sleeps, had spread a snare for this lamb of God, and had spued forth this female dragon, this devouring monster, maniac and demoniac, to swallow him up and destroy him in the torrent of calumny."

It is a time-hallowed and excellent custom to strangle monsters in the cradle. But why not in later life as well? The charitable advice of Girard's lady friends was to employ sword and fire on her with the least possible delay. "Let her die!" these religious ladies claimed insistently. Many high-born dames also desired her chastisement, deeming it the height of insolence that the creature should have dared to complain and bring to trial a man of Girard's eminence, who had done her only too great an honour.

True there were in the Parlement some obstinate Jansenists, who as enemies of the Jesuits were more than well-disposed towards the girl. But how could they feel other than beaten and discouraged, seeing ranged against them at one and the same time the redoubtable Society of Jesus, Versailles, the Court, the Cardinal Minister, and even the leaders of society at Aix? Were they likely to show a bolder front than the chief administrator of justice, the Chancellor d'Aguesseau, who had proved himself such a broken reed? The "Procureur Général" for his part displayed no hesitation; entrusted with the task of accusing Girard, he openly declared himself his friend and gave him his advice how to meet the charges of his accusers.

It was only a question of one thing,—to decide by what act of reparation, what solemn expiation, what exemplary punishment, the complainant, now accused in her turn, should make satisfaction to Girard and to the Jesuits. These latter, for all their gentleness and generosity, agreed that in the interests of religion an *example* would be useful as a warning both to the Jansenist Convulsionaries and to the swarm of scribbling philosophers now beginning to appear.

On two counts Charlotte Cadière could be assailed, and a hold obtained over her:

1. *She had slandered.*—But no law existed punishing slander with death. To get that length, it was needful to go farther afield, and say: "The old Roman text *De famosis libellis* (of slanderous libels) pronounces the penalty of death against such as have uttered libels injurious to the Emperors or *to the* religion of the Empire. Now the Jesuits are Religion. Therefore a document reflecting on a Jesuit deserved the last penalty of the law."

2. They had even a better hold than this.—At the opening of the trial the episcopal judge, the judicious Larmedieu, had asked Charlotte if she had not *divined* the secrets of a number of persons, and she had replied in the affirmative. Therefore she could be qualified, in the terms laid down in the formulary for trials of witchcraft, as a *divineress and deceiver.* This in itself merited death by all ecclesiastical law. She might even be qualified as a *witch,* after the statements made by the ladies of Ollioules, who described how at night-time she would be in

several cells at one and the same time, how she used to weigh softly upon them, etc. Their infatuation, their sudden and unexpected tenderness, had indeed very much the look of bewitchment.

What hindered burning her? Witch-burnings are still common everywhere in the eighteenth century. Spain in a single reign, that of Philip V., burns 1600 persons, even burning a witch as late as 1782. Germany burned a witch in 1751, and Switzerland one in 1781. Rome burns still,—on the sly, it is true, in the furnaces and cellars of the Inquisition.[5]

"But doubtless France at any rate is more humane?"— France is inconsistent. In 1718 a wizard was burned at Bordeaux.[6]

In 1724 and 1726 fires were lighted in the Place de Grève for offences which at Versailles passed for schoolboys' tricks. The tutors to the royal infant (Louis XV.), the Duke of Orleans and Fleury, so easy-going at Court, are terribly severe in Paris. An ass-driver and a nobleman, a M. de Chauffours, were burned alive. The beginning of the Cardinal-Minister's supremacy could not be better celebrated than by a reform of manners, by a severe example given the corruptors of public morality.—And what more appropriate example than a solemn and awful doom inflicted on this child of Satan, this girl who has assailed so fatally Father Girard's innocence?

The one thing needful to "thoroughly purge the good Father" was to establish the fact that (even granting he had done wrong

---

[5] This detail is sent us by a "Consultor" of the Holy Office still alive.

[6] I am not here speaking of executions the people carried out on their own account. A hundred years ago, in a village of Provence, an old woman, to whom a landowner refused an alms, flew into a passion and said, "You will be dead to-morrow!" He had a stroke and died. The whole village,—not the poor peasants only, but the most *respectable* inhabitants,—gathered in a crowd, seized the old woman and put her on a pile of vine-cuttings, where she was burned alive. The Parlement made a pretence of inquiry, but no one was punished. To the present day the people of the village in question are called *woman-burners* (brulo-fenno) by their neighbours.

and had imitated M. de Chauffours) *he had been the plaything, the victim of enchantment.* The law was perfectly clear on the point; by the forms of ecclesiastical jurisprudence and in strict accordance with recent decisions, someone was bound to be burned. Of the five magistrates on the bench, two only would have burned Girard, while three went against Charlotte Cadière. A compromise was the result. The three who formed the majority did not insist on the stake and faggot, waived the long-drawn, gruesome spectacle of death by fire, declaring themselves satisfied with death pure and simple.

In the name of the five it was resolved and recommended to the Parlement, "That Charlotte Cadière, after first undergoing the question, ordinary and extraordinary, be then carried to Toulon, and there in the Place des Prêchems, be hanged by the neck and strangled."

The effect was instantaneous and startling,—a prodigious reversal of public opinion. The men of the world, the scoffers, scoffed no more; their laughter was turned into shuddering. Frivolous as they were, they were not prepared to treat so appalling a piece of injustice lightly. They thought little of a girl being seduced, abused, and disgraced, treated as a mere plaything, driven by grief to death or madness; well and good, it was no business of theirs. *But* when it came to punishment as a criminal, when they pictured the wretched victim, the rope round her neck, being strangled on the gallows, their gorge rose. On all sides echoed the cry, "Never was seen, since the world began, so wicked an upsetting of common justice,—the law of rape applied back foremost, the girl condemned to death for having been corrupted, the seducer strangling his victim!"

A highly unexpected phenomenon in a town like Aix, made up almost exclusively of judges, priests, and fashionables,—the *people* suddenly shows itself alive, a violent eruption of popular feeling occurs. In serried ranks a crowd of men of every class marches with one impulse to the Ursuline convent. They call for Charlotte Cadière and her mother, and on their appearing

cry out, "Courage, mademoiselle, courage! We are with you
. . . fear nothing!"

The great eighteenth century, justly entitled by Hegel the
"reign of mind," deserves even better to be known as the "reign·
of humanity." Ladies of distinction, like Madame de Sévigné's
grand-daughter, the charming Madame de Simiane, took possession of the poor girl, and gave her refuge in their bosom.
More beautiful and more touching still, the Jansenist ladies,
women of a fanatic purity of life, so hard on each other and dis-
playing so exaggerated an austerity, sacrificed law to mercy in
this crisis, threw their arms round the neck of the poor terrified
creature, purified her with their chaste kisses and rebaptised her
with their tears.

If Provence is fierce and strenuous, she is only the more admirable at such moments,—fierce in her generosity and strenuous for great aims. Something of the same sort was seen during
the early triumphs of Mirabeau, when he had about him at Marseilles a million of men. Here, in anticipation of a grander revolution, was a gallant revolutionary episode, a mighty protest
against the imbecile Government of the day, and against the
Jesuits, the Minister Fleury's special protégés,—a unanimous
protest in favour of humanity and pity, a plea for the defence
of a woman, a child, so barbarously immolated. The Jesuits
conceived the idea of actually organising among their disrep-
utable hangers-on, their clients and the beggars depending on
their charity, a nondescript mob, which they armed with *hand-
bells* and cudgels to make head against the *Cadières,*—these
being the nicknames given to the respective parties. The second
named included practically everybody. Marseilles rose *en masse*
to carry in triumph the son of the advocate Chandon, while
Toulon declared so emphatically for their unfortunate com-
patriot that the populace was for burning the Jesuits' house
there to the ground. The most touching of all these testimonials
came to Charlotte from Ollioules. A plain simple boarder at
the convent school, Mademoiselle Agnes, young and timid as

she was, followed the generous impulse of her heart, threw herself into the war of pamphlets, wrote and printed Charlotte
Cadière's apology.

This deep and powerful movement reacted on the Parlement
itself. The enemies of the Jesuits were instantly encouraged and
fortified, so much so as to brave the threats of those in power,
the influence the Jesuits could bring to bear, the lightnings of
Versailles that Fleury might hurl at them.[7]

Girard's own friends, seeing their numbers decreasing and
their ranks thinning, called for an immediate decision,—which
was given October 11th, 1731.

No one ventured, in view of popular feeling, to propose confirming the savage recommendations of the Bench to have Charlotte Cadière strangled. Twelve counsellors sacrificed their honour, and declared Girard innocent; of the other twelve, certain
Jansenist members condemned him to the stake as a sorcerer,
while three or four, of a more reasonable temper, condemned
him to death as a villain. Twelve being against twelve, the President, Lebret, had to give the casting vote. He gave it for Girard.
Acquitted on the charge of sorcery and any crime involving
death, he was sent back, as a priest and confessor, for trial before the ecclesiastical tribunals, presided over by the Ordinary
of Toulon, his friend and intimate, Larmedieu.

The world at large, the crowd of indifferent spectators, was
satisfied. Indeed, so little attention has been paid to the terms of
the decision that even now M. Fabre states, and M. Méry repeats the statement, "that both parties were acquitted." This

---

[7] A grotesque anecdote symbolises and wonderfully well expresses the condition of the Parlement. The official reporter was reading his work, his con-
clusions with regard to the case as a trial for witchcraft and the share the
Devil might have had in the affair. Suddenly a crash is heard; a black man
comes tumbling down the chimney. . . . All fly in terror, except only the
reporter himself, who is entangled in his own gown and unable to stir. . . .
The man explains and apologises, being nothing more nor less than a chimney-
sweep who has made a mistake between different flues (Pappon, iv. 430).
In very fact it may well be said a great dread, that of the people, of the devil
of popular indignation, pinned the Parlement down, and held it motionless,
like the judge entangled in his gown in this story.

is to the last degree inaccurate. Charlotte Cadière was dealt
with as guilty of calumny, and condemned to see her memorials
and acts of defence torn up and burned by the hand of the
common hangman.

Moreover, there lurked a grim implication underneath. Cadière being thus marked out, branded as a slanderer, the Jesuits
were inevitably bound to push their endeavours, to continue
their intrigues subterraneously, to follow up their successes with
Cardinal Fleury and call down on her secret and arbitrary penalties. The town of Aix saw this plainly enough, and felt instinctively that the Parlement was really *betraying* her into the hands
of her enemies. Hence such a formidable burst of indignation
against President Lebret, and such alarming threats, he asked
that the Flanders Regiment might be sent for to protect him.

Girard fled in a closed carriage, but was recognised, and
would have been killed had he not rushed into the Jesuit church,
where the hypocritical scoundrel started saying Mass. He escaped eventually, and returned to Dôle, honoured and glorified
by the society, He died there in 1733, *in the odour of sanctity*.
The courtier Lebret died in 1735.

Cardinal Fleury did whatever he could to please the Jesuits.
At Aix, at Toulon, at Marseilles, he exiled, banished, and imprisoned. Toulon in especial was guilty as having carried Girard
in effigy to the doors of his *Girardines,* and having borne aloft in
ridicule the sacrosanct "tricorne" (three-cornered hat) of the
Jesuits.

Charlotte Cadière should under the terms of the judgment,
have been at liberty to return there and seek refuge with her
mother. But I dare affirm she was never suffered to come back
to the ardent stage of her native town, which had so loudly
declared itself in her favour. What became of her? To this day
no one has been able to discover.

If the mere crime of showing interest in her earned imprisonment, we cannot doubt she was not long in being imprisoned
herself; that the Jesuits easily procured a *lettre de cachet* from

Versailles to shut up the poor girl in a prison cell, and so stifle and bury along with her a business that had been so unfortunate for their Order. No doubt they waited till public attention was directed elsewhere, till people were thinking of other matters. Then the tiger's claw would seize her again, and she would be plunged in the abyss of some remote, unknown convent, and her voice stifled for ever in an *in pace*.

She was only twenty-one at the time the judgment was delivered, and she had always hoped for a short life. Pray God, she had her wish! [8]

---

[8] Persecution has gone on, both by means of the publication of falsified documents, and even in the pages of the historians of the present day. The *Trial* (folio, 1733) itself, our main source of information, is followed by an Index cleverly compiled to tell against Charlotte Cadière. Under her name is found noted consecutively and fully (as proven facts) anything and everything that was alleged against her, except that no reference is made to her retractation of what the drugged wine made her say. Under *Girard*, scarcely a word; for his doings the reader is referred to a crowd of passages he will never have the patience to look up.—In binding some copies care has been taken to place in front of the *Trial* itself, to serve as antidotes, sundry apologies and defences of Girard's, and the like.—Voltaire makes very light of the whole business, poking fun at both sides, particularly at the Jansenists.—The historians of our own day, who most certainly have not read the *Trial*, MM. Cabasse, Fabre, Méry, suppose themselves *impartial*, and sum up dead against the victim!

EPILOGUE

A woman of genius, in a very noble burst of enthusiasm, represents herself as seeing the two spirits, whose mutual struggle made the Middle Ages, coming at last to an understanding, drawing together, uniting. Examining one another at nearer hand, they discover, late in the day it may be, traces of kinship between them. What if they were brothers, and their age-long strife nothing more than a misunderstanding? The heart speaks, and they are melted. The proud and gallant outlaw, the tender-hearted persecutor, forgetting the embittered past, spring forward eagerly to throw themselves into each other's arms (George Sand, *Consuelo*).

Amiable fancy of a great-souled woman; and others too have entertained the same beautiful dream. The gentle Montanelli wrote a fine poem embodying the notion. Indeed, who would not welcome the alluring hope of seeing the combat here below end in peace and a reconciliation so touching?

What thinks the wise bard Merlin [1] on the point? In the mirror of his lake, whose depth he alone can plumb, what has he seen? What has he to say in the colossal *épopée* he gave us in 1860? [2] That Satan, if he disarm, will do so only on the Day of Judgment. Then, and not till then, pacified at last, both powers will repose side by side in one common death.

Doubtless it is not difficult, by a travesty of their true nature, to arrive at a compromise. The exhaustion of long-continued struggles, by enervating every fibre, makes way for certain combinations. The last chapter showed us two shadows agreeing to make covenant in falsehood; the shadow of Satan, the

---

[1] Victor Hugo.

[2] *La Légende des Siècles.*

shadow of Jesus, rendering little services one to the other, the devil posing as friend of Loyola, pious enthusiasm and diabolic possession going hand in hand, hell melted in the Sacred Heart!

These are mild times of ours, and hate far less virulent. Nowadays indeed men's animosity is pretty well confined to their friends. I have seen Methodists admire the Jesuits. I have seen those whom the Church throughout the Middle Ages brands as sons of Satan, whether legists or physicians, making prudent compact with the old vanquished spirit.

But, leaving mere fancies on one side, let us ask, Those who seriously expect Satan to come to terms and agree to peace, have they really weighed the problem involved?

The obstacle is not any surviving rancour. The dead are dead; the millions of victims, Albigensians, Vaudois, Protestants, Moors, Jews, American Indians, sleep in peace. The standing martyr of the Middle Ages, the Sorceress, says no word; her ashes are scattered to the winds.

Well, what is it, can you say, that protests, what is the solid barrier that divides the two spirits, and bars their coming together? It is a prodigious reality that has taken shape in the last five hundred years,—that Titanic work the Church has declared accursed, the vast edifice of the sciences and of modern institutions which she excommunicated stone by stone, but which each anathema only made more imposing and raised higher by yet another story. Is there one science you can name that was not originally a revolt against authority?

There is only one way to reconcile the two spirits and unite the two Churches. This is to demolish the new one, the one which, from its earliest beginnings, was declared sinful and damnable. Let us destroy, if we can, all the sciences of nature, demolish the observatory, the museum, the botanic garden, the school of medicine, every library of modern books. Let us burn our legal enactments and our codes. Let us go back to the Canon Law.

These novelties, one and all, were Satanic; no progress ever made but was his guilty work.

The same wicked logician it was who, heedless of clerical law, preserved and refashioned that of the philosophers and Jesuits, based on the impious doctrine of Free Will.

The same dangerous magician it was who, while Churchmen were disputing about the sex of angels and the like sublime questions, stuck obstinately to facts and created chemistry and physics and mathematics. Yes! Mathematics no less than the rest had to be begun afresh,—another revolt against authority, for had not men been burned for saying, three make three, and not One?

Medicine above all was truly and indeed Satanic, a revolt against disease, the merited scourge of an offended God. Plainly a sinful act to stay the soul on its road towards heaven and replunge it in the life of this world!

How expiate all this? How suppress and rage to earth this accumulated pile of successive revolts, which to-day constitutes the whole of modern life? To re-enter the path of the angels, will Satan undo this great work? Never! for it rests on three eternal foundation-stones,—Reason, Right, and Nature.

So triumphantly victorious is the new spirit, it clean forgets its previous struggles, and scarcely deigns to-day to give a thought to its own triumph. It has been no useless task to recall the pitifulness of its earliest beginnings, the humble shapes, so rough and barbarous, so cruelly grotesque, it assumed in the days of persecution, when a woman, the unhappy Sorceress, gave the first impetus to its scientific and popular vogue. Bolder far than the heretic, the doubting half-Christian, the man of knowledge who still kept one foot within the sacred circle, she eagerly fled from such constraints, and free on the free soil, strove to build herself an altar of the rude wild boulders of untrammelled nature.

She perished in her turn, as she was bound to do. But how? Mainly by the progress of those very sciences she first originated, by the hands of the physician, the naturalist, for whom she had worked so well.

The Sorceress has perished for ever, but not so the fairy. She will appear afresh under this form, which is immortal.

Woman, busied during the later centuries with men's affairs, has in requital lost her own true rôle,—that of *healing,* and *consoling,* that of the fairy that restores to health and happiness.

This is her true priestesshood,—hers by right divine, no matter what the Church may have said to the contrary.

With her delicate organs, her love of the finest detail, her tender appreciation of life, she is called to be its quick-eyed confidante in every science of observation. With her gentle heart and sweet pity, her instinctive kindness, she is a heaven-sent healer. Sick folk and children are very much alike; both need a woman to tend them.

She will pursue the sciences, and bring into their domain gentleness and humanity, like a smile on Nature's face.

Anti-Nature pales in death; and the day is not far off when her final setting will mark a dawn of blessed augury to mankind.

The gods wane, but not God. Quite otherwise; the more they wane, the more He waxes strong. He resembles an eclipsing light, that after each period of obscuration only shines out the brighter.

It is a good sign to see these things openly discussed, in the newspapers even. The feeling is taking root that all questions go back to the great fundamental and sovereign questions—education, organisation, the child, the woman. Such is God, and such the world.

All this proclaims the times are ripe.

So near is it, this religious dayspring, that again and again I thought I saw it dawning in the desert where I have completed this book of mine.

How bright and sunlit, how rugged and how lovely my desert home is! My nest was perched on a rock in the great roads of Toulon, in a humble villa, amid aloes and cypresses, cactuses and wild roses. In front, this vast basin of flashing sea; behind, the bare amphitheatre, where might sit at ease the States General of the world.

The countryside is quite African in general aspect, and has a steely splendour by day that dazzles the eyes. But on winter mornings, especially in December, the spot was full of divine mystery. I used to rise exactly at six, when the Arsenal gun gives the signal to begin work. From six to seven I enjoyed an entrancing hour. The keen, *steely* (if this is a permissible expression) scintillation of the stars put the moon to shame and stood out against the coming dawn. Before the day broke, and afterwards during the struggle between the two lights, the extraordinary translucency of the air allowed me to see and hear at incredible distances. I could make out every object at two leagues away. The smallest details of the distant mountains, trees, rocks, houses, contours of surfaces, all showed up with the most delicate and precise definition. My senses seemed multiplied, and I felt myself a new being, free, winged, emancipated. The moment was one of crystal clearness, of an austere beauty and infinite purity! . . . Involuntarily I would find myself exclaiming, "How now! can it be I am still a man?"

An intangible shade of blue—a blue the rosy dawn as yet respected and did not dare disturb, a holy ether, a sublimated spirit—made all Nature spiritual.

But a subtle change was in progress, a gradual, a gentle transformation could be felt approaching. A mighty marvel was at hand, soon to demolish and eclipse these quiet beauties. The impending transformation, the expected glories of the day, detracted nothing from the charm of being yet in the *divine night*, of lurking half-hid in the half-light, still enwrapped in the same enchanted wonderland. . . . Come, Sun! We stand all ready with our adorations, yet would fain enjoy yet another, a last, moment of waking dreams. . . .

The Sun is rising. . . . Let us await his coming in good hope and thoughtful reverence.

NOTES AND ELUCIDATIONS

Two only have been published in a complete form (see *Limburch*); the originals are at Toulouse, and extend from 1307 to 1326. Magi has taken extracts from two others (*Acad. de Toulouse*, 1790, 4to, vol. iv., p. 19). Lamothe-Langon has done the same for those of Carcassonne (*Hist. de l'Inquisition en France*, vol. iii.), Llorente for the Spanish Registers. These mysterious records were at Toulouse, and no doubt in all other cases, enclosed in bags suspended very high up on the walls, and, besides, sewn up on either margin in such a way that they could not be consulted without unstitching the whole. They afford us a valuable specimen, throwing precious light on all the Inquisitions throughout Europe, for the methods of procedure were everywhere precisely similar (see *Directorium Eymerici*, 1358). What especially strikes one in these Registers is not merely the vast number of those punished, but the multitude of persons *immured*, shut up, that is to say, in a tiny stone cell (*camerula*), or in a dungeon *in pace*, on bread and water. Another is the countless number of the *Crozats*, as they were called, who had to wear the red cross in breast and back. They were the best treated, and were allowed provisionally to live in their own houses. Only every Sunday after Mass they had to go and be whipped by the Curé of their parish (Ordinance of 1326, *Archives of Carcassonne*, quoted by L.-Langon, iii., 191). The most cruel part, especially for women, was that the common people and children used to jeer them unmercifully. They were liable, apart from any fresh offence, to be taken into cus-

tody again and *immured*. Their sons and grandsons were always suspect, and very readily immured.

In the thirteenth century everything is heresy; in the fourteenth magic. The transition is easy from one to the other. According to the rough-and-ready theory of the period, heresy
differs little from diabolical possession; erroneous belief of
every sort, as well as sin of every sort, is a demon to be driven
out by torture or the lash. For the devils are very sensitive to
pain (*Michael Psellus*). The *Crozats* and all persons suspected
of heresy are ordered to avoid any dealings with sorcery (*D.
Vaissette, Lang*). This change from heresy to magic is an advance in terror in which the judge was bound to find his advantage. In trials for heresy—trials of men for the most part—there
are assessors and others present. But in those for magic, almost
invariably trials of women, he has the right to be alone, tête-à-
tête with the accused.

Observe further how under the dread name of Sorcery were
included little by little all the minor superstitions, the time-
honoured poetry of hearth and meadow, Robin Goodfellow,
Brownies, and fairies. What woman can be held innocent now?
The most pious believed in all these things. On retiring to rest,
before making her prayer to the Virgin, every housewife left
out a drink of milk for her little friend. Maid and goodwife
offered at night a little bonfire to the fairies, by day a bunch of
flowers to the saints.

And for this she is charged as a sorceress,—brought up
before the man in black! He cross-questions her,—always the
same questions, always the same, those put to every secret
society, to the Albigensians, the Templars, all alike. Let her
bethink her; the executioner is near by, all ready in the vaulted
chamber yonder, the strapado, the wooden horse, the boots, the
iron wedges. She faints for fear, and says she knows not what,
"It was not I. . . . I will never do it again. . . . It was my
mother, my sister, my cousin, forced me, led me on. . . . What
was I to do? I was afraid of her, I went there all trembling in

spite of my own wishes" (Trepidabat; sororia, sua Guilelma trahebat, et metu faciebat multa,—"She was all a-tremble; her sister Wilhelmina betrayed her, and she did many things out of mere terror."—*Reg. Tolos.* 1307, p. 10, in Limburch).

Few were able to resist. In 1329 a certain Jeanne perished for having refused to denounce her father (*Reg. de Carcassonne, L.-Langon,* 3, 202). But with rebels of the sort other means were tried. A mother and her three daughters had successfully held out against the question. Then the inquisitor gets hold of the second daughter, makes love to her, and in this way reassures her to such a degree that she tells him everything, and betrays her mother and sisters (*Limburch, Lamothe-Langon*). The result is, all were burned together!

What broke down the spirit more even than torture was horror of the *in pace*. Women died of the terror of being walled up in the little black hole. In Paris could be seen the public spectacle of a dog-kennel in the courtyard of the *Filles Repenties* (Magdalen Refuge), where the Dame d'Escoman was kept immured (except for a slit through which her daily bread was thrown to her), lying amid her own excrements. In some cases their fears were worked upon till epilepsy supervened. For instance, the poor, weak, fair-haired fifteen-year-old child, Madeleine de la Palud, whom Michaëlis himself admits having terrified into denouncing her friends, by putting her in an ancient ossuary to lie on dead men's bones. In Spain, more often than not, the *in pace*, far from being a place of peace, had a door by means of which they could come every day at a certain hour to *work* the victim, for the good of her soul, by applying the lash. A monk condemned to the *in pace* begs and prays for death in preference to such a doom (*Llorente*).

As to the *auto-da-fés,* read in Limburch what eye-witnesses say of their horrors. In particular consult Dellon, who himself once wore the san-benito (*Inquisition de Goa,* 1688).

From the thirteenth and fourteenth centuries downwards such was the reign of terror that we find persons of the highest condition abandon rank, fortune, everything, the moment they were accused, and take to flight. This is what Dame Alice Kyteler, mother of the Lord Seneschal of Ireland, did when charged with sorcery by a mendicant friar who had been made bishop (1324). She escaped, but her confidante was burned. The Seneschal made apology, and was degraded permanently. (Th. Wright, *Proceedings against Dame Alice,* etc., 4to, London, 1843.)

The whole system takes shape from 1200 to 1300. It was in 1233 the mother of St. Louis founded the great prison of the *Immuratz* at Toulouse. What happens? Folk begin to give themselves to the Devil. The first mention of the *Covenant with Satan* dates from 1222 (Cæsar Heisterbach). People are no longer heretics, *half*-Christians, but satanic, *anti*-Christians. The wild *Sabbatic Round* makes its appearance in 1353 (*Procès de Toulouse,* in L.-Langon, 3, 360), on the eve of the Jacquerie.

Note 2. *Method of Procedure.*

The first two chapters, which are abstracts of my *Lectures on the Middle Ages,* explain by *the general condition of society* why humanity despaired, while chapters 3, 4, and 5 explain by *the moral condition of the soul* why women in especial despaired, and were led to sell themselves to the devil and become Sorceresses.

It was only in 553 A.D. that the Church adopted the atrocious resolution of damning the *spirits* or *demons* (the words are synonymous in Greek), inexorably, without room for repentance of any sort whatsoever. In this she followed the African harshness of St. Augustine against the more lenient advice of the Greeks, Origen, and antiquity generally (Haag, *Hist. des Dogmes,* i., 80–3). From that time on, theologians study and determine the temperament, the physiology of spirits. They possess or do not possess bodies, vanish in smoke, but are fond of heat, fear the rod, etc. Every detail is perfectly well known, and agreed upon in 1050 (Michael Psellus, *Energie des esprits ou démons*). This Byzantine writer gives precisely the same idea of them as that afforded by the Western legends (see numerous passages in Grimm's *Mythologie,* Maury's *Les Fées,* etc.). It is not till the fourteenth century all spirits are declared in so many words to be devils. Nodier's *Trilby,* and the majority of similar stories, are spoiled by the fact that they all stop short of the tragic instant when the goodwife finds her Robin Goodfellow or friendly Brownie suddenly transformed into a satanic lover.

In chapters 5–12, and onwards, from p. 41, I have endeavoured to investigate the question, *How did women become Sorceresses or Witches?* It is a difficult and delicate inquiry, and one that none of my predecessors have attempted. They pay no heed to the successive steps by which this humble state of things was reached. Their witch rises full grown, as if from the bowels of the earth, but human nature is not made that way. The investigation involved the most arduous work. The ancient texts are few and far between, and such as can be unearthed in the made-up books of 1500–1600 are hard to distinguish and identify. Having found the texts, how to date them, to say definitely, "This is of the twelfth, that of the thirteenth, the fourteenth century"? I should never have ventured on the ground at all if I had not already had in my favour a long familiarity with those times, my persistent studies in Grimm, Ducange, etc., and my book *Origines du Droit* (1837). All this has helped me enormously. In these formulas, the *Usages* that vary so very little, in the *Customs* that seem fixed everlastingly, nevertheless the historic sense must have its say. Other periods, other forms; these we learn to recognise, to date them psychologically. We can perfectly distinguish the sombre gravity of older times from the pedantic gossipy narrative of periods comparatively modern. If archæology can decide from the shape of such and such a Gothic arch that a building is of such and such a date, with how much more certainty can historical psychology demonstrate that a particular moral circumstance belongs to a particular century and to no other, that a particular idea, a particular passion, equally impossible in more ancient ages and in more modern epochs, was precisely what was to be expected at a particular date? Indeed, in this latter case the criterion is less liable to be misunderstood. Archæologists have on occasion been mistaken as to some pointed arch which has been cleverly reconstructed. Moreover, in the chronology of art certain forms may very well be repeated. But in the history of morals and manners this is impossible. The cruel record of the past which I here reproduce will never re-create its monstrous dogmas, its appalling dreams. In bronze, in iron, they are fixed in one and the same place for ever in the fatality of the ages.

Now for my especial sin, where criticism will be down on me. In my long analysis, historical and psychological, of the evolution of the Sorceress down to 1300, in preference to indulging in long-drawn prolix explanations, I have frequently taken a minor thread, biographical and dramatic, the lip of one and the same woman, as it were, down the course of three hundred years. This, please note, only applies to six or seven chapters altogether, and even in this short section it will easily be realised how everything is based on a firm foundation of historical fact. To give a single instance,—if I have given the word *Toledo* as the sacred name of the capital city of the magicians, I had on my side not only the weight of M. Soldan's deliberate opinion, not only the long passage in Lancre, but two very ancient texts to boot. We read in Cæsar von Heisterbach how the students of Bavaria and Suabia go to Toledo to learn necromancy. It is a master of Toledo who originates the crimes of Sorcery prosecuted by Conrad of Marburg.

However, after all, the Saracen superstitions, which came from Spain or from the East (as Jacques de Vitry alleges), exerted only an indirect influence, as did the old Roman cult of Hecate or Dianom. The mighty cry of pain, which is the true and inward meaning of the Witches' Sabbath, reveals quite a different state of things. It expresses not only material sufferings, voices, old miseries and wretchedness, but a very abyss of agony. The lowest depths of moral suffering are not sounded till towards the days of St. Louis, Philippe le Bel, particularly among certain classes which felt and suffered even more keenly than the old-time serf. Such must have been in especial the *good* (well-to-do) *peasants*, rich villeins, serfs who were mayors of villages, whose existence I have noted as early as the twelfth century, and who in the fourteenth, under the new system of imposts, became responsible (like the *Curiales* of antiquity) for the taxes, and are doubly martyrised by the king and by the barons, crushed under extortions,—their lives, in fact, made a living hell. Hence the fits of despair that send them hastening to the spirit of hidden treasures, the devil of money. Add in mockery and insult, who do still more perhaps towards producing the "Bride of Satan."

A trial at Toulouse, making in 1353 the first mention of the *Sabbatical Round,* enabled me to put my finger on the exact date. And what date more likely in the nature of things? The Black Death is heavy on the world, "killing the third part of all mankind." The Pope is degraded. The barons, beaten by the English and prisoners, are extorting their ransom from the unhappy serf, stripping him to the very shirt. Epilepsy is the great scourge of the time, succeeded by the Civil War, the *Jacquerie.* . . . The folk are so mad with misery, they set to dancing.

NOTE 3. *Satan as Physician, Love-philtres, etc.*

Reading the admirable works composed in our own day on the history of the sciences, I am surprised by one circumstance. The authors seem to think everything was discovered by the doctors, those half-schoolmen, who at every step were hindered by their cloth, their dogmas, the deplorable habits of mind due to their scholastic training. And others, who walked free of these fetters, the sorceresses and witches, did they find out nothing? It were unreasonable to think so; and Paracelsus states the very opposite. In the little we know of their recipes, a remarkably good sense is apparent. To the present moment the *Solanaceœ,* so freely employed by them, are considered the especial remedy of the dread disease which threatened the world in the four-teenth century. I have been surprised to see in M. Coste (*Hist du Développement des Corps,* vol. ii., p. 55) that the opinion of M. Paul Dubois as to the effects of iced water at a certain moment was in precise conformity with the practice of the witches at their Sabbaths. Consider, on the other hand, the idiotic prescriptions of the great and learned doctors of those times,—the marvellous effects to be expected from mule's urine, and the like (Agrippa, *De Occulta Philosophia,* vol. ii., p. 24, Lyons edition, 8vo.).

With regard to their love-potions, philtres, etc., it has not been noticed how closely the *covenants between lovers* resembled those between friends and brothers in arms. For the latter consult Grimm (*Rechts Alterthümer*) and my *Origines;* for the first, Calcaguini, Sprenger, Grillandus, and a host of other writers. In all cases they follow identically the same lines. It is invariably either Nature called upon and taken to witness, or the employment, more or less blasphemous, of the sacraments and holy things of the Church, or a feasting in common, such and such a drink, such and such a loaf or cake, shared between the contracting parties. To this add certain forms of communion, by blood, by this or that excretion.

But, no matter how intimate and closely personal these may appear, the sovereign communion of love is always a *confar-reatio,* the sharing of bread which has absorbed magic virtue. It does so, sometimes in virtue of the Mass pronounced over it (Grillandus, 316), sometimes by contact with, and emanations from, the beloved object. On the marriage night, in order to arouse love, the *bride's pasty* is eaten (Theirs, *Superstitions,* iv., 548). To rouse a similar feeling in the breast of the man *to be tied* (such is the phrase), the woman makes him consume a particular sweetmeat she has prepared for him, etc.

NOTE 4. *The Last Act of the Witches' Sabbath.*

When mankind has completely awakened from its prodigious dream of two thousand years, and can coolly and quietly take stock of Christian society in the Middle Ages, two astounding facts will become apparent, facts unique in the history of the world, viz. 1: *Adultery was one of its recognised institutions,* normal, established, esteemed, sung and celebrated in all the monuments of literature, noble and bourgeois alike, in every poem and every *fabliau,* and 2: *Incest* is the ordinary condition of serfs, a condition of things clearly manifested at the Witches' Sabbath, which is their one and only opportunity of freedom, the expression of their true life, where they show themselves for what they are.

I have questioned whether incest was officially and publicly displayed at these functions, as Lancre maintains. But I make no question as to the fact itself.

Economic in the main this state of things,—a result of the wretched state in which the serfs were kept. Women being less efficient workers, were regarded as so many useless mouths. One was enough for a family. The birth of a girl was lamented as a calamity (see my *Origines*); and the child received next to no attention. But many could possibly survive. The eldest only of the brothers married, so hiding under a Christian mask the polyandry that was the actual fact. Between them, a thorough understanding and conspiracy of infertility. This is the bottom of the mournful mystery, which so many witnesses attest without comprehending what it really implied.

One of the most weighty of these, in my eyes, is Boguet, serious, upright, and conscientious, who in his remote Jura country, in his mountain district of Saint-Claude, was bound to find the customs of older days better preserved than elsewhere, and faithfully followed with all the obstinate tenacity of peasant routine. Boguet also affirms two important facts: 1, incest, even incest between mother and son; 2, unfruitful, undelightful pleasure, child-bearing made an impossibility.

It is appalling,—whole nations of women submitting to such sacrilege. I say *nations* advisedly; these *Sabbaths* were enormous assemblages,—12,000 souls in one small Basque canton (see Lancre); 6,000 in one pretty hamlet, La Mirandole (see Spina).

A terrible revelation indeed of the insignificant moral influence the Church exerted. It has been supposed that with its Latin, its Byzantine metaphysics, barely comprehensible to its clergy themselves, it was Christianising the people. And lo! at the only moment when the people is free and can manifest its true nature, it shows itself worse than pagan. Self-interest, calculation, family consolidation, have more effect than all the empty teaching of clerics. Incest of father and daughter would have been comparatively useless in this direction, and less is heard of it. That of mother and son is specially enjoined by Satan. Why? Because among these uncivilised races the young labourer, on the first awaking of his passions, would have escaped from the family control, would have been lost for the common household, just when he was becoming of precious value to it. It was hoped to keep him to bounds, to nail him to the home, at any rate for a long while, by means of this strongly constraining tie, "That his mother incurred damnation for him."

But how could she ever consent to such a thing? We can only say, look at the cases, happily rare, which occur at the present day. The thing happens only under conditions of the extremity of destitution. It is a hard saying, but a true one: excess of evil fortune demoralises and depraves. The spirit once broken has small power of resistance left, it is weak and flaccid. The poor, in their half-savage life, so bare of everything as it is, spoil their children excessively. In the home of the destitute widow and the forsaken wife or mistress, the child is "monarch of all he surveys," and the mother has no strength, when he grows up, to oppose his will. How much more so in the Middle Ages! The woman was crushed to the earth on three several sides.

The Church keeps her down at the lowest level of degradation,—she is Eve, and sin incarnate. In the house she is beaten; at the *Sabbath* immolated, we have read how. At bottom she is neither of Satan nor of Jesus; she is nothing, and has nothing. She would die in her child. But they should beware of making a creature so unhappy, for under this hail of agony, what is not pain, what is sweetness and tenderness, may in revenge turn into the frenzy of despair. This is the horror of the Middle Ages. For all its spiritual aspects, it lifts from the hidden depths incredible things that should have never left them; it goes searching and scrutinising the muddy under-regions of the soul.

Still the poor suffering creature would fain stifle all this. Very different from the high-born lady, she can sin only out of submissiveness. Her husband will have it so, and Satan will have it so. She is afraid, and weeps at the idea; but her reluctance goes for little. But, for all the constraint she is under, the result is not less terrible in the way of perversion of the senses and degradation of the mind. It is a hell on earth. She is left horror-stricken, half wild with remorse and passionate revolt. The son, if success has been realised, sees an enemy in his own father; a breath of parricidal fury haunts the house, tainted with this abomination. One is horrified to picture what a society such as this must have been, a society where the family, so fatally corrupted and divided against itself, went on its way in gloomy dumbness, wearing a heavy mask of lead, under the rod of a witless authority that saw nothing and believed in nothing but its own supremacy. What a flock of spiritless sheep! What senseless, brainless shepherds! They had there before their very eyes a monstrous spectacle of calamity, grief, and sin, a spectacle unheard of before or since. But they only looked in the pages of their books, learned their lesson there, and repeated vain words by rote. Words! words! this resumes all their history. Their whole meaning was *a tongue;* phrasing and phrases, and nothing else. One name will be theirs for ever—*Talkmongers.*

NOTE 5. *Literature of Sorcery and Witchcraft.*

Its beginning dates from about 1400. The books composing it are of two kinds and of two periods—(1) those of the monkish inquisitors of the fifteenth century; (2) those of the lay judges of the days of Henri IV. and Louis XIII.

The huge Lyons compilation, composed and dedicated to the inquisitor Nitard, reproduces a crowd of these monkish treatises. I have compared them one with another, and sometimes with the old editions. At bottom there is very little in them; and the everlasting repetitions are wearisome to the last degree. The earliest in date (about 1440) is the prince of fools, a genuine Teutonic dullard, the Dominican Nider. In his *Formicarius* each chapter begins by drawing out a parallel between ants and heretics or sorcerers, the deadly sins, etc. This comes very near the confines of mere idiocy. He explains most satisfactorily the necessity there was to burn Jeanne d'Arc. This book possessed such attractions that the majority of the rest copied from it— Sprenger in particular, the great Sprenger, whose merits have elsewhere been insisted on. But how say all there is to be said, how exhaust this mine of asininities? *"Fe-mina* comes from *fe* and *minus;* because a woman has *less faith* than a man." And a few lines further—"She is indeed light-minded and credulous, always ready to believe." Solomon was right when he said, "As a jewel of gold in a swine's snout, so is a fair woman which is without discretion. . . . Her mouth is smoother than oil: but her latter end is bitter as wormwood" (Prov. xi. 22, v. 3, 4). But there, what cause for wonder? Was she not made out of a crooked rib, that is to say, a rib which is distorted, turned against man?

The *Marteau* (Hammer) of Sprenger is the representative work, the type, followed as a rule by the other manuals, the *Marteaux, Fouets, Fustigations* (Hammers, Whips, Cudgellings), issued later by the Spinas, Jacquiers, Castro, Grillandus, etc. The last-named, a Florentine and inquisitor at Arezzo (1520), has some curious particulars as to philtres, and gives some interesting stories. It comes out quite clearly from what he says that there was, over and above the actual objective Witches' Sabbath, an imaginary *Sabbath,* which many terrified individuals believed themselves to attend, especially women somnambulists, who would get up in the night and scour the country. A young man, crossing the fields at the first peep of dawn, and following the course of a brook, hears a very soft voice hailing him, but in timid, trembling accents. Looking, he sees a pitiful sight— a woman's white body almost naked, save for a scanty pair of drawers. Shuddering and shamefaced, she was hiding among the brambles. He recognises a neighbour; and she begs him to rescue her. "What were you doing there?" "I was looking for my donkey." He expresses incredulity, whereupon she bursts into tears. The poor woman, who had very likely in her somnambulism slipped out of her husband's bed and wandered away, starts accusing herself. The Devil took her to the Witches' Sabbath; while conducting her home again he heard a church bell, and let her fall. She tried to ensure the youth's discretion by giving him a cap, a pair of boots, and three cheeses, but the silly fellow could not hold his tongue, and bragged of what he had seen. She was arrested. Grillandus, being away at the time, could not conduct her trial, but she was burned, for all that. He speaks of it complacently, and says, the carnal-minded butcher, "She was a fine woman and plump" (pulchra et satis pingeris).

From monk to monk the snowball goes on, ever growing. About 1600, the compilers being themselves subjected to compilation, and supplemented by the later recruits, we arrive at an enormous book, the *Disquisitiones Magicæ,* of the Spaniard Del Rio. In his *Auto-da-fé* de Logroño (reprinted by Lancre), he gives a detailed description of a *Sabbath,* very curious, but one of the silliest productions to be found in writing. At the banquet, for first course, they eat children hashed: for the second, dead wizards' flesh. Satan, who understands his guests' little ways, conducts the company to the door, holding as a candle the arm of a child who has died unbaptised, etc., etc.

Does this exhaust the absurdities? Not a bit of it. The prize and crown of folly belong to the Dominican Michaëlis—in the Gauffridi affair, 1610. His *Sabbath* is undoubtedly the most improbable of all. To begin with, they assemble "by sound of horn"—surely an excellent way of securing their own capture. The *Sabbath* is celebrated "every day." Each day has its own particular crime, as well as each class of the hierarchy. Those of the lowest class, novices and folk of small account, get their hand in as a beginning by killing babies. Those of the upper class, the gentlemen magicians, are assigned the part of blaspheming, defying, and insulting God. They do not condescend to the trouble of evil spells and bewitchments; these they perform by means of their valets and waiting-maids, who constitute the intermediate class between the well-bred sorcerers and the clodhoppers.

In other descriptions of the same date Satan applies the nice grammatical tests of the Universities, making aspirants undergo severe examinations. After assuring himself of their scholarship, he inscribes them on the registers, and gives them diploma and patent. Sometimes he requires a lengthy preliminary initiation, a sort of semi-monastic noviciate. Or else, again, following the regulations of guilds and corporations of trades, he imposes an apprenticeship, the presentation of a masterwork, etc.

Note 6. *Decadence, etc.*

A fact deserving attention is that the Church, the enemy of Satan, far from vanquishing him, twice over gives him his success. After the extermination of the Albigensians in the thirteenth century, *did she triumph? Just the opposite:* Satan is found predominant in the fourteenth. After the St. Bartholomew, and during the massacres of the Thirty Years' War, *does she triumph? Just the opposite:* Satan is once more in the ascendant under Louis XIII.

The object of my book was purely to give, not a history of Sorcery, but a simple and impressive formula of the Sorceress's way of life, which my learned predecessors darken by the very elaboration of their scientific methods and the excess of detail. My strong point is to start, *not from the devil, from an empty conception, but from a living reality,* the Sorceress, a warm, breathing reality, rich in results and possibilities. The Church had only the demons. She did not rise to Satan; this was the witch's dream.

I have essayed to epitomise her biography of a thousand years, her successive periods, her chronology. I have described (1) *how she comes into existence* by the excess of her wretchedness and destitution; how the simple peasant wife, served by her familiar spirit, transforms this spirit in the progressive advance of her despair, is assailed, possessed, bedevilled by him, continually reproduces and incorporates him with herself, at last grows one with Satan. I have described (2) *how the Sorceress reigns paramount, but undoes and destroys herself.* The Sorceress, full of pride and fierce with hate, becomes, under success, the foul, malignant witch, who heals but yet corrupts, her hands more and more busied, her empiricism more and more in vogue, the agent of love and of abortion; (3) she disappears from the scene, lingering on, however, in country places. What remains, in evidence from famous trials, is no longer the witch, but the bewitched—as at Aix, Loudun, Louviers, in the case of Charlotte Cadière, etc.

This chronology was not yet firmly established in my own mind, when I attempted in my history to reconstitute the Witches' Sabbath in its several acts. I was mistaken about the

fifth. The true Sorceress of the original type is an isolated being,
a devil's nun, having neither love nor family ties. Even the
witches of the decadence do not love men. They submit to unfruitful, licentious embraces, and show it in their persons (*Lancre*), but their personal predilections are solely those common
to nuns and female prisoners. She attracts weak-minded, credulous women, who allow themselves to be enticed to their little
clandestine feasts (*Wyer,* chap. 27). The husbands of these
women are jealous, interrupt the pretty mystery, beat the
Sorceresses and inflict on them the punishment they most dread,
viz. to be got with child. The Sorceress scarcely ever conceives
except in her own despite, as the result of outrage and derisive
insult. But if she has a son, it is an essential point, so it is said,
of the Satanic cult that he become her husband. Hence, in the
later periods, hideous family groups and generations of little
wizards and witches, one and all cunning and malignant, ever
ready to beat or denounce their mother. In Boguet is to be
found a horrible scene of the sort.

What is less well known, but not less atrocious, is the fact
that the great folk who made use of these perverted races for
their personal crimes, keeping them in a continual state of dependence by means of their terror of being delivered over to
the priests, extorted heavy revenues from them (*Sprenger,* p.
164, Lyons edition).

For the decay of sorcery and witchcraft, and the latest perse-
cutions of which it was the object, I refer the reader to two
excellent works by Soldan and Thomas Wright respectively. In
connexion with its relation to magnetism, spiritualism, table-
turning, etc., copious details will be found in that curious book,
L'Historie du Merveilleux (History of the Marvellous), by M.
Figuier.

NOTE 7.

I have twice spoken of Toulon; but I can never speak
enough of a place which has brought me such happiness.

It meant much for me to finish this gloomy history in the land of light. Our works feel the influence of the country where they were wrought. Nature labours with us; and it is a duty to render gratitude to this mysterious comrade, to thank the *Genius loci*.

At the foot of Fort Lamelgue, which rises commandingly, though unseen, above, I occupied a small and very retired house situated on a sharply descending slope of healthy, rocky ground. The man who built himself this hermitage, a doctor, wrote within its walls a very original book, *L'Agonie et la Mort* (Death and the Death Agony). He died himself quite recently. Hot of head and volcanic of heart, he used to come thither every day from Toulon to pour out his troublous thoughts. They are strongly impressed on the locality. Inside the enclosure, a large one, of vines and olive-trees, in order to shut himself in within a double isolation, he had constructed an inner garden, narrow in dimensions, with encircling walls in the African fashion, and containing a tiny fountain. He is still present there by virtue of the exotic plants he loved, and the white marble slabs inscribed with Arabic characters which he saved from the ruined tombs of Algiers. His thirty years old cypresses have shot up into giants, his aloes and cactuses grown into immense, formidable trees. The whole very lonely, not at all luxurious, but with a great charm of its own. In winter-time the sweetbriar in flower everywhere, and wild thyme and aromatic scents of all kinds.

The roadstead of Toulon is, as everybody knows, one of the wonders of the world. There are some even greater in extent, but none so beautiful, so finely designed. It opens to the sea by an entrance two leagues across, this narrowed by two peninsulas, curved like crab's claws. All the interior, varied and diversified by capes, rocky peaks, sharp promontories, moorlands, vines, pinewoods, shows a singular charm, nobility, and severity of aspect.

I could not distinguish the inner portion itself of the roadstead, but only its two enormous arms—to right, Tamaris (henceforth immortal), to left, the fantastic horizon of Gien and the Iles d'Or, where the great Rabelais would have loved to die.

Behind, beneath the lofty circuit of the bare mountains, the gaiety and brilliance of the harbour, with its blue waters and its ships that come and go in never-ceasing movement, afford a striking contrast. Flapping flags and waving pennants, swift-flying despatch boats carrying admirals and other officers to and fro, all is animating and interesting. Every day at midday I would climb on my way to the town from the sea up to the highest point of my fort, whence opens a vast panorama, the mountains beyond Hyères, the sea, the roads, and in the middle of all the town which, as seen from thence, looks charming. Anyone seeing the sight for the first time, exclaims, "Ah! what a pretty woman Toulon is!" What an agreeable welcome I met with there, what devoted friends I found! The public institutions, the three libraries, the courses held in the sciences, offer numerous resources little suspected by the flying traveller, the passing visitor who is merely on his way to take ship. For myself, settled there for a length of time, and grown into a true Toulonnais, it formed a never-ending source of interest to compare together old Toulon and new, and note the happy progress of the centuries, a progress I never felt more acutely anywhere. The gloomy affair of Charlotte Cadière, the documents relating to which the learned librarian placed at my disposal, brought only this contrast for me in lively colours.

A certain building in particular daily arrested my attention, the Hôpital de la Marine (Naval Hospital), formerly a seminary of the Jesuits, founded by Colbert for the ships' almoners, and which, during the decadence of the French Navy, had occupied public attention in so odious a fashion.

It was well done to preserve so instructive a monument of the contrast between the two periods,—the former marked by ennui and emptiness disfigured by hateful hypocrisy, the present, bright with sincerity, ardent with activity, research, science, and science purely benevolent in this case, directed solely and entirely towards the relief of suffering and the consolation of human life!

Going inside, we shall find the house has been somewhat changed. If the decriers of the present say such progress is of the Devil, they must admit that to all appearance the Devil has altered his methods.

His magic nowadays is, on the first floor, a fine and well-selected medical library, which these young surgeons, with their own money and at the expense of their pleasures, are incessantly adding to, less dancing and fewer mistresses, more science and brotherly love.

Destructive of old, constructive now, in the chemical laboratory, the Devil is hard at work preparing what is to alleviate the poor sailor's pain and cure his ills. If the knife becomes needful, the insensibility the witches sought, and towards which their narcotics were the first essay, is afforded by the art magic of the immortal discovery made by Jackson in America (1847), and Simpson at Edinburgh.

Those days pondered and aspired; these realise. Their spirit is a Prometheus. In that mighty Satanic arsenal, I mean the well-equipped physical installation possessed by this hospital, I see realised in practice the dreams and longings of the Middle Ages, the most apparently chimerical fantasies of former days.—To traverse space, they say, "I would have force. . . ." And behold steam, which is now a flying wing, now a Titan's arm. "I would wield the lightning. . . ." And lo! it is in your land, docile, obedient. It is stored in a bottle, increased, diminished; sparks are drawn from it, it is called here and sent there. —We do not ride on a broomstick, it is true, through the air; but the demon Montgolfier has created the balloon. Last, but not least, the sublimest wish of all, the sovereign desire to communicate afar off, to make one from pole to pole men's thoughts and hearts, this miracle is accomplished. More than that, the whole round world is united by a vast electrical net-

'work. Humanity as a whole possesses for the first time from minute to minute the full consciousness of itself, a complete communion of soul with soul. . . . This is divine sorcery indeed! . . . If Satan does this, we are bound to pay him homage, to admit he may well be after all one of the aspects of God.

PRINCIPAL AUTHORITIES

GRAESSE, *Bibliotheca Magicæ,* Leipzig, 1843.

Magie Antique, collection of texts by Soldan, A. Maury, etc.

CALCAGNINI, *Miscell., Magia amatoria Antiqua,* 1544.

J. GRIMM, *Deutsche Mythologie.*

Acta Sanctorum,—Acta SS. Ordinis S. Benedicti.

MICHAEL PSELLUS, *Energy of Demons,* 1050.

CÆSAR VON HEISTERBACH, *Illustria Miracula,* 1220.

Régistres de l'Inquisition (1307–1326), in Limburch; and the Extracts of Magi, Llorente, Lamothe-Langon, etc.

Eymerici Directorium, 1358.

LLORENTE, *Inquisition d'Espagne.*

LAMOTHE-LANGON, *Inquisition de France.*

Manuals of the Monks Inquisitors of the Fifteenth and Sixteenth Centuries:—NIDER, *Formicarius;* SPRENGER, *Malleus;* C. BERNARDUS, *Lucerna;* SPINA, GRILLANDUS, etc.

CORNELIUS AGRIPPA, *Opera,* 8vo, 2 vols., Lyons.

PARACELSUS, *Opera.*

WYER, *De Prestigiis Dæmonum,* 1569.

BODIN, *Démonomanie,* 1580.

REMIGIUS, *Demonolatria,* 1596.

DEL RIO, *Disquisitiones Magicæ,* 1599.

BOGUET, *Discours des Sorciers, Lyons,* 1605.

LELOYER, *Histoire des Spectres,* Paris, 1605.

LANCRE, *Inconstance,* 1612; *Incredulité,* 1622.

MICHAELIS, *Histoire d'une Pénitente,* etc., 1613.

TRANQUILLE, *Relation de Loudun,* 1634.

Histoire des Diables de Loudun (by AUBIN), 1716.

Histoire de Madeleine Bavent, of Louviers, 1652.

Examen de Louviers; Apologie de l'Examen (by YVELIN), 1643.

Procès du P. Girard et de la Cadière, Aix, fol., 1833.

Pièces relatives à ce Procès, 5 vols., 12mo, Aix, 1833.

Factum, Chansons, etc., relatifs; MS. in the Library of Toulon.

EUGÈNE SALVERTE, *Sciences Occultes,* with introduction by Littré.

A. MAURY, *Les Fées,* 1843; *Magie,* 1860.

SOLDAN, *Histoire des Procès de Sorcellerie,* 1843.

THOMAS WRIGHT, *Sorcery and Magic,* 1854.

FIGUIER, *Histoire du Merveilleux,* 4 vols.

FERDINAND DENIS, *Sciences Occultes, Monde Enchanté.*

Histoires des Sciences au Moyen Age, by SPRENGER, POUCHET, CUVIER, HOEFER, etc.